COFFEE FIRST, THEN THE WORLD

COFFEE FIRST, THEN THE WORLD

One Woman's Record-Breaking Pedal Around The Planet

JENNY GRAHAM

BLOOMSBURY SPORT

LONDON · OXFORD · NEW YORK · NEW DELHI · SYDNEY

JENNY GRAHAM'S CYCLE AROUND THE WORLD

---⊙---

LEG 1: EUROPE TO ASIA

1   Start and Finish line at the Brandenburg Gate, Berlin, Germany

2   Poland, Lithuania, Latvia and onto Russia

3   Through Russia and Mongolia

4   Across China to Badaling

5   Flight from Beijing to Perth

LEG 2: SOUTHERN HEMISPHERE

6   Australia: Perth to Brisbane

7   Flight from Brisbane to Invercargill

8   New Zealand: Invercargill to Auckland, including a ferry crossing

9   Flight from Auckland to Anchorage, USA

LEG 3: NORTHERN HEMISPHERE

10   USA and Canada: Anchorage, Alaska to Halifax, Nova Scotia

11   Flight from Halifax to Lisbon

LEG 4: BACK TO EUROPE

12   Portugal, Spain, France, Belgium, the Netherlands and back to Berlin

---⊙---

18,000 MILES · 16 COUNTRIES · 124 DAYS

---⊙---

Routes are approximate.

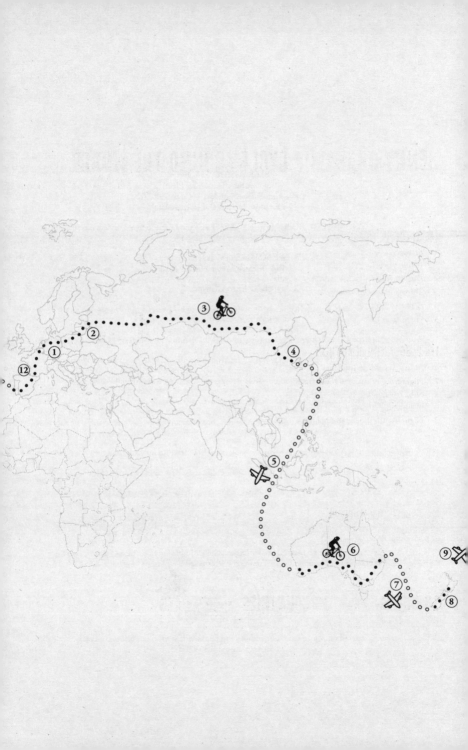

BLOOMSBURY SPORT
Bloomsbury Publishing Plc
50 Bedford Square, London, WC1B 3DP, UK
29 Earlsfort Terrace, Dublin 2, Ireland

BLOOMSBURY, BLOOMSBURY SPORT and the Diana logo are trademarks of
Bloomsbury Publishing Plc

First published in Great Britain 2023
Paperback edition published 2024

A catalogue record for this book is available from the British Library

Library of Congress Cataloguing-in-Publication data has been applied for

ISBN: PB: 978-1-3994-0104-3; eBook: 978-1-3994-0103-6; ePdf: 978-1-3994-0102-9

2 4 6 8 10 9 7 5 3 1

Maps on pp. iv–v, 20–1, 110–1, 178–9 and 242–3 by D.R. ink

Typeset in Adobe Garamond Pro by Deanta Global Publishing Services, Chennai, India
Printed and bound in Great Britain by CPI Group (UK) Ltd., Croydon, CR0 4YY

To find out more about our authors and books visit www.bloomsbury.com and
sign up for our newsletters

To the strong women in my life who have instilled a sense of freedom and belief in me from such a young age.

My top tier:

Mum, Nic and Aunty Lorna

CONTENTS

PART I
PREPARATION

15 June 2018 • Berlin, Germany • Time: 11.39 p.m. • Time until World Record attempt: 6 hours 21 minutes • Bed for the night: Airbnb

Well, we're doing it, then. We've made it to the start…

I'm not one for getting overly gushy about bikes, but as I lay on the cool, unfamiliar white sheets, I appeared to be talking to mine. She hadn't yet earned her name 'Little Pig' – that would come later – but the golden mustard steel frame of my Shand Stooshie bike had already become my companion. She'd been in my life for only four months, but during that time we had battled through snowstorms, crossed mountain ranges, skirted coastlines and spent every evening and weekend together, testing each other to the maximum as we trained and prepared for the Round the World project.

I looked her over. Every bolt on her chassis was familiar. Every component she held had weeks and months of thought put into it. With every decision came a list of pros and cons – durability versus weight versus price versus necessity versus mend-ability. She didn't hold one item that hadn't been meticulously considered.

The cockpit I'd set up on the handlebars would become my home – my front room and kitchen – for the next four months, holding all I'd need to navigate, collect data, charge equipment, light my way, carry clothes and food, and rest my weary body.

From the handlebars I'd attached aerobars, which sat proud both vertically and lengthwise. These were my armrests, with short poles that flipped up at the end for comfort. The poles were hollow and inside them I'd rolled up six different currencies in case of emergencies, to see me through the first leg of the route from Berlin to Beijing: euros for Germany, Latvia and Lithuania; zloty for Poland; roubles for Russia; tögrög for Mongolia; and renminbi for China. I also carried US dollars. I wouldn't need them for a long time, but they would be a good backup, because most places in the world recognise their value.

My friend Colin, from Craigdon Mountain Sports, had sacrificed the length of the shop floor's broom handle and sawn two small chunks from the top to wedge in between the bars. I then wrapped them up with tape – the perfect bodge. These would act as shelves and together with my bars, they would carry my essentials: my lights, a camera, a huge elastic hair band to stuff things under, my GPS Tracker, two water bottle cages with bottles, two wired speed sensor computers and my main GPS navigation tool – the Garmin Edge 1000.

I'd bought the GPS with the money I'd received from my very first sponsor, Evans Cycles, back in November 2017. They paid me £500 in return for three blog posts about preparing for my World Record attempt. I would need to raise a whole lot more than that, but it was a start and it represented a glimmer of hope among the piles of rejection emails I'd received from other brands and businesses.

That GPS would guide me the whole way around the world. Or at least it would if I actually downloaded any routes. I hadn't. I had thought about doing it lots of times and had even practised how, but had kept putting it off. It was a sit-down job; one I thought I'd do in the airport or sometime where there was a period of enforced rest, but there were always so many more pressing jobs to do and I'd never got to that point.

In only six hours' time I was due to start the ride of a lifetime. A World Record attempt to become the fastest woman to circumnavigate the planet by bike. I'd need to ride 29,000 km – or 18,000 miles – all on my own, over four continents and through 16 countries, and I'd just realised that I didn't even know the way out of Berlin.

The next hour passed in a fury of tech faffing. The routes were all saved on my Strava account and in my Dropbox as a back-up, but an issue with the Wi-Fi in the flat meant the routes wouldn't upload the way they had when I'd practised. I couldn't figure out what had gone wrong and instead panicked, assuming this was my tech incompetence.

Thomas Hogben and Mike Webster, both filmmakers, were in the next room. They had come out with me to Germany to film the start, in the hope that I'd make it far enough self-shooting for them to make a documentary.

I woke them up. Using his laptop, Tom eventually managed to download half the world on to a SIM card that I then plugged into my Garmin GPS. The issue was temporarily fixed, but it had just triggered every single fear and internal battle I'd had with myself about my ability to actually pull this off.

I was overcome by self-doubt, like I'd finally just proved to myself that I wasn't cut out for this World Record and was completely out of my depth. I returned to bed, replaying the time I had spent practising the uploads, internally beating myself up for not doing the job properly. I weighed up the likelihood of there being other, finer details of the trip I had also forgotten.

My alarm went off a few hours later. I opened my eyes and stared at the ceiling with my brow still furrowed and my jaw clenched. My chest was so heavy it felt like it was physically pinning me to the mattress.

• • •

It's hard to say when the Round the World project began for me. It had many different starts and stepping stones to get to this point. It could have been in the early 1990s when, as a 10-year-old, I obsessed over Cheryl Baker and Roy Castle's *Record Breakers* programme. Each week different people would attempt to break or set a Guinness World Record, from the sublime to the ridiculous. I was entranced by every single one of those attempts. Although I was more interested in competing with the man who had just sat in a bath of baked beans for 100 hours than I was about cycling around the world, it was the first time I remember questioning what action was needed between having the dream and then making it happen.

Perhaps it was in 2004 when I was about to turn 24 and a world of new possibilities was opening up to me. My son Lachlan had just started school and as a young mum with more time on my hands I enrolled on a six-month outdoor pursuits course at Inverness College. There I learned to ski, snowboard, canoe and kayak, navigate, rock-climb and embrace the technical skills of mountain biking with the overall aim of becoming an instructor.

Sport hadn't been a big part of my life until that point. I had never identified as 'sporty', but I enjoyed adventures in the outdoors and I instantly felt at home on a hillside. I'd been brought up in an amazing, working-class estate in the Highlands of Scotland. Inverness is a city now, but it was a town in the '80s and I felt I knew every street by name and each person who walked on them.

My mum's side of the family were all from the rural countryside, but had moved into town when they had kids. I had my sister, 10 cousins, two aunties and two sets of grandparents all within a few miles of my home. We'd spend our holidays, weekends and after-school time building dens, cycling to nice places for a picnic, having campfires, swimming in the sea and building tree swings. My Grandad Joe was a tinkerer and always had projects he was working on, including a seemingly never-ending supply of old bikes in the back garden that he'd fix up for us, so no one was ever short of wheels.

Learning to ride a bike is one of my strongest memories from early childhood. One Sunday morning we removed the stabilisers from my little red bike and drove to a big empty car park at the back of a local hotel. My dad ran behind me as I wobbled all around until I could no longer feel his hand on my back. I became hysterical with excitement taking those first few pedal strokes as my mum cheered me on loudly from the sidelines. It would be the first and last *really* happy memory I'd make with my dad. He and my mum had periods of separation after that and he'd go away to work. He'd remain present in my life into early adulthood, but there was a distance between us and we'd never share that joint euphoria again, which makes this memory all the more meaningful.

From then on in I didn't really stop riding my bike. Our neighbourhood was bustling with kids of all ages. We'd all be out playing for hours, especially in the summer with huge games of hide-and-seek, and full-scale water fights. We all rode bikes everywhere and when we weren't playing on them, we were using them as transport to get to the shops or visit family. Despite this deep connection with the bike, I hadn't given cycling as a sport much thought. I was aware of things like the Tour de France from clips on the TV or photos in papers, but what these men were doing on bikes didn't feel in any way connected to how I used a bike.

It was the six-month course that would expand my vision – and change the trajectory of my life. Overnight, I could see the Highlands for what they were: the greatest playground of all time.

But then came the end of the amazing course and there was, well, nothing. The college was developing an advanced course, but it wouldn't begin for another year. In the meantime, I wasn't qualified enough to be employable. With still so much to learn about the sports, but with limited funds and very little kit, it was going to be tricky.

The one piece of equipment I did have was a hardtail mountain bike, an ex-display Saracen which I'd bought from Halfords for £100 during the course. 'A bike for life,' I told myself. Along with my two very first adventure buddies from college, Ali and Charlotte, we kept the spark alive, meeting regularly for local rides.

I worried that this wasn't enough, though, and that this new world could slip away from me. A year felt like a long time to wait, so the day Lachlan returned to school after the summer holidays I got out the *Yellow Pages* (just writing that makes me feel quite old!) and called every outdoor centre within a 25-mile radius. I was looking for an opportunity to volunteer. They all said no – I didn't have enough experience, there were no vacancies, etc. The following day I did the same thing. Starting at the top I worked my way through them all again, asking if they'd had time to reconsider. Again, everyone turned me down – until I reached O.

A man answered: 'Ron Woodwark, Outdoor Education'. A little more confidently than the day before, I asked if there were any volunteering opportunities for my limited skills and abundance of enthusiasm. To my surprise he told me to come in for a chat later that week.

Ron Woodwark was the manager of a Lottery-funded project that came under the Highland Council Outdoor Education umbrella and shared the same building, clerical support and kit store. This was the Outdoor Education Response Team and its remit was to work with young people who were displaying challenging behaviours or were 'at risk' of exclusion or harm. There were two full-time staff on the team, Ron and his colleague Andy Clark, as well as a handful of freelancers. They ran six-week engagement programmes all over the Highlands of Scotland, giving groups a taster of a range of different activities, and the young people a chance to learn and develop in an outdoor setting.

I went out and met with the team. They agreed to take me on for a trial and that was it, I had my way in. Both Andy and Ron became great mentors. Andy's passion was coaching and mindsets, and we'd have long chats about philosophy and learning styles. He was skilful and physically capable at almost any sport. He was also generous with his time and until I learned to drive later that year, he would help with lifts, making sure I didn't miss out on opportunities. He'd even wait until I got Lach off to school and was really understanding when I'd accidentally sleep in – more often at first than I'd like to admit – while I adjusted to having a 'proper job'.

Ron had a lifetime of experience working in the outdoors, which was particularly evident when he was communicating and engaging with young people. I'd love our time together on long walks when he'd share stories of being a climbing bum in the Alps long before it was cool, sleeping under rocks, picking fruit and living as cheaply as possible. Ron had patience like no one I'd ever met before and was methodical about safety and in his practice. He made sure I didn't busy myself with the more technical parts of the job before I'd nailed the basics, and spent time building my foundation and understanding.

I worked part-time in an outdoor shop that paid me cash and then built up a kit allowance with the Outdoor Education team, earning credit for every job I volunteered on when they needed a female leader. Soon I could afford my own skis, hiking boots, waterproofs and paddles.

I returned to college for the year and when Andy left Outdoor Ed I applied for the position, and was successful. I worked alongside Ron for a couple of years until a nine-to-five job came up in Inverness, doing the same kind of work except within school hours. It also meant I'd work more intensely with the young people and their families, a part of the job I loved. I applied and became a Children's Service Worker at The Bridge – an intensive support unit educating 14 to 16-year-olds who had disengaged with mainstream schooling and were dealing with social, emotional and behavioural issues.

The Highland Council had a pot of funding that employees could use to build their outdoor qualifications if they were working with young people. The Bridge delivered outdoor education as part of their curriculum, so I continued developing my skills and gaining qualifications in the various sports. It was on one of those courses that I first became aware of the Round the World record. To be precise, it was in 2010, on a mountain bike leader assessment and in the middle of a conversation about managing saddle sores while riding back-to-back days. That's when one of the other students, Lewis, recommended Mark Beaumont's book, *The Man Who Cycled the World*. It's the story of Mark's record-breaking 2008 ride, where he circumnavigated the planet by bike in 194 days, solo and self-supported. I loved this book and it was the first insight I had into what a feat of endurance on this scale would take.

His stories of the kit choices he made and the physical effects he endured – including the saddle sores – fascinated me, along with his sleeping arrangements, finding culverts under the roads and being welcomed into Iranian homes. I was hooked by his journey and would debate with friends whether racing around the world at pace was a waste of a trip. Would you miss out on too many experiences along the way, or was it actually a purposeful adventure? I was leaning heavily towards the latter and boldly stated that one day I might 'consider doing just that!'

My life then was far from that of a round-the-world adventurer. Rides and hill days were squeezed around family life and work. It wasn't a dream that I held on to continuously, either. I was too busy living in the here and now to be planning something so far out of my reach, though the following year I did make a 10-year plan. This was out of character for me, but a good friend and colleague Simon had been training for a performance coaching course and needed someone to practise his technique on. I loved being coached, so I jumped at the chance and offered myself up as a guinea pig. Recently, while in the middle of a house move, I found my Life Wish List. It was funny to see some of the things that were important to the 32-year-old me. 'Having my own pigs' and 'Doing a ski season in Japan' both still sound great, but they wouldn't make the cut these days. I've still never owned even one pig or been to Japan.

Surprisingly, though, the majority of the list *has* come to fruition: dreams about where I'd be living, who I'd like to have around me, where I'd be in my career and my relationship to the outdoors all have great big ticks next to them. Perhaps the biggest tick of all would be next to 'Having a MASSIVE cycling adventure. Around the world maybe!'

If I hadn't found this list, I'd have answered the question, 'When did you start thinking about around the world?' in terms of more recent events. Perhaps it's fairer to say that I'd been subconsciously chipping away at the skills and building experience for many years. It's astounding the power that can come from writing things down – putting your hopes on to paper so you can get on with the day to day of life.

In 2014 I encountered the niche world of bikepacking races when a friend had a Trackleaders web page open on his computer and I happened to notice. It was showing what looked like a virtual race with a pre-plotted route layered on top of a map of the Highlands of Scotland – 500 miles through glens and over mountain passes. Some I knew well and others I'd never seen before. What brought the route alive was the moving dots on the screen. This was my introduction to the notorious bikepacking race the Highland Trail 550 (HT550). The riders carried a GPS spot tracker with them that then transmitted a location back to this page. Each of the riders were identified by their initials and a dot that represented their gender. I'm afraid it was blue for boys and pink for girls, and out of the 25 or so blue dots on the screen only one of them was pink: IE. Iona Evans. She wasn't just the only woman out there, but also the first ever to compete. I was fixated on her and couldn't believe that more women didn't want to be part of this clearly really cool event. This was also my first experience of dot watching, the term given to the highly addictive spectator sport that allows ultra-endurance races to unfold on your computer screen.

Iona's pink dot changed things for me. Along with this new community of people, I was inspired to turn all my focus from mountain climbing to mountain biking. The following year I would make it to the start line. In fact, I'd make it to four HT550 start lines over the next five years, but the first one, in 2015, was the baptism of fire. A saying that I first heard from Red Bull athlete Ross Edgley – 'You need to be naive enough to start, but stubborn enough to finish' – summed up my first HT550 efforts beautifully, except for the finishing part. I didn't make it the whole way around and I kept going far longer than I should have. On Day 8 of that race I woke up in a campsite shower block and, after squeezing my shoes on over my swollen feet, I used the wall and sinks to help me hobble over to my bike by the door. Looking in the mirror as I passed, I was taken aback by the mess I was in. Pretending I was okay to carry on was much too like Monty Python's Black Knight insisting, ''Tis but a scratch.'

I pulled out at that point; it was my first ever bitter taste of sporting failure. I wallowed in self-pity for some time, but I knew that couldn't be the end. The ride had ignited something and would become a driving force for me to make sure my body was strong enough for future missions.

A few days before I'd scratched (withdrawn from the race), I'd been stuck trying to cross a remote river. It took 20 hours for the rain to stop and the water to drain enough. During this time, I hobbled up and down the bank making four or five attempts on the crossing, but the water currents and depth were always too strong for me to get myself and my bike over to the other side. This meant that my JG dot had been pinging in different places on the river. It created a bit of a stir among the people watching it play out. The GPS signal updates every 10 minutes or so. If it pinged as I was mid-river, anyone watching had to wait another 10 minutes to see if I'd crossed or not.

It would take years to forget that scratch. If songwriter Cat Stevens had been a racer, I'm sure he'd have changed his lyrics to, 'The first scratch is the deepest'.

And yet, three things came out of that moment in time. Firstly, someone on Twitter made my river-crossing track into a meme – as a meme lover, I was quite proud of it. Secondly, the bike I'd built for the ride was made from a Stooge frame. Andrew Stevenson, aka Mr Stooge, got in touch to say he'd been watching the river crossing and admired my grit. Then he offered me a brand new frame for free! Thirdly, Mark Goodwill from local bike shop OrangeFox Bikes shortly after offered me free workshop time and kit as a way of supporting my next challenge. I couldn't believe the encouragement I was receiving from the race. I was feeling like a bit of a loser and yet these people were congratulating me.

I continued working in social care, but went part-time so I could get involved with a community bike project with Velocity Café and Bicycle Workshop. I was now surrounded by bikes and people who loved them, which fitted my newfound obsession for building miles and strength. There was a mountain bike group that rode out from the café each week and I soon found what would become lifelong friends within it. I rode further, both at the weekends and by taking part in different bike-packing events. I loved the purity and the ethos, the simplicity of riding as hard as you can while keeping enough energy reserves to look after yourself in wild places. By 2017 I had put thousands of miles into my legs and was beginning to looking into 'actual' training. It was then that things started becoming a bit more focused.

On an Adventure Syndicate training camp in Girona, I met John Hampshire – just a year and a half before I found myself on the start line of the world. I'd never been on a training camp before, but relished the idea of getting fitter and faster. John was offering one-to-one sessions throughout the week to talk about training and goal setting. I'd never had any individual time with a cycling coach like that and I made the most of his knowledge, booking in as many sessions as I could. We clicked with each other and got on really well. The camp was a great success; everyone learned so much and strong bonds were made between the 30 women who attended. It was that feeling of finding like-minded people and having an absolute hoot as we went.

I left a day early so I could make it back home in time for work and as I arrived into Edinburgh Airport an email from John came through on my phone. He wrote: 'I've come up with a scheme to offer a year of coaching to selected people as part of a social experiment. Are you interested in being one of them? You would get one-to-one coaching along the lines of my Silver level and in return you would have to write a blog once a month about your experience.'

My heart skipped a beat as I read it over and over with a rush of emotion welling in my eyes. This. Was. It! I didn't yet know what 'it' was, but I did know it had the potential to be life-changing – and I was so ready for life-changing. Not that I didn't have an amazing life. I really did. But there was something sitting within me, at my very core; something I'd been struggling to articulate, but I felt that John could see it. Now, more than just the coaching that he offered me, he was offering me his belief.

I replied excitedly, accepting immediately. The following day I went into work at the council and received an email about voluntary redundancies. I messaged John to tell him I'd applied and, although I didn't get the redundancy, this set the tone for the year to come. I felt as though I'd been at a junction in my life for a while. Lachlan was preparing to leave school and had secured an apprenticeship, and when your only child reaches that stage there's a natural refocusing of time, money and purpose.

I had a deep curiosity about how much more I had within myself. That Easter I was due to race across Arizona – the AZT750, 750 miles from the Mexican border up to Utah – in the longest single track race in the world. It was like nothing I'd ever ridden before. The route had a mandatory 40-km hike-a-bike through the Grand Canyon, where you need to carry your bike on your back. I completed the race in 11 days, finishing joint sixth with a lovely couple, Fiona and Paul, also from the UK, who had crawled out of the Grand Canyon at the same time as me. We rode the final day as a team.

We then hitched a lift to Las Vegas, almost 1000 km away, and lay by the motel pool with the kind of satisfying fatigue that only endurance events can bring. My face was swollen and sunburned, and I had deep cuts on my lips from the wind. My waist was bruised and disfigured from carrying my bike, and my legs and mind were capable of only the simplest tasks. Yet I was consumed, both by contentment and the simplicity of the adventure I had just had. I lay scrolling on my phone, dreaming of what was going to be next. I was a mountain biker at heart and had only just bought a second-hand road bike to help with training, but through my Google search for 'endurance rides' I saw it: the Guinness World Record for the fastest woman to circumnavigate the planet by bike. She did it in 144 days, supported.

This couldn't possibly be my destiny, could it? Yet little over one year later, I was at the start line.

Day 1: 16 June 2018 • Berlin • 5.05 a.m.

There was a 10 km ride from my Airbnb to the start line at the Brandenburg Gate. The sun had just come up and the long straight pavements of the Strasse des 17 Juni were empty. I was battling to let go of the previous evening's GPS issue. My internal dialogue had gone dark and I continued tearing myself down for the mistake. Had I made a fool of everyone by having them believe that I could pull this off? Filmmakers Tom and Mike had driven to the start in a hire car. They must have been questioning me too after my inability to make the tech work the previous evening.

I'd felt the fear of failure in the build-up to the trip, but had always been able to rationalise it and work through the concerns. Accepting that I might well fail was part of the process, as was knowing that I'd done everything within my power to get to the start line physically and mentally prepared. It was much easier to rationalise from a distance – but now that I was actually here and could no longer be sure how prepared I was, I felt helpless and panicked. It was as if I was driving a car full-speed towards a cliff and couldn't take my foot off the accelerator.

The last few months had been pretty full-on while preparing for the trip. I was juggling lots as I continued to work full-time. I trained around 20 hours per week alongside managing the project and the fundraising, but it wasn't the project tasks that proved the most taxing. What was hard to keep on top of were the less glossy parts of adulting: the everyday monotonous jobs of finding car insurance, getting shopping, replacing the broken cooker or cutting the grass. I built up an impressive number of parking fines and late payment fees as my capacity to 'adult' slipped away from me. I struggled getting enough sleep at night as my head processed all the jobs that needed to be done. I was overwhelmed and this had just tipped me over the edge.

I was snapped out of these thoughts by my phone ringing. I couldn't answer it. I couldn't bear to hear anyone's excitement right now. Then a message popped up: 'Jen! We're in Berlin! We've stayed up all night to come and wave you off.' These chirpy, drunken words came from a couple I knew back in Inverness, Alice and Craig. They were friends of friends really, but I had spent a bit of time with them at festivals and barbecues over the years. They were great fun, but there was not a chance I could deal with them right now. It was 5.30 a.m. so they'd have been up partying in Berlin clubs and were now coming to meet me, this ball of anxiety. No, no, NO!

I called the number back. A loud, enthusiastic Scottish voice bellowed down the phone: 'Jennnnnnnny, we're trying to get into the Brandenburg Gates.' The Brandenburg Gate is an outdoor structure. Surely there was no inside? 'Wait, wait, here's a security guard.'

More shouting was going on down the phone. I was really worried now – I hoped they wouldn't find me. 'Ali, mate, please don't come! I've had a really bad night and feel really stressed out, and we're filming the start.'

'Oh, wait, what?' Alice sounded just as panicked as I felt. 'I don't want to be on the telly, I'm hammered, Jenny. Bye bye bye, love youuuuu. So sorrryyyyy, so sorry. Good luck, chick!'

Ah, the relief. A television crew wasn't actually going to be there (sorry, Ali!). It was just Tom and Mike who could have easily edited them out, but I felt far too fragile to deal with the messiness. I was left feeling guilty – albeit a relieved guilty. Who had I become lately that I was actually turning people away from this special moment?

I'd tussled over the years with the number of personas I'd built up in my life and wondered if I could unapologetically be all of them. Did they slot together? I was a mum and had been my whole adult life. I was embedded in my community with the work I did and cherished time spent with my family of generational Highlanders. I had kept hold of old school friends. We loved music, festivals, camping trips and parties. We would often take things too far, staying up all night making memories on dance floors and fields all across the country.

I was also a thrill-seeking adventure buddy, obsessive, single-minded and focused. I could plough all my time and more into projects I felt passionate about. I was a team member in the Mountain Rescue and I could sometimes lose my way and forget those parts of life that didn't have my attention.

But right now, I wasn't any of those. I wasn't a caring, fun friend and I certainly wasn't a hardcore adventurer. This was really bad timing for an identity crisis.

• • •

The Brandenburg Gate is an iconic landmark in the heart of Berlin, and it would be the start and finish of my route. With a history spanning well over 200 years, it has represented both unrest and division, and peace and hope, in Germany and indeed Europe. The eye-catching neoclassical monument stands 26 metres high and is more than 60 metres wide, dominating the space. Made up of 12 large sandstone columns, it divides the street into five passageways, each wide enough to drive a car through, although it is now a traffic-free zone. Its roof is decorated with carvings of Greek mythological figures and it is crowned with an impressive bronze statue known as the Quadriga – a winged goddess of victory driving a chariot pulled by four horses.

I have deep respect for the Brandenburg Gate and what it represents, but the choice to be here was not mine, but Lachlan's, and I'm not sure the architecture had anything to do with that decision. He had suggested meeting me somewhere en route, but I'd worried about the dynamic and change of focus, so I asked him to choose the finishing point, perhaps somewhere he'd like to go to for a holiday. It made sense for it to be somewhere in Europe, to minimise the number of flights needed during the ride. We looked over the maps and he said quite confidently, 'It's got to be Berlin, Mum. It looks like such a cool city and Germany does have the best beer!' So, there it was. We had a start and finish location.

The Football World Cup was underway and in three days' time the Germany versus Mexico game would be projected live on to the Brandenburg Gate. In preparation for this, the whole structure had been surrounded with scaffolding, which stopped me riding through the arches. Instead, I skirted around the edge of them, passing through the old gatehouse and into the square called Pariser Platz.

It was 5.36 a.m. Tom and Mike were capturing shots of the area and I stood by a post, re-zeroing my bike computers. I carried two of these computers in case one stopped working and I was trying to decide whether to keep them both counting in kilometres or change one to miles. I went with kilometres. It made for easier maths and the majority of the world worked in metric too, but because I'd been brought up with an imperial system in my head I often switched between kilometres and miles (something you might spot throughout this book and in the audio diaries). However, I could feel Tom wanted me to just make my mind up and start getting some pictures taken. There were only 20 minutes to go, so I stopped fidgeting and got involved.

I had decided to have no family or close friends at the start line. We were all carrying our own stresses, concerns and excitement about the trip, and I felt I'd probably stay more focused without them. Although, now I was here, it felt strange not to have a loved one close by for such a monumental moment. I wasn't alone, though, as some local bikers and shops had found out about my attempt and a small gathering of supporters was beginning to form in the square. It included a couple called Joachim and Melanie Rosenlund. Joachim was a bikepacker and had invited me round to the family home in Berlin the day before, where we looked over routes and went for a ride. Melanie made eye contact with me, came straight over and embraced me and, for a moment, I didn't let go. It was a hearty and meaningful hug, which made me feel again like things were going to be okay. And she hadn't just come for the cuddles; she'd baked a carrot cake and made a flask of coffee to have with it.

Speaking of coffee, I've always enjoyed it, but, as reflected in the title of this book, coffee stops quickly became an essential motivator for me on my Round the World trip. It had to be coffee first and I had to have one before I could really get on my way. Pretty much every day, as soon as I woke up, finding one would be my sole focus. The further I got, the more this became apparent. In fact, it got to the point where I'd plan where I slept around how far I'd need to ride for coffee the next morning. On days when I camped within 5 km of a coffee stop I found it much easier to roll out of my bivvy bag and get going. On days when the nearest coffee was further away I was much more tempted to hit the snooze button. It worked and I never had any trouble justifying staying for a second cup either.

There was a bit of a buzz now. I could feel the excitement building and chatted to the well-wishers who all spoke much better English than my German. There were also two witnesses who had been asked along to sign off the beginning of the ride. Guinness states that these people need to be independent and not linked in any way to the project.

Melanie and Joachim's neighbour was a lawyer and agreed to come along with them. I'd also reached out to the Scottish government in Germany; an office had been set up in Berlin earlier that year. The director Dr Alexandra Stein excitedly accepted the invitation to come along, even at that time in the morning. As well as an abundance of enthusiasm, she brought a big Scotland flag with St Andrew's cross on it and wrapped it around my shoulders. The minutes were passing so quickly and just as I'd almost forgotten what we were here for, Mike gave me the nod. 'One minute to go, Jen.'

I'd decided 6 a.m. would be the official start time. I was already straddling my bike, leaning over my bars, chatting. I stood upright, clipped into my pedals and began riding back towards the gates. I then U-turned and cycled towards the warmth of the assemblage of supporters. I was aware of the long deep breaths I was taking and as I got closer to the small crowd, I could sense the noise, but was preoccupied with the chemical reaction currently making its way up through my body. It started at the very end of my toes and quickly rose up my legs. The energy continued at pace. I shot my fist up in the air and the release followed. It was extraordinary, like nothing I've ever felt before. If there was a visual representation, I'm sure it would have looked like that emoji whose mind has just been blown open; all my emotions came spurting out of my head into the air.

'YAAAAAAS!' I shouted and carried on riding, beaming a ridiculous smile. The relief was immense: no longer was I talking, thinking or worrying about this. I was just actually doing it. I, Jenny Graham, was riding around the *actual world*! This thing that had consumed my life for the past year was happening and all I needed to do was ride my bike. Lots.

There was a comedy moment 200 metres down the road, when I was stopped by a red light. We laughed. Tom and Mike were in their hire car, filming out of the side windows, and Joachim was driving. He had his bike in the car, so that he could drive the lads for the morning and then ride back into Berlin.

A couple of local riders rode with me for the first hour or two out of Berlin: Gerald Hilderbrandt, an experienced long-distance cyclist, and another lad whose name I forgot in all the excitement, but his story stayed with me. He was riding to see his grandparents who lived 100 km away and this would be his longest ride ever. I was so happy for him. That feeling – of pushing the kilometres and hours that you can sit on a bike for – is what had got me here. He was happy to be part of my day and I was equally happy to be part of his.

PART II
EUROPE TO ASIA

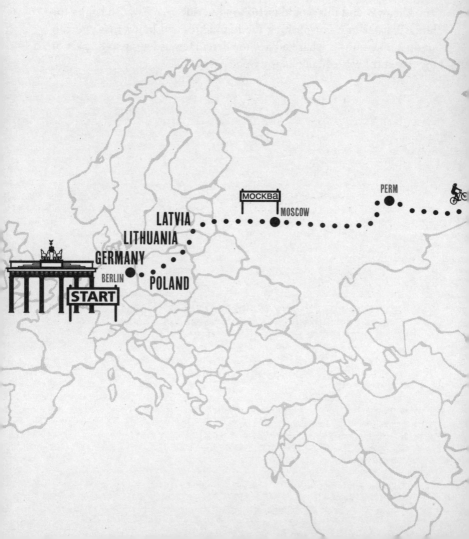

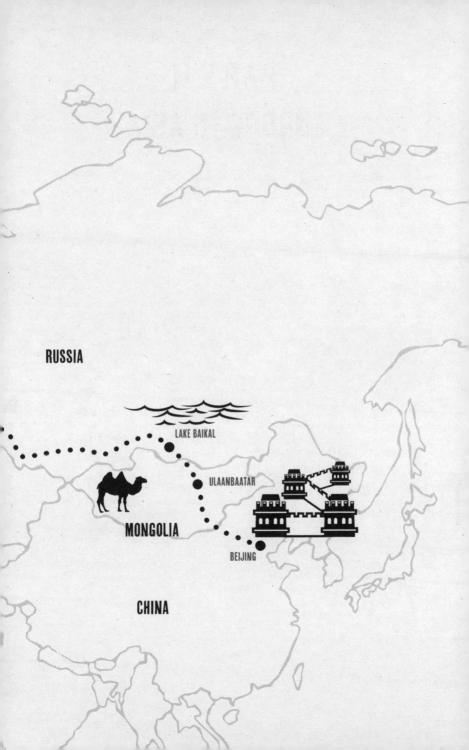

RUSSIA

LAKE BAIKAL

ULAANBAATAR

MONGOLIA

BEIJING

CHINA

Day 1: 16 June 2018 • Brandenburg Gate, Berlin to Wylatowo, Poland • Ride time: 15 hours • Ride distance: 321 km • ODO: 321 km (odometer reading or overall distance travelled) • Bed for the night: Bivvy by the side of the road

The morning was full of trip firsts: my computer screen flashed up the first 100 km, then the first 100 miles. I crossed my first border crossing from Germany into Poland and I met Tom and Mike in the first McDonald's. I didn't realise then what a staple they would become of the trip. Not that I'm a fan of the food day after day, but free Wi-Fi, clean toilets and screens where you can order a meal without speaking to anyone proved a draw too good to turn down the more fatigued I became.

The guys had dropped Joachim off already and were spending the day filming with me before heading back to Scotland. I was pleased when they joined me for the stop. It all felt so relaxed in comparison to the previous 24 hours and it was nice to share some laughs with them again.

Mike had been one of the first people I'd told about my Round the World dreams. I bumped into him in the supermarket not long after I was home from racing the AZT750 in Arizona. Mike worked at the local theatre, running filmmaking and media groups with young people, and had often worked with some of my students. We kept in touch on social media and he saw some of my pictures of Arizona. He asked if I had any more trips planned, as he was doing a bit more freelance projects with a particular interest in the adventure film sector. We met for a coffee the following week. Admitting my Round the World ambition – and that I thought I might even be good enough to pull it off – wasn't something that came easily and I cringed at the thought of telling him. I worried that by admitting my ambition I was going a step too far and that I really wasn't of record-breaking pedigree.

Mike has a gentle and relaxed personality. I thought then that he'd always seemed kind and open, so if I was going to share this dream with anyone outside my inner circle, he was the person. He was so excited for me and offered his support straight away. He quickly got his friend and colleague Tom involved and between them they became the Round the World film crew. We chatted briefly about them spending time on the road with me, but soon realised that this would impinge on the solo and self-supported aspect of my journey too much. Instead, we decided that I would self-film from the road, using my mobile phone for video logs and a 360-degree lens camera that was attached to the top 'shelf' of my aerobars. They would collect footage from home, including interviews with family, and track me on the lead-up to leaving.

Tom matches Mike on enthusiasm and any time we met to film they radiated belief that, 'This was a thing'. They spoke in the tense that suggested it was real: 'When we're in Berlin' rather than 'If we get to Berlin'. It was these small subtleties from the people around me that made an enormous difference. The pair didn't get involved with any of the planning or fundraising, but having them on board with the film became an integral part of getting to the start line.

The rest of Day 1 was spent with the boys leapfrogging me, getting shots hanging from the car window, tooting as they passed. We were all big waves and smiles. If things continued like this, I was in for a dreamy trip.

I ended the day on 15 hours of riding time and with a distance of 321 km. 'That's 200 miles down and only 17,800 left to go!' I chirpily told Tom as he filmed my sleeping set-up. It was 11 p.m. when I found a small green area just off the road, surrounded by bushes and trees, and for the first time began pulling out my sleeping equipment. This all lived inside a 17-litre, waterproof Apidura Saddle bag that hung below my saddle rails and attached to my seat post. It was the biggest volume bag in the range and it needed to be large because it would carry the majority of my life-on-the-road kit: sleeping equipment, warm clothes, waterproofs, medicine and some larger repair items like my pump and inner tubes. The rest of my kit was spread out between much smaller bags.

On the top tube I stored all my electrical items (power bank batteries, cables and plug sockets) as well as easy-access stuff like sun cream, lip balm, mini pliers and my multitool. Two food pouches that hung from my handlebars would be continually filled with snacks. The most I'd ever need to carry, I thought, was one and a half days' worth of food. I imagined that to be around 6000 calories.

On my bike's frame I carried a large water bottle, which was held in place by a side-release bottle holder. This gave me room in the top of that space for a partial frame bag, which I could use as food overflow, as well as for some smaller bits of my maintenance kit, wet wipes and gloves. On the opposite side to the storage pouch was a documents pocket where I kept a photocopy of my passport, insurance and visas, as well as spare cash and bank card. It was a backup in case I lost my skinny beige bumbag that I would wear discreetly under my top. In there I carried my actual passport, cash and bank card. Looking after this bag was on my mind daily. If I lost it, I could expect major delays, which might even stop the show.

• • •

When choosing my sleeping equipment, I had to balance weight versus packability versus warmth to arrive at my perfect sleeping set-up. In my final choices I compromised the warmth of each item in favour of packability. I thought it would be more useful to fill the space in the bag with warm layers of clothing that would have more versatility: I could wear them on and off the bike, whereas a chunky sleeping bag only had one practical use.

There were three key items that made up my sleeping equipment:

- The sleeping bag – a Cumulus X-Light 200: A two-season, down-filled sleeping bag with a comfort rating of 4°C and a limit rating of 0°C. It weighed just 350 g and could be stuffed snuggly into a three-litre Exped waterproof packsack, with enough room for my super-lightweight Haglöfs L.I.M. Essens down jacket to be squeezed in with it. The sleeping bag saved weight by having no zip or hood. Instead, it had a drawstring cord around the neck, which I could pull tight if I tucked my head down into the bag.
- The roll mat – a KLYMIT X Lite: A peculiar-looking, ultra-light and compact sleeping pad, which was only 103 cm long

and supported me from my shoulders to hips (I used stuffed dry bags under my feet and head). The pad had large chambers cut from the material, leaving it with a structure like a skeleton. The major selling points of this mat were that you could blow it up in just four breaths, it weighed only 145 g and packed down to the size of a banana. It was surprisingly comfortable, but wouldn't be durable enough to last the whole trip.

- The bivvy bag – a Terra Nova Moonlight: The waterproof sleeping bag cover weighed just 180 g. The bag itself was made from ultra-light material and the top section around my head had a mesh hood that could be zipped closed.

• • •

Tom seemed to have a more romantic notion of what bivvying might be. 'Oh, is this it? Is this you bivvying?' he said as I got ready to lie down near the bushes. 'Yup, this is it.' We were saying our goodbyes. We had no plans to see one another until my return to Berlin and were all wishing each other safe journeys, Tom reminding me to film everything! We hugged and they were off.

It felt okay to see them go. The day had been long, and mostly pretty good. I was keen to feel what this was going to be like on my own.

• • •

When it comes to Round the World records, it's difficult to lay out the progression of the Round the World female record without going back in time. I mean way back. To the invention of the bicycle...

The term 'bicycle' was first recorded in 1860 as the high-wheeler penny-farthings became popular. Before that there were many forms of two-wheeled vehicles that required balance to stay upright, but this was the first to be called a bicycle. It came along at the start of a huge shift in society as travel and communication were making massive advances in the late 1800s.

In 1872, in his book *Around the World in Eighty Days*, Jules Verne introduced the world to Phileas Fogg and with him came the concept of global travel. Ten years after Phileas, history was made when Thomas Stevens returned from a two-year trip, having ridden his penny-farthing bicycle for 13,000 miles across the United States, Europe and Asia to lay claim to the first ever circumnavigation of the world by bike.

This kind of journey, an adventure for adventure's sake, was also highly unusual for the time, because most large expeditions had previously been undertaken as a political, scientific or colonial enterprise, whereas Thomas's drive was simply to witness other cultures from his saddle and immerse himself in them.

The Safety Bicycle soon followed and was to be the blueprint for the bike design we are familiar with today. It revolutionised the world, particularly for women. Although women were riding and even beginning to race the high-wheelers, they were doing so at a time when they were expected to be seen in restrictive corsets and large, flouncy woollen skirts. Neither were designed for ease of movement and the calls for dress reform were only just coming into play.

This new design of bike, with evenly sized wheels, was not only much closer to the ground, but it also had a drive chain (enabling the transmission of power from one place to another). This meant that the pedals were now placed underneath the frame, as opposed to being part of the front wheel, as it had been on the farthing. This made the bike far safer – hence the name Safety Bicycle – as the likelihood of getting clothing caught up in the wheels was dramatically reduced. And if it did get caught up, you now had much less of a distance to fall.

There was strong momentum in the women's equality and suffrage movements at this time, but women were still very much considered second-class citizens. Married women didn't have the right to own a house, sign a contract or keep their own wages, assuming that they were 'lucky' enough to be allowed to work (for poor women, of course, working was a necessity).

But in 1894 Annie Cohen Kopchovsky, better known as Annie Londonderry, would challenge those norms by becoming the first woman to lay claim to cycling Round the World. A 26-year-old married mother of three, living with her family in Boston, she was an unlikely candidate to do so. Her journey around the planet is thought to have come about as a result of a wager between two wealthy men and a debate over whether a woman was capable of such a feat. They imagined not, but set the guidelines for any woman bold enough to try: she would have 15 months to complete the ride, following a route very similar to Stevens's journey, crossing the United States, Europe and Asia. She had to leave with no money, but could work and sell her story along the way. She wasn't allowed to ask for food and boarding for free, and she'd need to come home with $5000 in earnings.

The facts surrounding Annie's ride are murky, but it's thought that she cycled about 7000 miles. She crossed America twice (due to bad kit choices and a turn in the weather) and then caught a steamer boat to France, where records show she shared 500 wintery miles with a few French cycling escorts. This seemed to be the end of any substantial riding for her. The timings of her trip suggest she took three months to get from France to Japan – exactly the same time she took to ride across the United States. Add in the hold-ups to be expected in foreign lands and it's fairly well accepted that Annie most likely stayed on a steamer boat all the way to Japan, missing out Asia completely.

She didn't let this little detail stop her and created her very own media storm everywhere she went. She became a human billboard for sponsorship, sewing patches and ribbons on to her outfit in return for money from businesses. On her bike she carried a billboard for Londonderry Spring Water Company, which paid her $100 in return for her agreement to call herself 'Londonderry'. She sold pictures of herself and carried published pamphlets telling her story. She turned up at public events and gave talks, and was extremely well received in most places she went. Her entrepreneurial skills can't be knocked: she telegraphed ahead of major towns and cities, telling officials of the welcome she had received elsewhere – which applied a certain pressure.

It is deeply unfortunate that Annie was a *completely* unreliable witness to her own account. Despite the embellishments – she probably rode about half the distance she claimed – she clearly pulled off a great achievement and most definitely did travel around the world *with* a bike. The bizarre and sexist stipulations about timings and generating funds were not things that had hampered Thomas Stevens. I can't help but wonder what would have happened if she hadn't been obliged to stick to them. In any case, for whatever reason she was either unable or unwilling to tell the real story.

If she were a modern-day woman telling such tall, outlandish tales, I'd be deeply disappointed and fearful of her undermining some of the hard work that's gone into the fight for women's equality across the century. Perhaps it's the gap of 130 years, or empathy because of the times she was living in, that have softened me towards Annie. I've listened to several podcasts about her story and there is something in her spirit that always makes me smile.

In the late 1890s there were many other women showing incredible and more authentic athleticism. For example, Tilly Anderson collected the 100 miles record of 4 hours, 47 minutes and 30 seconds and Louise Armaindo set the American long-distance record of 600 miles in 72 hours. The bond between women and bikes was clearly instantaneous. One of my favourite quotes is from the American suffrage activist Susan B. Anthony:

> Let me tell you what I think of bicycling. I think it has done more to emancipate women than anything else in the world. It gives women a feeling of freedom and self-reliance. I stand and rejoice every time I see a woman ride by on a wheel... the picture of free, untrammelled womanhood.
>
> https://bikeleague.org/content/march-womens-bike-history-month

Despite the achievements of these women and their clear athletic ability, society would be slow to accept women competitors. In fact, it would take a whole hundred years for the International Olympic Committee to let women race in Olympic cycling events. The first one was in Los Angeles in 1984 – when I was four years old. It would take a further 30 years until the Olympic Games created an equal amount of cycling disciplines for women and men.

Guinness World Records started recording records in 1955, so when I began looking at the history of Round the World, I was surprised to find that the first women's record hadn't been officially certified until just a few years ago, in 2012, when the wonderful Juliana Buhring completed the distance in 152 days. This was 31 years after the first man to set the record.

Juliana is a British-German cyclist with a humbling backstory. She found herself taking on the world after a year of heart-breaking grief when she lost her partner in an accident. A friend suggested she rode with her across Canada as part of her recovery. Juliana felt that if she was going to ride across one country, she might as well go for the world. Eight months later, she did just that.

She left her home in Italy with minimal cycling experience, closely accompanied by a friend in a van in case of emergencies, but it would take her only a couple of weeks to realise that she had what it took to go it alone. Sending the friend on their way, she completed the world circumnavigation solo and self-supported.

Italian cyclist Paola Gianotti followed with a fully supported ride just two years later, in 2014. However, her ride is not without controversy. She was hit by a vehicle while crossing the United States and broke her fifth vertebra. The Guinness World Record team decided her clock could be stopped for her to recover, which resulted in a four-month break in the middle of her ride. There is no argument that the accident must have been a hugely traumatic experience – thankfully, Paola made a full recovery – but stopping the clock caused a lot of contention.

That simply doesn't sit within a race format and it is hard to agree that a broken ride should take the record from an uninterrupted one. There are many examples of external factors that can and will affect your ride. Being hit by a vehicle is an extreme one, but the endurance world has a code of conduct that expects you to embrace your ride whatever comes your way.

That's my two cents' worth, but it's not my opinion that counts. Guinness World Records are the organisation managing the rules and their certification establishes the record. So, when Paola rolled across the finish line eight calendar months after starting, she set a new official World Record time of 144 days – and that would be my time to beat.

Let me give an insight into the official rules. They have gone through some changes over the years, but they are currently as follows:

- The route should follow a primarily east to west or west to east direction.
- The total distance ridden must exceed 18,000 miles or 28,968 kilometres.
- Two antipodal points – approximate opposite places on the planet – need to be passed through. I decided on Wellington in New Zealand and Madrid in Spain.
- You are allowed to fly to cross the ocean (thankfully) and your total trip distance including these transits must exceed the length of the equator: 24,900 miles or 40,075 kilometres.
- The same line of longitude can't be ridden twice. This would affect my route because the east coast of China's longitude overlaps the west coast of Australia's, so I would end my ride at Badaling rather than Beijing, 50 miles or 80 km short of the city and then start riding again from Perth, Australia.
- No drafting is permitted of vehicles or riders, meaning you can't tuck in behind them to gain help from a slipstream.
- Only the use of publicly chartered flights or boats is permitted.
- The start and finish should be in the same location.
- The clock never stops. The moment your ride starts, everything you do between then and the finish line is included in your overall time. Which means, of course, time spent sleeping, eating, faffing, riding and in transit.

The inclusion of transit times was the newest of the rules, introduced in 2012. This makes a huge difference: previously you could stop the clock to rest and reset at the end of each leg, usually at an airport. In the new rules, your resting period is also timed.

In the same year that the rules changed, Mike Hall famously won the inaugural Round the World Cycle Race, where 10 adventurers set out to try to break the record. Mike was the first person home on that race, with a staggering ride time of 91 days and 18 hours. He was two weeks faster than the previous record holder and had ridden completely unsupported. The rule change happened on his return and meant he would need to submit his time including his transit, which would have taken it up to 107 days, 2 hours and 30 minutes.

Mike chose not to submit his ride to Guinness World Records, possibly because of this late rule change. But it should be said that, regardless of the official certificate, his ride is celebrated and recognised across the world.

• • •

Nine men have held the record since 1981, when Nick Sanders completed the first official record lap, with a time of 138 days covering 13,609 miles. At that point there was no distance or southern hemisphere stipulation and most people attempting the record chose the same kind of route as the original trailblazers, covering the United States, Europe and Asia, and sticking to the northern hemisphere.

It was in 2015 that Andrew Nicholson completed the first circumnavigation under the new stipulations of riding 18,000 miles and passing through two antipodal points on the planet. His ride took 123 days, 1 hour and 6 minutes, and it's fascinating to look back and see the progress of the record as men began chipping away at the time.

The current holder is Mark Beaumont, not for the ride that had inspired me so many years before, but for his second pedal around the planet. On that occasion he put together an extraordinary crew of experts to support the circumnavigation and completed it in a mind-blowing time of 78 days, 14 hours and 40 minutes. Mark took 44 days off the previous record and made it around the world in under 80 days, a feat that Phileas would have been proud of! I had followed sections of Mark's trip and was casually impressed with his daily averages, but it wouldn't be until I started riding it for myself and got a feel for the terrain and environment that I truly began to appreciate the scale of his achievement.

I reached out to Mark in the planning stages of my ride and, to my delight, he messaged straight back and set up a call. From that moment onwards, he has been a great support, generous with his time and knowledge as well as being a reliable ear.

A map of Mark's 80-day route shows a satisfying line around the globe, and he rode across continents and flew only when he reached the next ocean. Historically, riders have flown over sections of land mass too, particularly over Asia, where it's a bit more difficult with border crossings and there can be more safety issues. However, I loved the clean lines of Mark's route and would adopt nearly all of it for my own attempt, changing only the start and finish, and adding in detours for food and bike supplies and shelter. The route was as follows:

- Leg 1: East from Central Europe through Russia to Lake Baikal, and then onwards to Mongolia and China;
- Leg 2: Australia from west to east, followed by New Zealand from south to north;
- Leg 3: North America – Anchorage, USA, to Halifax, Canada;
- Leg 4: Back to Europe, from the Iberian Peninsula through to Central Europe again.

The only issue I had with this route was the large section of Russia. I researched the roads and knew they were dangerous, with huge amounts of fast traffic on them. I'd thought about adjusting that section and dropping further south into Kazakhstan and entering China from the west. Mark shared his own research with me, which suggested the winds would be more stable going through Russia and that I could expect many more headwinds on the lower route I was proposing. Riding into headwinds for even a few hours, let alone weeks, is soul-destroying, not to mention slower. I was still torn, and I'm not sure if it was the wind predictions or the comfort of it already having been planned and ridden the year before by Mark and his team that made me stick to Russia. I suspect it was the latter as there were already so many unknowns in Asia.

• • •

There is no distinction made between supported and unsupported rides when it comes to the Guinness World Record. Individual records only stand for female, male and tandem, so regardless of how you choose to race the world, you are competing for the same record. There are, of course, real-world distinctions and I will lay them out below, but please don't assume bias on my part. I have so much respect for supported rides and really admire the drive towards athletic achievement. I put far more value on the transparency of riders throughout their race than I do on people's individual preferences.

Whether supported or unsupported, the jobs you need to do on the road are stripped back to fairly basic tasks, but each is vital to maintain forward momentum. The rider needs to:

- Remain fuelled and hydrated;
- Have shelter/a safe space to sleep;
- Maintain body temperature throughout different climates;
- Keep body and mind in working order;
- Keep bike in working order;
- Manage travel logistics, such as flights;
- Navigate;
- Collect evidence of the ride, such as witness statements and GPS files;
- Keep electrical items charged;
- Make decisions on a tired brain; and
- Carry enough equipment to fulfil the above tasks.

Think of a spectrum with supported at one end and unsupported at the other. On the purest supported ride, the cyclist travels with a crew close by in at least one motor vehicle to deal with all these jobs. For example:

- Preparing and handing you what you need to eat and drink when you need it;
- Providing a bed, most likely in a campervan, wherever you need to stop;
- Handing you spare warm clothes, drying wet kit and washing the smelly stuff;

- Massaging and bandaging up any sore bits on your body;
- Providing hugs (vital!);
- Charging all your electrical items and carrying spares;
- Having spares such as wheels, components and even a bike on hand, plus a workshop repair kit;
- Undertaking mechanic duties and handling those spares as well as bike maintenance;
- Dealing with all the logistics and saving you from decision-making; and
- Transporting all your equipment.

It's pretty easy to see that a good support team will enable a rider to sit on the bike for the maximum amount of time each day, while helping to maintain bodily strength and well-being. On the other hand, the purest unsupported rider carries out all these jobs themselves:

- Finds, carries and eats enough calories and water throughout the day;
- Finds a safe place to sleep and sets up camp, or locates and books accommodation;
- Carries enough clothes to avoid hypothermia in colder climates and is okay with riding in dirty or wet kit;
- Keeps on top of charging equipment with a dyno hub and battery packs, and plug sockets whenever stopped;
- Books flights/ferries;
- Stays happy or at least motivated;
- Manages aches, pains and injuries;
- Fixes the bike with the spares carried or rides a broken bike to the nearest bike shop;
- Carries all equipment for the duration of the trip;
- Communicates with the public and navigates language barriers; and
- Uses only services that are available to the public, i.e. bike shops and post offices.

It's fair to say that Mark's 80-day ride and mine pretty much lived at opposite ends of the spectrum, but there are many riders who opt for somewhere in the middle. They might have a support team join them for the more remote sections or during some of the colder, wetter months. Maybe they will have people doing logistics from home or stay with friends along the way. It's perhaps because of this sliding scale of possibilities that Guinness have avoided taking on the task of monitoring such details.

There are clear time-saving benefits to a supported ride, but it comes with its own pressures: having people around you when you're suffering deeply; being held accountable to such a strict schedule; and never having the opportunity to keep your mind busy with the admin and logistics instead of the monotony on the road.

The differences in the financial costs of these two ways of racing are significant too. Again, these are extreme examples and there is a middle ground for sure, but Mark's highly skilled team and all the logistics meant his ride cost £500,000, while mine came in at around £15,000 (both included a lot of favours).

I budgeted for the ride through a series of educated guesses on the back of an envelope one Sunday morning. I averaged the price of food and accommodation in every country I would visit, costing for three meals a day and staying indoors every third night. I included a budget for three complete bike overhauls when I reached a new continent and then last-minute flight prices.

The figure I came up with was £15,000, which was a substantial amount of cash for me to get together. I felt fairly confident that I could raise it through sponsorship at first. I mean, it was such an amazing idea, who wouldn't want to sponsor it – right? Or not.

I sent out dozens of emails pitching the project, using all my contacts and those of friends and *everyone* turned me down. The ones that did reply all said the same thing: that they received many of these emails every year and couldn't support everyone, so sorry, but no.

The rejection was awful at first; I wanted to crawl under a rock. I already had so many doubts of my own about the trip that seeing what I perceived to be other people's in print was hard, but it also gave me a resistance to fight against. By the time I'd received about 30 knockbacks it was just too embarrassing *not* to make this happen. Imagine meeting these people next year and telling them that I didn't go as I couldn't convince anyone to believe in me! No, I needed to pull this off – to save face if nothing else. Our precious little egos are not always pretty, but they do get us places sometimes.

I'd gained some clout in the bikepacking world, but it was still a fairly niche scene and this was a big claim I was making. I needed the backing of people with profiles bigger than mine. And that's just what happened, courtesy of the Adventure Syndicate.

The Adventure Syndicate had been set up two years previously by endurance riders Lee Craigie and Emily Chappell. Lee once represented Scotland at the Commonwealth Games and was the first professional athlete I knew personally. I greatly admired her drive and vision to break free from the norm. She and I both lived in the Highlands of Scotland and over the years had shared many adventures.

I'd met Emily at a bike event in Edinburgh, the Capital Trail, in 2015, and had bonded with her over a plate of cheese scones and coffee as we tried to mend her broken bracket at the roadside. I was impressed by the way she told a story with such charm, both in her written work and speaking in public about her life and adventures crossing great expanses of the planet by bike.

The Adventure Syndicate was born with the tag line 'to encourage, inspire and enable others' – particularly women and girls – to believe they may be capable of more than they think they are. In essence, this was done by bringing together a diverse collection of female riders and adventurers to share stories through a variety of mediums and deliver workshops, courses and camps. Emily and Lee had gathered some impressive female athletes from a range of disciplines: people like Kate Rawles (known for her North and South American adventures on a bamboo bike), Rickie Cotter (a talented endurance racer) and Sarah Outen (a Round the World adventurer).

I had supported the Syndicate during their launch event in 2016, when they succeeded in getting a team of woman around the North Coast 500 in a record-breaking time, as well as at various other events, both personally and through the Syndicate. Both Emily and Lee then knew I was a team player and had the determination to make this happen.

In November 2017, after hearing of my plans, they asked me in a pub in Kendal if I wanted to come on board as a sponsored rider. I was elated. Being part of this already established team of women gave me and my ride the integrity I needed to appeal to funders. It also meant I had access to more potential sponsors.

I pitched the Round the World project at an Adventure Syndicate film launch in London in February 2018 and by March I started receiving some promises of cash, which was a relief – I was leaving in June! I gained about a third of the budget, as well as the majority of the kit I'd need from the relationships the Syndicate had with Leigh Day (a law firm), Komoot (a mapping company), Shand (bike builders), Endura (a clothing brand) and Apidura (a bike luggage brand).

A friend, Joss Evans, was a solicitor for Unitas Global (a global communications company) and around the same time introduced them to me. They loved the Round the World project and came on board as a named sponsor. This was an incredible boost, but I still had to raise about £7000 to meet my target. I decided to go public with my dreams and raffle off my swanky carbon Niner mountain bike (I'd won it the previous year when I put in a successful application to become a Blackburn Ranger). Across my social media feeds, I wrote:

> I'm raffling off this beautiful Niner bike so I can race around the world – chasing the World Record – and it could be yours for the price of a £10 raffle ticket!

And that was it, along with a silly picture of me looking happy beside the bike. The responses came flooding in. As well as buying raffle tickets, people inundated me with lovely messages of support and the project began gathering momentum.

I made about £4000 on the raffle tickets, and to top it up Lee and I hosted a fundraiser evening in Inverness for the Adventure Syndicate to launch the project and unveil the winner of the bike raffle. It was a huge success and the way everyone around me pulled together to make it happen was humbling to say the least. And we'd done it. I'd met my £15,000 target to go around the world.

It's with this in mind – the struggle to get that budget together – that I hope one day the two categories of supported and unsupported records will be recognised. The harder the times become to beat, the more likely it is that riders will need to be supported. While that will bring an element of professionalism, the massive price tag also means we run the risk of it becoming an elitist sport.

Day 2: 17 June 2018 • Wylatowo to Myszyniec • 15 hours • 328.8 km • ODO: 649.8 km • Bivvy by the side of the road

Poland so far had mostly consisted of long straight highways, often surrounded by lengthy sections of dense forest that limited my view. It was busy at times, though this morning it was quiet, but then it had only just gone 4 a.m.

After Day 1's extremes of emotions I was feeling a bit flat. I recognised that I was being fidgety on the bike. My concentration would come and go and I'd need to work hard at not stopping too often throughout the morning, as I could always find a reason to faff with my kit.

My body and mind would need some time to settle into the routine. My brain had been going at pace for months now, so it was no surprise it felt a little frazzled. The last big admin job I needed to do was find a team to help with my social media posts. I had a volunteer lined up to take on this role, but when I got in touch to say I'd started and to query the lack of posts about it she let me know that actually she'd overpromised and would have to pull out.

This was quite a big deal, because brands sponsoring me were expecting regular updates from the road, which would raise the profile of the ride and gain more publicity. Over the next week I'd recruit my sister Nic, filmmaker Tom and fellow endurance rider and all-round helpful guy Ian Fitz. They would do one post a week across Facebook, Twitter and Instagram, each using the information that I'd dump in a WhatsApp group and my daily stats that Nic would begin to collect further into the trip. They were so kind taking that on at such short notice and I am deeply grateful. Organising things from the road felt stressful at the time, but having jobs to do from my tribar 'office' was probably good for weaning my busy mind gently into finding some flow.

To gain the official record of 144 days I'd need to average more than 200 km per day. At first I was happy with just trying to beat it and see how I got on, but my coach John had suggested setting a goal to keep me motivated on tough days. So I went in high.

Each day I aimed to average 15 hours' ride time, five hours' sleep and one sit-down meal, where I could also wash and manage charging. That amount of time on the bike would equate to a daily average of 290 km and along with four days' travel time and six days' contingency, the plan was to complete the world in 110 days.

I include my daily stats throughout the book so you'll get a sense of how I'm doing. I don't include stats for the less eventful days. Place names are approximate as often I'd stop at the side of the road in an unnamed location. I've included my ride times and distances for the day, my bed for the night, and an odometer (ODO) reading which shows my total distance travelled.

110 days was my own personal target and when I describe 'feeling behind target' I am referring to the 110 days as opposed to the record itself. Right now it was difficult to imagine anything could get in the way of achieving that – I wasn't really comprehending how extreme the enormity of the task was – but there would be plenty of time for that to hit me.

• • •

I first met Pennie Latin, a Senior Content Producer at BBC Radio Scotland, when she came along to the Round the World fundraising event I held in Inverness. She sat in the front row with her denim jacket, wild curls and huge smile, and continually asked fascinating questions. I remember thinking: 'Who is this woman? I need to bottle her up!'

We arranged to meet for coffee the following week, where she then suggested I send back audio diaries of my trip. She would edit them into audio bundles to be played on BBC Radio Scotland's *Out of Doors*. There was nothing high-tech on my end, just a simple audio recorder on my phone and instructions to stay out of the wind. The magic would happen on Pennie's side, as she picked out the gold from my daily ramblings to play twice-weekly on the show throughout the whole trip.

This was a last-minute addition to the media I'd need to collect on top of video diaries and general riding shots. Meeting Pennie, and feeling her genuine excitement and passion for the work we would create, was very similar to how I felt about Tom and Mike. She was another person invested in the trip and in me. It would have been a lonely time if not for these invisible hands and I had many of them along the way.

I'm also a big fan of radio – it's such a powerful communication tool – and I was delighted to think that my story would be shared across Scotland. Even friends and family who had already received messages from me would tune in every week. My mum would get people stopping her in the shops saying they'd heard me on the radio and wanted to send their support. I think she found it really comforting.

I wasn't well practised in collecting audio or video at this point, and for the first week I'd talk nervously and self-consciously into my phone, but as the trip progressed there was nowhere to hide – when you're that fatigued, the rawness seeps in and the truth comes out. Eventually the recordings were no longer a task, but more of a roadside therapy session – someone to talk to, even if it was just myself.

🎧 **Audio diary:** *I had a beautiful sunset and nice roads to end the day. There was this garage I arrived at around midnight. They had mashed tatties in a tub, and they had hot water that you could fill it up with, so I just had a tub of mashed tatties, some Babybels and an Earl Grey tea. I've been eating sugar and bread all day long, so this was just the ticket. I was looking for a motel, but it was too late by then. No rooms left, so I'm just going to sleep in this go-kart field.*

**Day 3: 18 June 2018 • Myszyniec to Aukštadvaris, Lithuania •
15 hours • 287.6 km • ODO: 937.4 km • Bivvy by the side of
the road**

I woke up muggy inside the bivvy bag at 4 a.m. It was already so warm.
My face felt weird. I could sense my head hanging over the top of my
eyebrows. Rubbing my hand across the swelling, I felt my forehead
protruding considerably. It was huge!

I had two big bags of fluid filling the entire length of my forehead.
This was impressive, as I have a fairly big forehead. We're talking four
fingers deep! They were the result of mosquito bites. I started packing
up the sticky sleeping bags, continuing to prod at my lumps. There
were two bites, one on each side, and where the swellings met they had
merged with a crease down the middle, making it look remarkably like
a bottom. Great. Day 3 and I had a butt on my head.

I didn't need to look in my medical bag; I knew I had forgotten to
pack any antihistamines. How silly of me. This seemed like a ridiculous
oversight, but I could pick some up in the next town, Kolno.

I unscrewed the cradle of my helmet, making it as large as possible,
and then squeezed it over my gigantic forehead. By the time I reached
Kolno a couple of hours later, the pressure of my helmet had pushed
the bulges of fluid down my face and they were now surrounding my
eyes like a bandit mask. My eyelids had filled up and were sagging over
the tops of my eyes.

The antihistamines did make a bit of a difference, but the swelling
took over a week to subside. I'd stop throughout the day for ice lollies
to place on my face, but I'd forget what I looked like and take off my
glasses to see the cashier's horror as they took in my sausage face.

The weather had been on and off thunderstorms with humidity in
the air all day, but it cleared up by late afternoon. As I rode through
Lithuania, I was instantly struck by the contrast in the landscape. I was
now surrounded by lush open green hillsides, bright yellow crops lined
the roads, and the quaint little towns often had large storks nested on
top of chimneys, an impressive sight.

The roads were much quieter and also less reliable. A few times the
surfacing would just run out. And for no apparent reason, there would

sometimes be large areas of tarmac gouged out and the road destroyed. At times these would be passable and I'd teeter down nearly sheer drops with my loaded bike and inappropriate, gripless cycling shoes, and then clamber out the other side, but other times I'd need to backtrack and find an adjacent road.

One section took this to the extreme: with no notice, the tarmac road turned to gravel and stayed like that for 10 km, mostly rideable with the road tyres, but occasionally the gravel would get too deep and I'd have to get off and push.

🎧 *I'm coming along this dirt track and listen to this … it's just alive with crickets! On the right of me is a field full of rapeseed and it goes on and on for as far as I can see. Aw, there's a baby deer just crossing over the track. How cute!*

Well, I'm not doing so well for distance today. Think I'll get 280 km, just with having that extra-long break for my eyes swelling this morning. I'm not going to get hung up on that. I'll just ride for another hour and a half. It's 10 p.m.

I'll just get off this dirt track and head into the next town. I'd love to get some accommodation and recharge everything, batteries, wash myself and, yeah, get a nice sleep.

Day 4: 19 June 2018 • Aukštadvaris to Malta, Latvia • Approx. 15 hours • 302.3 km • ODO: 1239.7 km • Bus stop

I didn't find any accommodation that night. Instead, I slept in a field by the side of the road on the outskirts of Adincava and woke up to an ant infestation in my food bags. Some sweet macaroon bars, stashed right at the bottom of the feed bags, had attracted them. I didn't realise the extent of the issue until I was a few kilometres down the road and a constant stream of ants were appearing in lines, marching from the bags and then falling from my handlebars, like lemmings.

I rode into the town of Semeliškės and stopped at a petrol station, where a friendly woman in the garage smiled at me and spoke in English to tell me where I could find a hose to clean out the bags and remove the ants. I was taken aback by her warmth. No one had smiled at me since I left the boys on Day 1. I was only on Day 4, but they had been long days!

Outside I threw away all the food that was open and salvaged what I could. Hundreds of ants were now crawling about in the bin, on the ground and on me.

In preparation I'd imagined that horrific weather, endless miles and huge mountain passes were going to be the elements that wore me down. I'd overlooked insects. They were relentless. I was *covered* in bites and puffy bits.

My body always reacts extremely strongly to bites and, although one bite isn't a huge disaster, they do subtly wear you down. They're probably my Achilles heel. Perhaps because they always come with the heat, which just adds to the irritation.

BBC News picked up on my Round the World story and one of their favourite pictures to use was my big puffy face, with me squinting. It made me laugh. I couldn't believe that had become my hero shot!

Day 5: 20 June 2018 • Malta to Navoloki, Russia • 14 hours 35 minutes • 359.2 km • ODO: 1598.9 km • Bivvy by the side of the road

I arrived into Latvia yesterday evening and spent the night in a bus stop in the middle of a tiny village called Malta. Then this morning I cycled into Rēzekne for breakfast at a hotel. So far, the thing that has struck me about Latvia is the quality of the roads: massive, double-lane highways with barely any traffic and super-fast rolling tarmac. I'd take one turn in the road to head east out of the town and that was me for the next 63 km until I came to the Russian border.

With Russia looming, I had visas on my mind. As a European I had the luxury of passing through the majority of the countries with little more than an online form. The three big borders for me were Russia, Mongolia and China. Gaining these entry visas had been a mission in themselves, just a couple of weeks before I left. Each country has its own T&Cs, but basically:

- You can't order your visa too far in advance.
- You need an entry date and proof of intention to exit the country, i.e. a flight booked.
- You can only stay within the borders for a set number of days.
- You need to supply a name and address where you will stay on the first night.
- Russia and China both require a resident native to invite you to visit their country.

Each embassy system was completely different and, much as I wish it weren't so, did seem to fit their traditional national stereotype. At the Russian Embassy the process was efficient and there was zero small talk. I was served by a tall, blonde woman with excellent cheekbones, who caught me out when, after a very uncomfortable 20-minute grilling, she asked for my email address. 'Jenny Graham is @ hotmail dot co dot uk' I told her. She then looked me in the eye and without cracking a smile said, 'That is funny.'

The Mongolian Embassy was welcoming, laid-back and busy. After the initial shock of the embassy being in London and not Edinburgh, and taking an emergency flight down one morning to make the very specific opening times of Tuesday and Thursday, 1 to 3 p.m., I joined the queue that lined the street outside. There was only one man working from a tiny little office, behind a Perspex window with papers piled high all around him. Although 3 p.m. came and went, eventually it was my turn to stand at the desk to be welcomed by his smile.

When I told him I would be cycling there, he lost it with excitement. 'YOU'LL BE CYCLEEENG!' he proclaimed.

'Yes, I'm cycling around the world.'

He was so pleased I was visiting his country and assured me that I'd be welcome.

The Chinese Embassy was very official, professional and strict. It was the only embassy where I needed to book an appointment – and the only one that refused my request. I had all the information I needed, but there was something wrong with the way I'd filled in the forms. I panicked. I was running out of time, starting the ride in 10 days, so in desperation I called an agency, who charged a ridiculous amount of money to sort it out.

I had all three of the visas I needed so rationally I knew crossing the border shouldn't be an issue, but the closer I got to Terehova border control the more I spooked myself with all the reasons the Russians had to not let me in:

- My face – still sausage-like. Did I look enough like my passport picture?
- My invitation – I needed an official invitation into Russia from a resident, but it was a fairly slack system and you appeared to be able to buy them for £10 on the internet, which is what I had done. And which now felt a little dodgy.
- My accommodation – I'd need to prove where I was staying for the next couple of nights, so I'd booked a couple of Airbnbs with free cancellation policies, as I had no intention of staying in them. What if they knew that?

🎧 *I've just come through the Russian border, which is very exciting because I have built these border crossings up so much! I mean, people do them all the time. But I keep dramatising it, like they'll be looking for an excuse not to let me in, but actually it was really easy. I was there for about forty minutes and had to go through three different checkpoints and get everything signed off.*

I think the nerves come from not knowing the language and being conscious that if I get held up here, then it would have a massive impact on me. So, I was trying to be cool and calm to the guards, but obviously on the inside I was pretty much pleading with them to let me in!

I got through the first two gates all right and accidentally skipped the third one, which was the customs one, and had to go back and get that. And then you have to fill out the form about where you are going to stay and who your host is. I was sweating it on that, but anyway it was all fine.

They were lovely, really, like, they didn't really care. When I said I was Scottish, they were making fun of me about the football, which I laughed at more out of relief than actually caring what was going on with the World Cup.

So yeah, I'm chuffed about getting into Russia!

This was my fifth country in five days. Ticking off a country a day had been very satisfying, and the borders gave me great milestones and kept me focused mentally. However, that would be the last of the quick wins for a while, as I entered the humongous mass that is Russia, with Mongolia and China stretching out after that, those three countries together amounting to over 8000 km of riding.

Blue signs with Москва (Moscow) written in white writing, followed by its distance in kilometres, would become the most familiar sight on the road as it counted me down at regular intervals, starting at 620 km from the Russian border. Moscow was my first and last point of familiarity; Russia had another 6100 km for me to ride east, but all of it was a complete unknown. I was filled with curiosity to know what Asia would bring, but for now I was on one long very straight road, travelling east, Moscow-bound.

I'd pass by the odd little town and petrol station, but mostly this corridor cut through an extensive forested area, with very little variation until I got closer to the city. There were a lot of roadworks going on. New surfaces were being laid with an asphalt finish, and during the day the heat meant the tar wasn't drying off and remained quite sticky. Small pieces of stone kept melting on to my tyres. I'd have to lean down with a gloved hand and rest it on the wheel as it spun to knock all the chips off.

I quickly found myself in battles with the oncoming traffic – battles I could only lose. Lorries would pull out to avoid roadworks on their path and drive full speed towards me on the wrong side of the road. There was no recognition of my right of way and no indication that they might slow down. This wound me up at first, being forced into the verge, and I assumed it was just one or two crazy truck drivers – but I soon realised this was how it was going to be.

I'd hoped for accommodation this first night in Russia. I'd planned to stay indoors every third night if I could, but was currently on night 5. The thing I was craving most was a shower. I was covered in bites, mainly from mosquitoes, clegs (horseflies) and ants, and was beginning to feel quite worn down with it. I'd been able to have some sink washes in restaurants and service stations, which did help and would have to do, as by the time it got to 11 p.m. there was no sign of any accommodation and I was too tired to keep going, so I made my way off the road and into a small overgrown junction.

Day 6: 21 June 2018 • Navoloki to Shakhovskaya • 9 hours 4 minutes • 248 km • ODO: 1846.9 km • Motel

My morning routine so far had consisted of waking up after four or five hours' sleep, packing up camp and riding in the clothes I'd slept in until I found somewhere to stop for breakfast. I called them my PJs, but really they were my sleeping, travelling and spare layers for emergency, all in one: Lycra shorts, merino wool base layer, down slippers and hat.

I'd usually find a petrol station within the hour and they nearly all had seating areas, charging points and toilets so I could wash, change into riding kit and top up while having breakfast. That day, though, I lucked out with a hotel for breakfast. The coffee was black, sugary and instant and I had my first plate of blinis – buckwheat pancakes, served with melted butter. Both tasted delicious. I'd pointed to the pancakes by accident and didn't really know what I was ordering, but I'd spend the next four weeks trying to remember their name.

I was using a Russian translator app on my phone. The camera function could be swiped across a menu and an English translation would appear. However, I'd overlooked the small fact that I'd need the internet to use it. Sometimes I could log into the Wi-Fi, but loads of places didn't have it or didn't understand my request. That meant relying on 4G, but I hadn't yet managed to pick up a Russian SIM card (and never would).

I had a UK (GiffGaff) top-up SIM card rather than a billed contract to avoid huge costs on my return home, but I was now getting charged for receiving as well as sending messages. So my newly topped up credit would often disappear after a handful of well-meant messages had come through. Then I would be back to pointing at the menu and hoping for the best.

Russia continued to be the same on that one straight road, but I was pleased with my progress. I averaged 310 km per day that week, so when I passed a motel two hours earlier than I had planned to stop, on the outskirts of Moscow, I took it.

I made a cup of tea, took it into the shower with me and stood for ages letting the heat penetrate my bites. It was an intense feeling of pleasure and pain. I'd scratched some of the bites the night before in my bivvy bag and they had burst, leaving open blotches that had then filled up with dust on the road. It was unbelievably good to feel clean again.

Day 7: 22 June 2018 • Moscow to Nokpob • 11 hours 22 minutes • 248.5 km • ODO: 2095.4 km • Motel

I was riding on a five-lane carriageway when my rear wheel punctured. The lanes were stacked with morning traffic moving slowly towards Moscow. I walked on the hard shoulder for a couple of hundred metres, down to a petrol station, and with an ice-cold can of Coke I sat in the sunshine mending the hole and soaking up the busy industrial scene.

I had spent days counting down the kilometres into Moscow and the ride into the city didn't disappoint. Grand bronze and copper statues, turreted cathedrals and palaces with gold tops came into view, contrasted with Soviet blocks and dilapidated buildings, telling two very different stories. It felt a bit like being at an art exhibition where you are most definitely in awe of the work, but equally have limited knowledge of the deeper story being told.

For now, though, I had more prosaic thoughts at the front of my mind. Making decisions on mechanical spares to take with me had been a difficult task. With big miles expected and rural locations, it was easy to find a reason to fill my bag with every tool in the workshop.

So, if you don't know one end of a bike from another, here's where I explain that a bike is a brilliantly engineered feat of moving parts – and those parts can all snap, break or fall off. Some pieces would need replacing through wear and tear, others might survive the trip. I expected to change my tyres, chain, brake pads, drive chain and cables. Plus, I also tried to expect a whole load of things I couldn't yet imagine going wrong. Bike shops across the world would supply the big overhaul of parts, but I needed to be self-sufficient enough to keep rolling over big rural expanses.

To help me figure out what to take, I went through a process of whittling down. I started with a wish list – and didn't hold back. I just collected up everything, from every place in the shed, and if it remotely resembled a bike tool or bodging solution, I laid it out on the kitchen table. Large workshop tools too big to carry, obscure mounting bolts never ever used, chunky sets of Allen keys and a large selection of homemade tyre boots were quickly consigned to a corner of the kitchen. I was happy I could do without them.

Now I moved on to the realistic list. Looking at each item, I asked myself two questions: what was the likelihood of needing it and would not having it stop progress, or would I just have to ride a broken bike for a long time? That removed the full spare chain, chain whip, spare tyre and brake fluid. All were useful tools, sure, but I needed to think rationally.

Next, I moved on to the 'that'll have to do' list. This was when I went to pack my bags, certain that I couldn't possibly take any less, and realised it wouldn't all fit. That's when things became dialled down to *actual necessity*.

In the end, I narrowed it down to a fairly standard repair kit and just made sure each tool was high quality. I also mostly chose reliability over weight and was left with the following:

- A mini-track pump (for pumping tyres to high pressure with ease), which I'd wrapped in electrical and duct tape to save on space
- Tons of puncture repair kits (glue and patches)
- Tyre boots (an old piece of toothpaste tube that could act as a patch for a slash in the tyre)
- Two spare tubes
- Three heavy-duty tyre levers (to take the tyres off and put them on again)
- Four brake pads
- A cassette locking nut (to remove cassette)
- 4 mm and 5 mm Allen keys
- Mini pliers
- A multitool with chain break

- Two magic links for chain (single chain links)
- A small section of spare chain
- Chain lube
- A small rag to clean chain
- 10 large zip ties
- A couple of bolts
- Four spokes
- Mech hanger (an attachment designed to limit damage; placed between your chain and frame, it should brake or bend before your frame does)
- Spare dynamo (pedal-powered charging device), hub connectors and wires
- One gear cable
- Sugru™ (mouldable glue)
- Spoke key (to repair a buckle in the wheel)
- Heavy-duty sewing kit

There was one more thing to consider. Punctures were the most likely and common repair I'd have to make on the road, so the question 'To tube or not to tube?' was a big one. To tube, the classic option, is to insert an inner tube made of latex or a synthetic rubber inside your tyre and inflate it with air. The downside to this is that they can puncture easily when foreign bodies from the road enter the tyre. The inner tube then needs to be repaired or replaced. To go tubeless, on the other hand, is to use a pneumatic system that replaces the tube with a latex solution. When a hole is created in the outer tyre, the solution is forced into it and congeals almost instantly, creating a plug. No repair required. The hole may sometimes be too big for the sealant, so you can carry little fibrous sticks of rubber-coated cord that can help with the plugging process, but usually it's a much smoother and faster system.

All tyres can run with tubes, but you need a 'tubeless-ready' tyre to run with the solution. The difference comes from the beading systems that lock on to the rim more snuggly, creating a tighter seal. At the time, there was a limited choice of tubeless tyres that catered for my very specific Round the World needs: durability plus good rolling resistance. The rolling resistance is the amount of drag created between your tyre and the riding surface. I was looking for that perfect combination of having enough grip on the road and a smooth tread to minimise friction.

I used training rides to try out all the tubeless-ready road tyres I could find. I monitored how many kilometres they would give me before failing, which was typically between 1600 and 2400 km. This was a lot less than I'd get from a tubed tyre because of the type of rubber used. A tubeless tyre needs to be made with more lightweight material, so that the side walls can be air-penetrated in the absence of the inner tube. I needed tyres that could manage at least double that distance, so I hesitantly went with a tube set-up. The Continental 4000 was the most reliable I tested: it felt good, had just the right amount of grip and lasted well.

The decision not to take a spare tyre with me was a difficult one, but I'd opted for the lighter option of a sewing kit that I could use to make a repair on a burst sidewall. The reality of how big a deal a tyre blowout would be for me when riding through a remote section (as I was about to do) hit me after my first puncture.

At least in this instance I was near civilisation. Crossing the Borodinsky Bridge, I detoured along the river and found myself at an extremely cool, hipster bike shop on one of the city's back streets. It was brilliant and well stocked. I bought my replacement tyre of choice: a Continental 4000.

The late afternoon ride out of Moscow was a little more chaotic than the morning traffic. I was sandwiched between thousands of vehicles and that continued into the late summer night. The hard shoulder was a huge dirt track filled with cars undertaking the main flow, creating seven lanes at some points. The good news was that the sheer volume of traffic made the speeds they travelled more manageable for me. A dusty sunset cast a beautiful light on this surreal motorway scene. I rode for another five hours, covering a little over 100 km, until 2 a.m. while the roads remained congested. I found 24-hour accommodation at Nokpob.

I carried my bike up the 10 steps into the reception and found a woman asleep at her desk. Gently, I woke her up. Waving at her, I smiled and nervously said, 'Krovat', meaning bed. She looked at me puzzled, so I said it again, this time more slowly and a bit louder, pointing at myself: 'Me K-R-O-V-A-T.' It was the correct word, but obviously the wrong pronunciation and in a strong Scottish accent. The woman was still perplexed and was now talking at me quickly in Russian. I panicked and leaped into a game of charades, making a pillow gesture with my hands and resting my head on them. It worked.

I was shown to a room across the hallway and wheeled my bike into a three-bedded room with wooden clad walls, and a massive pink curtain and pelmet covering the window. I was delighted to get a quiet space to lie down away from the chaos of the streets.

Day 8: 23 June 2018 • Pokrov to Dzerzhinsk • 13 hours 22 minutes • 320.88 km • ODO: 2416.28 km • Motel

I'd hoped that it was just city traffic I had encountered, but the next day the Trans-Siberian Highway was relentless, mostly with trucks. Massive convoys of them passed in both directions, 10, 20, 30 at a time, all nose to tail with one another. Throughout the day, the safety of the hard shoulder became less reliable as it narrowed from the width of a car to barely as wide as my handle bars. There was just enough room to ride in it as long as the trucks kept to their own carriageway and didn't cross over the white line separating the two.

This wasn't always the case. They hugged that line so tight that I'd hold my breath as they hammered past me, just millimetres from my arm. Some lorries drove so fast that they would create a speed wobble and I'd watch their back end swerve over the line – it would have been enough to take me out, had I been just 10 seconds faster. I'd even pass some that hadn't been able to hold their speed and had overturned. They now laid across the space that I would have been occupying, had we been there at the same time. It was terrifying. Sometimes the shoulder disappeared completely and I was just on the road. None of these drivers expected to see me there and even when they did see me, they didn't know what to do about me.

I'd hear a loud blast behind me and I'd jump off the road into the gravel, bushes or whatever happened to be there. Seconds later, the swoosh of a lorry would go by. There was no way they could stop or slow down because they drove so close to one another. I was tense the whole time. It was taking my full concentration to keep making the correct decisions. I'd stop every couple of hours to drink some water and to give my head a rest from the relentless near misses. Right then, I had no idea how long it would last. There was another 5919 km of Russia left. Surely it couldn't be like this the whole way?

When I pulled into garages or cafés, people were lovely, smiling, the drivers speaking to me in all sorts of languages and laughing in a kind way. It was welcoming and they were warm people, but as soon as they were behind their steering wheels, all connection and compassion disappeared. There was a clear hierarchy on the road. This is true in most parts of the world: getting into a vehicle closes you off from the physical environment and comes with an element of entitlement to the road. I'd never felt it to such an extent before, though.

As the least important person on the road, I was the pawn that could be sacrificed at any moment. Adding to the heaviness of the day were the regular memorials to people who had lost their lives on the highway: steering wheels, bumpers and number plates were decorated in flowers, pictures and teddy bears. Death on that road wasn't just accepted, it was expected.

Day 9: 24 June 2018 • Dzerzhinsk to Cheboksary ring road • Approx. 12 hours • 235.8 km • ODO: 2652.08 km • Motel

Breakfast at the motel wouldn't be served for another 20 minutes, but despite waking up hungry, I decided not to wait and cycled away with no food.

I had stopped for five hours the day before, so I was keen to stay focused and squeeze some more bike time into my day. There had been plenty of food stops until this point, so I was sure this wouldn't be an issue, but it was a further 50 km until I found a petrol station. I bought a hot savoury pastry, two yogurt drinks, and bottles of fresh orange and fizzy water that I mixed together. Then I sat out in the forecourt, looking over at the trucks that were parked at the pumps and wondered where the hell they were all going.

In the afternoon the road became a series of gradual and steady undulations. At the lowest point, the side would narrow, with no hard shoulder and a barrier on either side, meaning there would be nowhere for me to bail to if the convoys came. I had to time these sections, checking behind me first. I'd sprint down the hill and as far up the other side as I could until the road rewidened, where I'd relax into a normal pace. And then I'd do it all again.

Late in the afternoon I had another stream of close calls that ended with me leaping from the road on to a gravelly track and falling with the bike still attached to my feet. Feeling pretty stupid, I picked myself up and walked along the gravel track for a kilometre until I reached a roadside café. I walked through the door and burst out crying when the woman behind the counter smiled at me. She and another guy were trying desperately to communicate with me and all I could do was say, 'I'm fine, I'm fine,' as the tears streamed down my dusty face. A bag of gingerbread buns appeared along with a cup of tea and a pat on the back. I felt bad meeting them like that, but was so grateful for their warmth. I took my tea and buns outside, and sat on the ground, resting against the café wall, watching the traffic go by.

I'd cycled 518 km since Moscow, but wasn't sure I could – or should – keep going on this road. I began thinking about rerouting to avoid any more near misses, but I was slap-bang in the middle of a big highway. It was going to be a mammoth task to calculate the distances and navigate on smaller roads, and that was assuming they were actually tarmacked, but I couldn't get any 4G signal to take a proper look. No, I'd need to stick with this awful plan – but something would have to give.

After a half-hour stop and rest, I got myself together and started off again, riding into the evening. Things began feeling much calmer by the time the sun was going down. I had my head up, looking around at the gorgeous horizon, and it actually felt peaceful. Maybe I just needed to be on the road more during the night.

There was a definite decrease in traffic at night. The vehicles had their lights on, so it made it easier to see them coming from behind as they lit up the road. I had mine on too – two flashing and one solid beam at the rear made me way more visible.

Over the last couple of years I'd discovered a love for riding through the night. It started during a self-supported, bikepacking challenge in my local mountains, the Cairngorms. I'd found myself in a remote area during a snowstorm as night fell. I was too cold for it to be appealing to lie down and try to sleep, so I just kept going until the sun came up and I reached the village of Blair Atholl. I'd never done that alone before. The urge to stop, get safe and close my eyes had always overruled my ability to keep going, but now, once I pushed through that first night, it was as if I'd discovered a secret, like I was riding through the stolen hours.

When planning for Round the World, though, I gave myself a rule. I'd even written it down: 'Don't ride all through the night in the first few weeks.' Now, here I was on Day 9, just 2500 kilometres into a 29,000-kilometre challenge, and that was the master plan!

I was confident that it would get me out of the immediate nightmare, but I was worried about the impact it would have on me for the rest of the trip. Would I lose too much time readjusting my body's sleep pattern? Would I get a proper rest through the day? I was relying on finding accommodation that would be willing to take me in at 7 a.m. And was it even what other Round the World riders would do? I thought back to conversations I'd had with my coach John on the lead up to the trip. I'd often berate myself for feeling like 'my way' of training wasn't the same as other (successful) athletes. I would postpone the session for so long that I'd end up doing many of them late at night or in ridiculously bad weather as I'd miss the dry spell. But John always brought things back around and reminded me that this was 'my ride' and doing things 'my way' seemed to be working out okay so far.

I knew it was way past John's bedtime at home, so when I found a 4G signal, I messaged my pal Emma, who would still be up. It was funny I chose Em, because although she is one of my most favourite people on the planet, she knows little to nothing about endurance riding.

We'd met 10 years before working together in Children's Services, and bonded over our love for pick 'n' mix and belly laughs. We've been inseparable ever since. She'd kept me grounded throughout the year of intense training, and kept me going with the normal life chat, sharing funny memes and recounting old stories. We talked about the 'World', but often I was so exhausted from living, breathing and thinking about it all day and every day that I appreciated having a tiny space free from it all.

I let her know the night cycling plan by text, not to receive any advice but just to say it out loud. It helped. I signed off: 'Right, I'm gonna go, but whatever I do, I'll be safe 😊. No.1 – come home safe. No.2 – cycle around the world. No.3 – break the record. #priorities 🖤 xoxoxox.' Emma replied: 'Fking love those priorities!'

It's interesting looking at the order I wrote them down in. I'm not sure breaking the record had ever consciously been at No. 1. Or perhaps I'd just taken coming home safe as a given up to that point, but with those priorities well etched in my mind, riding through the night had to be worth a shot.

🎧 *It's Monday morning about 3 a.m. after that horrendous day I had yesterday when I kept getting run off the road. So, I decided, 'Let's just ride at night, it'll be nice and I won't spend so much time in ditches.' The best bit about Russia for me has been the sunset because things are getting quieter, it comes alive. It's so pretty, not very dark and not covered in trucks. But now I get to see the sun rise too – how amazing is that? I'm well chuffed. Yeah, I think I'm onto a winner. And I ride really well at night anyway, so it'll actually be nicer and safer and it's going to be way more fun – and that's important because it needs to be FUN too!*

I found a bed in a motel on the outskirts of Cheboksary sometime around 6 a.m. The receptionist, although not sharing a language with me, was noticeably friendly when I walked through the door, her short curly blonde hair perched on top of her head. She wore a tight blue skirt suit and killer stiletto heels, which made her walk with purpose. I was impressed that she could walk so well in them, particularly, for some reason, because it was that time in the morning.

It was the first location I had stayed at that wouldn't let me take my bike into the room with me. I felt really nervous about leaving her, but the car park compound was my only option. There were two guards controlling the gates who didn't speak English, but signed to me that they would keep an eye on her. It was horrible at first, but the lure of a bed soon took over.

Day 10: 25 June 2018 • Cheboksary ring road to Mamadysh • 14 hours 30 minutes • 321 km • ODO: 2973.08 km • Motel

I thought that I should be able to ride for four nights before it would really start affecting my efficiency and recovery time. I based this on friends who worked on night shifts and remembered that they would often do so in blocks of four, so it seemed reasonable enough to me. Now the first one was done, I had three left, which I estimated would take me to the city of Perm, 1000 km away. From there I could reassess the situation.

I would try to find a bed sometime between 6 and 8 a.m. each morning and get back on the road between 2 and 3 p.m. There were still a couple of hours in the afternoon that would be busy, but I'd be fresh from sleep and could stay alert knowing that I had a quiet night ahead. It was midsummer now and my location was quite far north, almost on the same latitude as my home in Inverness, so there was darkness for only a couple of hours, between around 11.30 p.m. and 2 a.m., with hours of twilight either side of that. Really this was the perfect time of the year to be riding at night, because there was some visual stimulation to help me stay awake.

This had been the part of the world I was most worried about in terms of resupplies, but I needn't have been. The volume of long-distance traffic meant there had been a constant supply of roadside services, all 24-hour. The hotels charged in four-hour blocks and drivers could get off the road at any point, so they didn't mind me arriving to sleep as the world was waking up. There were also restaurants serving home-made hot food. I preferred to stay out of these restaurants during the night. I felt safe enough riding alone. I was just a figure appearing, then disappearing between the moving vehicles, but I didn't want to draw attention to myself going into establishments where people were more likely to notice I was on my own. I did occasionally call in to a petrol station, but didn't hang around. In the morning before I slept, I'd eat plates full of pre-chopped vegetables, individual bowls with grated carrot, tomato and cucumber, cheese and lettuce that sat covered in chilled cabinets. Then when I woke again, I'd fill up on a rice and meat dish. The fresh food was such a treat and a change from the packaged food from the service stations.

• • •

The Russian traffic police had been scattered across the country, stationed fairly regularly every 150 km or so, pulling over lorries and cars to check documents at any time of the day or night. I'd initially been a bit nervous of them, but they barely even noticed me, so I soon became pretty blasé about passing by them.

It was early evening on a quiet section of road. I was sitting up, riding no hands, and eating from my food pouch. The sun was shining on my back and music was coming from my headphones when a guard signalled me to pull me over. Oh no.

There were two of them: one lad with short dark hair and brown eyes, and a taller, lighter-haired man who would do all the communicating. I could smell their aftershave as soon as I got close to them. They seemed so clean. I'd been riding for only two weeks, but I felt feral in comparison. I was waiting for a fine of some kind, but instead I was offered tea. They had a Portakabin and the blond man put the kettle on.

We didn't share a language, so instead we both spoke in our own, just a little louder than normal, and used lots of hand signals. He pointed to my knees, which were all cut from constantly jumping into the verge, so I stood up and gave them a run through of the truck scenario from the day before. Things like 'Beep' and 'Argggh' are universal and go a long way towards setting the tone of a story.

Then the blond guy began warning me about thieves and to be careful (I think). When he did his impersonation of a robber running out the door on tiptoes with a pretend swag bag over his shoulder, I lost it. It was so funny.

He put his number in my phone, followed by *Nee-Naw, Nee-Naw* and his finger swirling in a circle.

I asked them for a picture before I left and they reached for their gigantic visor hats and truncheons. They instantly wiped all the smiles from their faces and stood perfectly straight for the camera.

🎧 *Managed great distance through the night – 321 km! Found a hotel this morning, but had to walk across a flyway to reach it on the other side of the road. It was a pain lifting my bike all the way up. Then they made me leave it in an unlocked shed again at the back of the hotel. I was really concerned and locked it up with my mini padlock, but the staff were oblivious to bikes being stolen. Had a restaurant too, so ate pasta and salad with tea. Tired!*

Days 12 and 13: 27–28 June 2018 • Yakshur to Aynt via Shadeyka • 21 hours • 451.3 km • ODO: 3699.49 km • Hotel and bus stop

It was 4.30 a.m. and I'd been riding since 3 p.m. the previous day. Ideally, I'd be hoping to finish around this time because, although I loved the nightime riding, I would get a little lull in energy in the early hours. You might think I'd be in awe at the sun coming up, but it was more a case of 'ah, I've not even been to bed yet and now the sun's coming up!'

It was already 24°C, although I had just cycled through this dip and it had gone down to 10°C. I was riding in the fog past some hay bales in a field and it was absolutely gorgeous, not what I expected Russia to look like at all. It had been rolling hills today, which I liked, because it gave me something to get my teeth into, but I had a bit of a sore knee on my right side. My saddle kept slipping, so I thought it might be that. I was really paranoid about getting an injury. My right knee and left Achilles were a little twingey, but I was 3249 km in to the Round the World ride. That was 2000 miles! Whoop whoop!

What's more, I'd covered 1200 km riding through the past four nights. Despite the change from days to nights feeling seamless, it was now taking its toll as my body and mind battled against natural rhythms. I'd been struggling to stay awake through the night and had crazy indigestion after most meals.

I was looking forward to getting a hotel in Perm, sleeping a little longer than normal and then beginning to gradually shift back to riding days. I hadn't banked on the ring road around the city being so busy when I arrived at 6 a.m. Commuters filled the four-lane carriageways.

My planned detour into the centre to find accommodation would use up too much time in this traffic, so I just kept riding, assuming there would be something in the suburbs, but just as I was leaving the ring road, I hit some major roadworks, which diverted me on to country lanes, far from anything.

It was midday and I'd been awake for 23 hours by the time I rolled into the rural settlement of Shadeyka. The roadside stop had a dusty car park that was filled with trucks and lined with a choice of places providing basic food, drinks and accommodation. I peered into a café bar. The Mediterranean colours and dim lighting were just the vibe I needed to hide from the bright midday sun.

There was a sign for beds pointing upstairs, so I ate, slept and ate some more before leaving at 8 p.m. Most places I stayed were basic accommodation. Clean and cheap, perfect for my budget. The only downside was that everyone made me leave my bike either at reception or in a shed at the back of the building. I'd plead with them to let me take her to my room with me, but the answer was always a definitive no. I'd become used to it, but still locked up the back wheel to the frame and then on to any piece of furniture I could. It was just a tiny combination lock that could be cut through very easily, but if nothing else at least the staff might notice a small commotion. Watching me, the hotel staff were always bewildered. One man told me in broken English that no one would want to steal it, because they'd have to ride it – and then he laughed.

There were major advantages to staying indoors. As well as a more restful sleep, I had access to a shower. I'd find a sink to wash in most days, but a full body and hair wash in this hot and dusty climate were welcome and helped me keep on top of the saddle sores that were developing.

Saddle sores are an abrasion created from friction between the delicate skin on your undercarriage and your clothing. They develop on a scale of seriousness, from a red dimply rash right up to nasty abscesses. Most cyclists will be familiar with them and, because I was wearing my cycling shorts for many hours a day and was not always able to wash them well, I was also at high risk of picking up a bacterial infection that would exacerbate the problem. To manage the situation, I'd use a mix (not at the same time) of Sudocrem (to create a thick barrier between my skin and shorts) and also to sooth sores while I was sleeping and bib free, and talcum powder (to dry the area out if it became too damp). The two were meant to counterbalance each other.

I would wash my bibs daily, either in a sink or with water from my bottle, and leave them hanging off my saddle bag or tribars as I was riding. This was the only item of clothing I had brought two of and I very nearly removed the spare pair when I was repacking in Berlin. Now, I was so grateful that I hadn't.

●　●　●

The right saddle can make a huge difference to your comfort on the bike, but finding a companion for your bottom to spend thousands of hours on is no easy task. I had been looking for the perfect perch for the last 15 years to no avail. I'd find saddles that were comfortable for a few hours at a time, but in reality I had just become good at being uncomfortable.

The advice you mostly get is that everyone's fit is individual and you just have to try them out for yourself. This is true, but isn't very helpful. There seemed to be a lack of discussion around the basics of female anatomy and the alignment of specific saddle designs, although it's worth mentioning there have been great advances and recognition of the issues, even in the short time between riding the world and writing this book.

I'm sure it's not a gender-specific issue, but taking into account the amount of soft tissue women have and the historic lack of industry research into woman-specific saddle solutions, it didn't take long before I felt I'd need to tap into some black magic to get this one right.

I went through at least eight saddles in the nine months lead-up to Round the World. Some were bought, some borrowed. I visited a lot of shops and trawled a lot of blogs for any glimmer of useful information. Some brands offer your money back within 30 days if you return it 'like new'. These schemes are great for other people I imagine, but I can barely leave the shop with it 'as new'. If there's a wall to scrape it along or a dent to be put in it, it's guaranteed I'll have it done by the time I get home, so the collection of reject saddles began to mount.

I tried out a saddle fitting service at a well-known cycle chain store (that shouldn't be named). The shop floor was busy with male staff and customers. I sat in the corner on a bean bag device to measure the width of my sit bones. When the assistant saw the results he shouted across the shop to his colleague, 'She's the widest size. Can we get the widest saddle possible?' I'm generally pretty good at laughing off embarrassing situations, but in that moment it was clear to me why so many women I knew were riding uncomfortable saddles.

I had a breakthrough when I tried out my friend Penny Phillip's time trial bike. A TT saddle is a funny-looking contraption with the nose completely cut off and two padded prongs coming out from the widest part of the seat. It's designed to work best when the rider is in an aerodynamic position with the pelvic bone rotated forward, so when I leaned forward on to my tribars I had never been so comfortable on a bike. With no nose to cause friction or the dreaded 'flap mash'.

During Round the World I would need a variety of positions on the saddle to minimise injury and to keep me pedalling for as long as possible. The TT design didn't give me that, but it was a good start to narrowing down the selection.

I then came across a company in England that provided a saddle library service in association with Selle SMP saddles. This was perfect for my klutz tendencies as the saddles weren't new and wouldn't need to be returned as new either. After the bike shop assistant's not-so-subtle assessment, I ordered the widest option they had, with a dropped nose to simulate the TT design. They sent me the Selle SMP Pro model. I used it on a week-long trip with the Adventure Syndicate when we rode for 100 miles a day between Bristol and the Pyrenees. It was a great success and unbelievably comfortable.

When I returned from the trip (five weeks to go until Round the World) I was keen to order one ASAP. They were so expensive, though, that I held off as Fiola who worked at Komoot said she could give me a slimmer, narrower and firmer model that she no longer used.

Fiola kindly sent the saddle. I rode it for a week and decided not only that it wasn't as comfortable as the Pro, but spending a couple of hundred pounds on such an integral component should have been a given in the build-up to cycling Round the World.

Despite starting my saddle search nine months previously, I didn't receive my saddle of choice until I was almost three weeks out from the start. The delay didn't worry me, though, as I had complete faith in my choice. The thing I failed to take into account was that the saddle I had used in the Pyrenees had been broken in by the many bums that had sat on it. My fresh new leather saddle had not. And it would take me until I reached Australia until I felt truly bedded into it… Classic error.

• • •

It was around 8 p.m. The roadside café felt different now. It was busy. People were milling about, drinking. There was music playing. A Spanish man approached and in broken English asked if he could cycle with me. This was surprising, because I hadn't met any other cyclist on the road since Berlin. Part of me wanted him to, just for fun, but the other part judged him by his loose clothing, open-toed sandals and windswept, long, wavy hair. Although he looked like a great craic, he also looked like he wasn't in a hurry to get anywhere. After this morning's blunder of staying up so long and now sleeping for the rest of the day, I planned to ride one more full night before beginning the readjustment to days, hopefully without losing too much ride time. We worked out with our fingers that I'd be riding twice the distance he would tonight, so we exchanged names and he waved me off.

This wouldn't be the last I saw of Roma. He turned up twice in the next week, each time appearing from parked lorries at the side of the road, the drivers of which he had persuaded to give him and his bike a lift. He'd come running towards me, excitedly waving his arms in the air and shouting at me. There would be a couple of days in between seeing him, so I was always startled that someone was *that* excited to see me. At one point as he galloped towards me I thought it must be my mum, because of the level of enthusiasm he was showing, but for now, as the sun faded, he just shouted after me, 'Goodbyeee, Jenny!' I'd soon miss those safe, feel-good vibes.

🎧 *I've not really had a lot of hassle from men until now, but tonight this guy driving a massive articulated lorry with a Kyrgyzstan number plate wouldn't leave me alone. He kept leapfrogging me, driving alongside me when he could and leaning out the window, laughing and signalling for me to get into the truck. It felt pretty intimidating, because it was 2 a.m. I kept shooing him away and telling him no.*

He then drove about 10 minutes ahead and got out of his van as I was riding towards him. It was on a fairly lonely stretch of road, so I wasn't going to hang about, but as he walked towards me he pulled a lighter from his pocket, which made me jump, then lit a cigarette, before writing 500 in the dirt with his finger. I think he was trying to tell me in the most menacing way that there was 500 km to Yumer, the next big city, and that I should take his offer of a lift. I declined, rather abruptly, and rode off up a dirt track that would be too small for his truck to get down. I waited until I saw the lights disappear.

I sat in a bus shelter until some drunk teenagers turned up. It was bizarre – all this on such a lonely stretch of road. I carried on riding until I couldn't keep my eyes open and it all became too much. I slept in a bus stop north of Aynt for three hours. Pretty tired.

Day 14: 29 June 2018 • Aynt to Beloyarsky • 12 hours 45 minutes • 277.68 km • ODO: 3927.17 km • Hostel

I pulled into a petrol station around 8 a.m. My head felt cloudy this morning and my systems were a mess, with clothes hanging off them and layers stuffed in the wrong places. I had wrappers in all my food bags and none of my electricals were where they should be. In order to refocus, I went through a sort of primitive grooming ritual – for myself and for my bike.

I changed into fresh bibs and applied a slathering of Sudocrem to help with the saddle sores. I sink-washed my body and face, and applied sun cream for some moisture. I brushed my teeth extensively, then finger-combed (as I had no brush) my hair before replaiting it.

I pulled everything out on to the pavement of the garage forecourt and repacked in an orderly way – the way I had planned for it to be.

All the sleeping equipment was compressed to the very bottom of my saddle bag. I binned all the empty wrappers, got my cables where they needed to be, and refilled with snacks and drinks. Keeping on top of hydration was always difficult. I carried three water bottles on the bike, one in the frame and two under the tribars. Regardless of how cold the water was when I filled my bottles, it soon warmed up and drinking litres of lukewarm water from plastic bottles is unappealing. The only thing that makes it more palatable is to add some flavour or change the texture. I'd pick up carbonated water whenever possible, then mix it with a still fruit juice. Up until now I'd managed to buy hydration tablets from petrol stations too. These were my favourite with fizzy water and I also bought a tiny, highly concentrated orange juice tub for diluting. This gave me plenty of options for flavours.

The coffee tasted pretty weak from the petrol station machines, and I'd need more and more of it to get me going in the morning. I began adding an extra shot of espresso to the cappuccinos, which really helped, although I could find myself too wired if I wasn't careful.

🎧 *After a hard start to the day, I kept cycling through until about three o'clock this morning. It was raining, a proper thunderstorm, so rather than bivvying I continued on to this little village and found a hostel. I couldn't see anyone in it, so I went upstairs and saw there was a room open. I lay on the bed. About 20 minutes later I could hear a bit of a kerfuffle and the next minute the light was on in my room and this really angry woman appeared. She'd just come in to show some other people the bed and I was lying there like Goldilocks. She was raging, but paying her helped.*

Then two people had come in – it must have been nearly 4 a.m. by that point – a young kid about eight years old and a man; I think he was male but couldn't be sure. I could hear them shuffling about. I kept drifting in and out of sleep. One of them went for a shower, they were talking quite loudly. I was thinking, 'Aww, shut up!' I looked up to go and put the light off, but had made eye contact with the guy, who said 'Oh, hi. I'm so-and-so,' and I said 'Hi, I'm Jenny,' but I was just so zonked out, I put the light off. I don't know how long I was sleeping for, but he woke me up with this Google Translate in my face, either offering sex or asking for sex. I don't know which, but there was going to be a hundred roubles involved.

I sat up with my crinkled, puffed-up head and pointed at where the man should be and shouted, 'Get to your bed!' It was all I had. My body lay exhausted. I weighed up the situation and whether I was in danger. The urge to sleep was so strong that I continued drifting in and out of it, hearing phone calls, loud conversations, rustling of bags, lights on and off.

When 8 a.m. came I was up and out. The café downstairs supplied my traditional breakfast of sugary coffee and a meat pastry I later worked out was called a *chebureki*. It was a bit like a flattened Cornish pasty that had been deep fried and then left out to cool. Before serving it would be reheated in a thin plastic bag in the microwave, which meant it always arrived soggy. I was never aiming to get a *chebureki* when I ordered. Instead, I was hoping for a plate of the sweet pancakes I'd ordered by accident on Day 1 in Russia, but it was the meat pastry that people most liked to bring me. Before I set out on this trip, I'd had a romantic image of learning Russian on the move and even downloaded a phrase book. Hilarious! I barely had enough energy to string a sentence together in English, let alone learn a whole new language. However, I'd nailed the Russian for 'coffee', which was thankfully pretty easy even for me: *k-waffi*. Even if it was black, sugary instant coffee, I felt a comfort from it.

As I was leaving, I saw the family from the night before. I locked eyes with the grown-up, who looked sheepish at first, but soon gave a hearty wave and smiled over. I felt a bit sad about the whole thing. Who were these people and what was going on in their lives for them to arrive in the middle of the night, perhaps desperate for money? With a child to take care of? Surely they had to have been high on drugs, as it was such peculiar behaviour.

I couldn't help but compare our lives that morning. I had a day full of opportunities to thrive, a privilege that can only be tapped into once surviving is a given. I had a constant stream of messages flowing through my digital world, assuring me that I was courageous, brave and just an all-round awesome human being. Those words of encouragement from my family, friends and now complete strangers who were following my journey gave me a strong sense of belonging and complete trust in those who supported me from afar.

I sat uncomfortably aware of my own comfort and the support of others, and I wondered who was messaging this family to tell them how strong they were for keeping going, and to remind them to love and respect themselves. Of course, I had no idea how empowered or connected these people felt or what the actual situation was, but I did know that while I rode a bike with a total rig costing over £6000, these people were selling their bodies for less than £1. It was a stark reminder of my privilege.

Day 15: 30 June 2018 • Beloyarsky to Borovskiy • 11 hours 45 minutes • 267 km • ODO: 4194.17 km • Back of a bus shelter

Riding past a sign that read 'The Jewel of Siberia' was one of those OMG moments. I was actually in Siberia! The only reference point I had to this place was from back in the day when German techno band Scooter remixed Supertramp's No.1 hit 'The Logical Song'. I was in my early twenties and, having worked my way through both the grunge and indie years, I could have danced and sung all night long to some happy hard core. The song – and Scooter's lyrics proclaiming that the place to be was, in fact, Siberia – rang through my head and I smiled at the image of 20-year-old me dancing about like a loony.

I wondered what she would have thought of me now, 20 years on and cruising through Siberia on a world tour. To be fair, she would probably have been right up for it, always gunning for an adventure and looking for ways to push boundaries; she just hadn't been exposed to this world yet. I sent a quick video message home to Lachlan as the sun set behind the sign, reciting the lyrics that had made me smile.

The volume of traffic had become way more manageable over the last couple of days. I knew that it was still a main road and that came with risks, but the impending sense of doom had gone and I was now enjoying my surroundings again. It took a few hours to drop down into the city of Tyumen. With over half a million people living here, there was an impressive array of lights, but one in particular caught my eye: an intense, bright orange ball on the skyline. It sat just above the horizon and, although it was much bigger than the other lights, my perspective suggested that it belonged there. That had to be a billboard, surely? It was mesmerising and I looked about for something similar. Then, scanning the sky for the moon, it slowly dawned on me: it *was* the moon. A gigantic, orange blood moon was rising up into the sky behind the silhouette of the city. WOW! It stopped me in my tracks as I stared, transfixed by the sheer magnitude of its natural wonder. I tried to take a picture, but my £100 Motorola phone's 'moon function' wasn't up to much, so I just stared and ingested the magic. The night sky was becoming a constant companion on the road. This wasn't the first or the last occasion I'd spend time gazing up at it, feeling completely connected to my environment.

I skirted around the huge city, hoping to find some food, but the ring road had nothing to offer. The last thing I needed was to get gobbled up in the vacuum of time that was city life, so I continued on the now dark and empty dual carriageway, leaving the city behind me.

Eventually, at about 11.30 p.m., I saw a dimly lit motel-type building just off the street. I made my way through the dingy reception and followed the noise of a television. A man stood smoking at the bar. He was short, round, with greasy slicked-back hair, and it looked like he would be my chef for the evening. I always tried to order food that I felt had the best chance of avoiding contamination – something fried is always a good shout, as the hot fat is going to kill all the germs that could be breeding in the kitchen.

I ate and had a coffee, but while I was tired and keen to get somewhere to sleep, this was too early to stop. I went to pay and the man started gesturing that I should stay. He told me a terrifying-sounding story using Google Translate and a mime about wolves that apparently liked to kill female bike riders. It seemed fairly specific, but after the long-winded, animated story I thought perhaps I should just get a bed and hope that it would reset my body clock. I'd lose a couple of hours of ride time today, but I could get five hours' sleep and be back on the bike for 6 a.m.

I went to pay – and my card wouldn't go through. And I had used all my cash up at my last stop. Kicking myself, I started trying to set up an internet bank transfer for £3.50 with the limited Wi-Fi connection. The man was very chilled out about the whole thing, but I was watching all of today's progress slip away and it was frustrating.

At some point during dinner, one of his Google Translate messages had insinuated that I should come to his bed with him. I laughed out loud – must be a mistake! A mix-up in the translation. I mean, that's a weird thing to ask. Now, sitting here trying to make this tiny transfer between my bank and his, I received another suggestion of the same variety. Ah. This *wasn't* a Google issue. He took the definite rejection well, barely even acknowledging it. I asked him for his bank details again in case I'd made a mistake. He took my phone to put them in, but instead he dialled his own number and saved it as 'Alke'. Great. Just what I needed!

Clearly I now had to get out of this situation, but another hour passed and I still hadn't resolved my banking issue. I wanted to cycle away, but he had fed me and I owed him the money. Eventually, idiotically late, I remembered the dollars stashed in my handlebar tubes for this very situation. The smallest note was $50, but I wasn't going to hang around for change. I paid for dinner and bed just in time for Alke to inform me that I couldn't take my bike to my room. There had already been so many hold-ups here, and what if he started being a nuisance and wouldn't give it back to me?

By this point Alke's woman friend was part of the scene. She was an angry-faced Russian woman, with deep wrinkles and gaunt cheekbones. Without any exaggeration, I can say that she looked like she wanted me dead. She stared at me, long and hard, and I could only guess that Alke was her partner. Since he seemed to be mixed up in some bizarre interaction with me, I was getting the brunt of her coldness. I just wanted to sleep.

I was standing with my bike, about to submit to the no-bike rule and take my bag off for the night, when my new admirer hit me with another 'come to bed' translation that I didn't spend too long trying to work out. I packed my bike and escaped into the dark night. It was past 2 a.m. The sun would soon begin to come up and I still hadn't slept. To say I was stressed out by the poor decisions of the evening would be an understatement.

🎧 *I was just raging with myself, raging with him. I needed to get to bed. There was nowhere open, so I rode out of town and then saw this shelter. I looked round the back and there was this ledge, and a ditch I could put my bike in, so it was out of sight as well as me. I did that and lay down, turned around on my side. There was this little slit just underneath the bus shelter, so I lay facing towards looking across the road, and all I could see for miles was the sunrise coming up over the horizon. Behind this little bus shelter I just had the best view ever of the sunrise.*

After a few hours' sleep, I thankfully had a settled morning on the bike. The sun was shining brightly. Mid-Russia was as flat as the eye could see, and would remain this way for the next 600 km: to my right lay Kazakhstan, whose border I would come within 100 km of, and to my left lay the great expanse of Russia. It has 17 million km² of land, over 200 times larger than my homeland of Scotland. I had heard these figures before and I knew that it was by far the largest country in the world, but still I would look around in surprise and shake my head. Bloody hell, this place was huge – and such a mixed bag. I was still fighting to ride 15 hours a day on relatively easy terrain, while the culture continued to be both an inspiration and a challenge.

Day 17: 2 July 2018 • Abatskiy to Omsk • 13 hours 11 minutes • 309.9 km • ODO: 4835.57 km • Motel

🎧 *I came through Omsk at one in the morning and there were all these mental stray dogs, gangs of them hanging out at bus stops. They were just looking for food and scavenging about. Any time you went past they would give you such a chase, so you had to be properly giving it some welly going past them. This one corner I turned, I was going pretty slow and the dog clocked me – there was a split second when I was like 'Dog!' and he was like 'Leg!' He barked and put the chase on and there was no way I was going to accelerate in time. He was big, a decent-sized dog, but I had been eating a cereal bar and I just managed to get it and chuck it at him and I think I shouted 'Food, food' or something like that. He just stopped and ate the cereal bar instead of me.*

After nearly regaining my daytime riding hours, I'd slipped back into the habit of being out on the road late. This would be a pattern throughout the trip and I'd eventually go with it, but coming so early on it was frustrating.

I was struggling to start early enough in the day to warrant finishing before midnight. Or I would be on track for a midnight finish and then something would happen that would keep me going much later, like a storm would come in or I'd get hit on by one of those forward men. And here I was again at 3 a.m., arriving at a vibrant motel on the outskirts of Omsk.

It wasn't all bad, though, as I do enjoy riding at night. In fact, I'd rather stay riding into the dark than I would go to bed earlier and have to get myself up in the morning before the world was awake, so I guess in some way it suited my riding style. And in this part of the world, 24-hour accommodation and food was a thing, so rolling into the motel and all-night café I was served up some Eggs Benedict, which felt like such a treat.

I didn't know it at the time, but this would be my final night of nasty behaviour from men, because for some reason it suddenly stopped just as quickly as it had started.

Day 18: 3 July 2018 • Omsk to Tatarsk • Approx. 7 hours • 202 km • ODO: 5037.57 km • Bivvy in the woods behind some sheds

🎧 *Didn't start till after midday. I faffed about so much in that motel/café. Aw, my bodyclock is all over the place. Once I did start I stopped again in a café 50 miles down the road and stayed way too long. I really needed to coax myself onto the road today.*

On days like these I needed to forget about the enormity of the bigger picture, whether that was the end of the day, the stage or the whole ride, and instead focus on the next few miles. I'd think about all the riding I do at home on a daily basis, whether it's cycling to work, the shops, visiting friends, or my favourite two-hour loop. That gave me a range of distances between 5 and 50 km, and I'd set the target and mentally visualise what that looked and felt like at home. I'd remember a happy and joyful time I had on that ride, perhaps with friends or in good weather. I'd remember feeling strong and fast at home, then apply it to the road I was on now.

Riding into the unknown when you are unmotivated, or exhausted, or both, is difficult. You can talk yourself into it being too hard or unenjoyable, but having a tried-and-tested route that you enjoy makes it easier to break those barriers down.

The most effective distance and place I chose to ride to in my mind was a little village on the outskirts of Inverness called Kirkhill. I have some good friends who live there and often enjoy riding to visit them. It's 14 km from my house to the village, so across the world I would mentally ride to Kirkhill. I found this particularly useful at night when, if I wanted to get another hour in on the bike, I would go 'visit my pals'.

Day 20: 5 July 2018 • Chulym to Oyash • 9 hours 33 minutes • 234.3 km • ODO: 5593.3 km • Bivvy behind a pile of stones by a café

🎧 *Today was mental for punctures. I think it was eight by the end of the night, although three were down to me not fixing them properly. The culprits were tiny little shards of metal, which spin off the hubs of motor vehicle wheels and are left as debris on the road.*

In fact, fixing the punctures was no problem, but getting the tyres reseated, getting them to sit in the rim and create a seal, was tricky. I was often left with a wobble, which felt like I'd buckled my wheel and wasn't very reassuring when you're hammering along the road.

So, I spent a lot of time and energy I didn't have pumping the tyre up to as high a pressure as I could get, before letting it all back out and trying to manipulate the tyre into place, before repumping. Going through this process each time was frustrating and now my thumbs are skinned from the pressure.

I was about to start fixing my latest puncture when I heard a distinctive howling followed by the sound of an animal running towards me. I stood frozen, then screamed. I assumed it was a wolf and hoped they didn't like loud noises!

Alke, the creep from the hotel, had been doing impressions of wolves sneaking up on me and killing me in my sleep. I thought that was a bit drastic at the time, but now I was here I really wished I knew more about their behaviour.

I told myself it was probably just a stray dog, but it was enough to give me the heebie-jeebies and I backtracked to a restaurant a kilometre and a half away and sat on the porch, using the restaurant's outside light to see what I was doing. However, I was more tired than I realised and woke up a while later with glue all over my hands and my tube with a hole in it still.

Giving up on the situation, I bivvied behind a mound of gravel at the back of the car park. In the morning I got some coffee and sat in the sun, fixing the puncture with more ease. I was soon joined by two Russians. The older man was doing the gardening and a younger, more sprightly lad was working in the restaurant. They brought over a bucket of water then stood with roll-ups hanging from their mouths, telling me in Russian where I was going wrong. It was all very light-hearted and fun. At one point the young boy took my phone off me and took a selfie of us all under the porch.

Day 22: 7 July 2018 • Uspenka to Achinsk • 13 hours 9 minutes • 296.9 km • ODO: 6112.2 km • Hotel

🎧 *Wow! Russia is just going on and on! It's been lumpy today, but a nice wee tailwind. I'm somewhere between Moscow and Lake Baikal, just riding endlessly east. I'm late for my initial flight, which I guess was always going to happen, but I was feeling a bit down about having to cancel it, and then I went on to Instagram and my friend had just posted the Trackleaders' map of where I am. I've not looked at the big-scale map for ages, and it just hit me how far I'd come – waah! – chuffed!*

Day 23: 8 July 2018 • Achinsk to Kuskun • 11 hours 5 minutes • 227.8 km • ODO: 6340 km • Hotel

There'd been a massive change in landscape over the last couple of days. I'd moved away from the long flat western Siberian Plains and was back onto undulating hillsides and high plateaus. I found myself drifting off to sleep just before midnight and would stop regularly to rest my head on my handlebars. The roads were quiet at this time so I put in my headphones and played the *Best of Meatloaf* at full blast. A bike ballad was just what I needed and it worked to completely shift my energy. I was still singing my heart out as the sun rose on the hills ahead. It was morning again, 4 a.m., as I pulled into the dusty parking lot of a 24-hour petrol station.

The moments at the start of the trip when my head had been buzzing with to-do lists were well gone. At times like this I'd found my flow, riding with such contentment, especially around twilight. It wasn't all singing, all dancing. Russia had been hard work at times, but I felt that I'd lucked out with the weather. A few heavy showers, headwinds in places, but mostly warm and dry. The clear skies allowed for incredible sunrises and those big moons all helped with morale.

I leaned my bike against the petrol station wall and looked at her. She was such a great companion. She'd been through it all with me – the treacherous traffic, the sleazy men, the night rides, and the sleeping in ditches and bus shelters.

She had been built especially for me. I'd gone to the Shand factory in Livingston, Scotland, in March to meet with Steven Shand and Russell Stout, the owners. Russell oversaw marketing and Steven was the engineer. It was his job to measure me up for my new steed.

I'd taken my current road bike with me as an example of the fit that I *didn't* want! It had been my first ever road bike. I saw it hanging in the window of a local bike café, for sale for £300. It was a large frame and completely unsuitable for all five foot five of me, but it seemed like such a great deal that I bought the second-hand Revolution road bike and cycled it into the ground as I developed my love for long road miles. However, the overstretch left me with a really sore lower back.

Steven is an understated man, as was his bike fitting. He watched me do a couple of laps on it around the car park, then got his tape measure out briefly – and that was about it. I'd never had a bike fitted to me before, but could that really be it? Surely not.

Over the next month I received picture updates from the workshop of the building progress. First came the bike fit drawing and the frame diagram with all the measurements around it – oh, wow! Then came the photo of steel tubing in a cardboard box with Shand Stooshie Graham written on the side. Next was the welding of the frame. Only on my return did I find out that this was Stuart Allan's first-ever bike weld. His love of bicycles had brought about a recent change in jobs, from welding aircraft carriers down at Rosyth Dockyard, and after my return from Round the World he would tell me about watching my progress with fingers crossed that he hadn't mucked it up. I would never have known: the joins in the steel were a masterpiece.

My bike was one of four built by Shand that year for the Adventure Syndicate team and we'd left the colour scheme to the experts. My only desire had been for it to still look nice in the rain. Perhaps it was my Scottishness coming out, but I'd had dark-coloured bikes before and on a miserable wet day they do nothing for your spirits. And they never stand out in a picture. The paint design had come from Euan: glossy mustard gold with my name printed in Sign Painter font down the left-hand fork and a thistle for Scotland above it, and the Adventure Syndicate logo on the other.

Lastly, Frazer the mechanic had built it up using some pretty high-end carbon components supplied by Richie Logic, along with 45 mm, deep section, carbon rim hand-built wheels by the well-established Scottish craftsman Derek McLey: The Wheelsmith.

I went to pick her up one Friday evening at the beginning of April – and the moment I set eyes on her I was in love! She was the picture of beauty. I cycled her around the car park and it felt like we'd always been together. She fitted absolutely perfectly, to the point where I didn't know a bike could feel this great. Wow, how had Steven done that? The black magic of bike engineering is not something I will ever be able to get my head around, but there was no question or doubt that we were perfectly suited.

I looked at her now with the rising Siberian sun glinting off her frame and felt a pang of affection. 'That'll do, Little Pig, that'll do,' I said, patting her top tube. The line came from the film *Babe*, which I'd not seen in about 20 years, so I have no idea why I thought of it just then. But she had been just as capable, strong and reliable to me as that little sheep-pig had been to the farmer – and in that moment, my Little Pig was christened.

Now I really needed some sleep!

• • •

I love capturing snapshots of cultures and the changes that happen at such a gradual pace. A bike lets me travel fast enough to make progress, but slow enough to get images of the people and places, and enjoy the sights and smells. The most significant change on this trip was coming into Asia, as I rode through Siberia, then Mongolia and into China.

I was instantly struck by just how busy the Siberian people were. Men worked on the roads from sunrise, digging, painting and cutting the grass. Women and children worked in the fields, picking berries and selling them to passing traffic, mostly truck drivers. They gathered by the railway crossing as the incredibly long, unhurried carriages chugged on by.

Traditional houses soon turned to huts: small, simply built homes painted in beautiful bright colours, often with vegetable gardens, which were sometimes communal, multiple homes standing around one patch. Smoke from open fires filled the air as people cooked.

The homely smell of a campfire felt incredibly familiar in these new surroundings, not least as the everyday details became more unfamiliar. The quality of my toileting experiences, for instance, varied greatly throughout Asia.

I'd often just pull over into a field if I needed a wee, but I looked forward to an actual toilet stop in garages or restaurants; there was something comforting about having a moment off the bike and sitting down. However, I quickly learned to manage my expectations: the flush was soon a thing of the past, replaced by a long-drop structure as seats made way for a simple squatting system. Hovering over a small hole was a straightforward skill, but not easy with my tight quads. Still, it certainly helped speed up loo breaks; if things are too comfy, it's easy to linger longer than needed. Some of these toilets, as I'm sure you can imagine, were a fairly traumatic experience. Most were well maintained and cleaned, to control the flies, but some weren't and these did stay in my mind for the next few hours of riding.

It was common for petrol stations to have a toilet out the back of the forecourt – a concrete base and walls surrounding the pit. Sometimes there were two entrances – one female and the other male – which made me smile as ultimately each contributed to the same pile. There were no doors to close, just a staggered concrete wall to provide a bit of privacy. The floor was a slab of concrete with a rectangle hole in the middle, small enough to catch you if you slipped, but big enough for a fairly relaxed aim.

The more I used these toilets, the more grimly fascinated I became by what lay beneath my feet. While I could close my sense of smell off, the same couldn't be said for my vision. I'd stare astounded down the hole: wow, all that shit! I wondered how many humans it took to create such an impressive heap and how often the toilet was cleaned out. Who did it? It must be by hand (and a shovel, oh God!). How did they deal with it? Could it be used on the fields or was it dumped in rivers? I was tempted to take a picture, but thought that was probably a bit weird. Kind of wish I had, though.

I sat out the front of a garage one afternoon, eating my lunch under the baking sun, and I watched people on their way to the loo. I was struck by the diversity of folk using the concrete block. Young local children would run in playfully while the community elders, in no hurry, would stop for a chat with neighbours. Visitors like me, passing through, were also directed to the 'bathroom'. A smart, slender woman with high heels tottered in at one point and an out-of-place businessman exited an even more out-of-place sports car to use the modest facilities. It didn't seem to matter who you were, your social status, age, wealth or gender – everybody's shit would end up in the same pile. Simples!

I come from a culture where en-suite bathrooms are quite normal in some homes; where we spend time and money decorating our private bathrooms, and sometimes even change the colour scheme just because we feel like it. I had spent my life in ignorant bliss. I had been on the road for only a few weeks and already my perspective was changing.

Days 25 and 26: 10–11 July 2018 • Tayshet to Tulun and Kutulik • 27 hours 31 minutes • 550 km • ODO: 7202 km • Bench in café and pipe under the road

Cycling through time zones was exciting at first; I felt like a time traveller skipping over invisible boundaries. Now, though, I was just a woman who'd lost out on an accumulated seven hours of sleep.

I had thought about different ways to manage these skips in time. During Mark Beaumont's ride, his team moved the clock forward by a nominated time each day – mostly 15 minutes and then 10 minutes as they got closer to the equator. This meant they never had to contend with any big losses in time and were essentially in their own time zone (expedition time). It made a lot of sense to work like that, but I couldn't fathom how to make it feasible for me to do. It would rely on me doing something semi-thinky each day and simply taking care of the basics (sleeping, eating, riding) was enough. So instead, I decided to just go with it.

I didn't realise how annoying this was going to be and I soon came to wish I'd taken notes of the areas where the time changed. Then at least I'd have known when to expect them. Instead, I'd just look down at the GPS and see that the clock had skipped forward an hour. If it happened in the morning, I'd have some chance of making that hour up throughout the day, but if I jolted forward in time during the evening, there was no way of making up my ride time – and ride time was my main daily motivator. Along with coffee, it was the thing that got me up in the morning, that prized me away from cafés and kept my brain ticking over, as all day I'd be constantly estimating.

When this happened it was difficult to stop riding at the planned time and I was more inclined to just ride into the early morning – 3 or even 4 a.m. – to make it up. Technically, this wouldn't make any difference and would just result in a later start the next day, but mentally it helped. That night, I did just that and realised I'd hit a milestone:

🎧 *Tonight, I found a great big pipe under the road to sleep in. It's 3.30 a.m., but it should actually only be 2.30 a.m., because I crossed another timeline. There has been plenty of accommodation available until this point, but it's getting a bit sparse now. This was big enough to get my bike into, and really clean and dry.*

I sat looking out at my porthole window view and took note of my ODO, congratulating myself for hitting the quarter-way mark. I had travelled a quarter of the way round the world – in 25 days! Whoop, whoop!

So far, I had ridden for 312 hours, climbing 37,980 metres and averaging 278 km a day. If I could keep that up, it meant I was scheduled to complete my circumnavigation in 110 days, which would be on target and amazing.

Day 27: 12 July 2018 • Kutulik to Moty • 11 hours and 40 minutes • 250 km • ODO: 7452.45 km • Wooden cabin

I'm eight years younger than my sister Nic. As adults that doesn't get in the way of our relationship, but as children it was a bit of an awkward age gap. I was too young to play with when she was young enough to want to, and by the time I was four or five and ready for action she had become a teenager, and a pretty cool one at that. Her room was pristinely planned out, with matching Pierrot the Clown bedding, curtains and ornamentals and quirky touches like giant cat footprints, which she'd sponge-painted on the wall and across the ceiling. I was mesmerised by the way she could make her space so inviting, while I was busy in my own room, picking at my Mickey Mouse wallpaper and peeling it off the wall.

Although she was past the playing shops stage (this didn't stop me trying), she dealt with me following her around everywhere pretty well. She'd take me for walks, sometimes to the park, and we'd dance on our Lolo Balls (a squished rubber ball with a plastic disc around the middle – an '80s classic) in front of the sitting room mirror, singing to Yazz's 'The Only Way Is Up'. We had animals in common too: a couple of hamsters, Tom and Jerry, and then a cat.

Nic was smart enough to use my youth to our advantage (mainly hers), knowing that I'd be more likely to get away with things. This included her convincing me that Mum wouldn't mind if I took a kitten home from our grandad's friend. Which I did. And when I arrived home with that little white ball of fluff tucked up in my jacket, Mum absolutely *did* mind! But by then the kitten was in the house and would never be returned. She became our family cat, MooMoo. Nic left for university when I was 10 and we would never live in the same city again, but she would make sure I came to stay with her regularly, wherever she was.

She was much sportier than me as a child, but had never gotten into outdoor adventure sports in the same way as me. This meant that when I'd relay tales of big hill days or plans for an EPIC, they would be missed, or at least get limited interest. There was one major exception to this: bikepacking events with spot trackers. The minute I had a dot to follow, Nic switched from unaware to an out-and-out dot-watching fanatic, obsessing about the race field, moving times, check points – you name it, she knew it.

If I was riding, she would have the Trackleaders page up on multiple screens in the house and would message Mum (and me) regular updates. Because the dot on the map showed only the initials of the riders, I'd test Nic after races by calling out initials and waiting for her to relay the rider's full name each time. Yup, she'd found her calling as a dot watcher.

On the build-up to Round the World, she had been very big sister about the whole thing, quizzing me on safety aspects and asking me lots of 'what if' questions, needing to know how often I'd call home and what I'd do in an emergency. My safety was Nic's biggest concern.

Given her previous dot-watching fixation, maybe it shouldn't have been such a surprise that by the time I'd made it to Moscow, Nic had set up her very own Round the World spreadsheet: she knew where I was at any given moment; how far I'd ridden; the distance between me and the next town, city and airport; my daily averages; and my expected arrival time back in Berlin.

I found out about the spreadsheet by accident when I told her in a voice message about dropping my spare tyre a few days back. I was surprised when she returned with some info on a bike shop just 50 km away. 'How do you know that?' I asked. She told me it was on her spreadsheet. What spreadsheet?

I cycled for a bit, mulling things over. I knew there was a bike shop there before she told me as I'd found it on Google that morning, but should I use it now that she had shared the information? I wasn't sure what that meant for the integrity of my self-supported rules. Also, if she started helping with some of the logistics then I'd surely become reliant on her. I rode with it for a while longer before calling her and going into a heartfelt explanation about how much I appreciated her and how moved I was, but I couldn't have her sharing information with me. It was too much assistance and I wanted to be as 'pure' as possible. I had been talking for a fairly long time when she chirped in with 'Hey Jen, I'm just in Boots buying a new mascara. I'll message you back later, yeah? No stress, though. I knew it might be a bit much for you.'

I decided to miss the bike shop, just so that I hadn't taken advantage of Nic's support. I'd later regret that.

🎧 *Went for a Subway today and met this lassie who learned English in school – about my age. She was like, 'Where you from? Scotland? Oh wow!' And everyone came around that worked there and they were all leaning over the salad bar bit. She was like – 'from Scotland! What are you doing in our little town?' She was super-chuffed. It was really nice. They gave me free coffee.*

It was so interesting meeting the people working in hotels and eateries along the way. Their reactions to me, this untamed woman alone on a bike in the middle of Siberia, varied greatly. The woman in Subway wasn't the first person I'd met there who could speak English. Earlier in the week I'd spent a couple of hours with a 14-year-old girl, Nastia, who was fluent in English and had translated everything available in her mum's café for me, before showing me all the pictures on her phone of the beautiful places she goes camping.

I also met a young man named Stepan, who was the same age as Lachlan and worked in a petrol station. I was buying some evening snacks and, once I'd paid, he asked to speak to me outside. He looked really serious and a little annoyed. I didn't have much choice as I was going back out to my bike anyway, but when we got there his face lifted. He was excited and a little nervous to ask if he could practise his English on me.

We talked about our lives. I had naively assumed he, like the others, had learned English so that they could travel and leave their town, but all three of them said this wasn't the purpose. The poverty here was stark and they lacked choices. I had been exploring what I could physically and mentally achieve on this ride, and I saw now that I was incredibly lucky to have that luxury.

Most people I met didn't share a language, so we used other methods to communicate. Three little boys – I guessed between eight and 12 years old – were playing outside the shop this morning. They loved the bike and I took my phone out to look up Google Maps and show them where I was from. It was common that people didn't recognise Scotland, but when I said 'United Kingdom' they could usually work it out from there, but these kids just shook their heads. I pointed on the map, starting from the town we were in and zooming right out. Still they didn't recognise it. I started pointing to European countries and the only one they knew was France. For some reason, they were incredibly excited about France!

I'd cycled from the centre of Europe in just under a month and had found communities with no idea about our existence. It's easy to be all wrapped up in yourself, particularly when you're taking on a challenge like Round the World and achieving that goal becomes your sole purpose. Being reminded that nobody knew who I was or where I came from was extremely grounding.

Day 28: 13 July 2018 • Moty to Il'inka • 17 hours 30 minutes • 350.8 km • ODO: 7803.25 km • Bivvy in pipe

I'd ended the previous night in a wooden cabin that was a restaurant and B&B. My motivation had been low as the rain came down, and the road twisted and turned, climbing relentlessly in the dark. This morning the mountainous climb continued, but with fresher legs and some sunshine it was easier to take. As I finally topped out of the seemingly never-ending climb, I came head to head with a family of three Chinese bike tourers coming the other way. 'Heeeeey,' I shouted out to them excitedly, as if they were long lost friends – and they waved back, just as surprised to see me. The two women and a man were pushing their mountain bikes laden with panniers on the back and dry bags hanging from the handlebars. This hill was hard enough work on my lightweight road bike; the grind for them must have been huge.

I crossed the road to see them and as I reached the first woman we threw our arms around each other in the biggest hug, squeezing tightly and laughing at the absurdity of meeting one another here. There was no one cycling on this road; the only suggestion of someone on a bike had been Roma a few weeks ago (although, come to think of it, I'd never actually seen him on his bike!). We did lots of chatting in completely different languages. Our attempts at sharing where we were going and where we had been were lost on one another, but it didn't matter. That detail wasn't important, it was just so cheering to be with other cyclists.

We had all climbed a mountain, carrying our lives on our bicycles, and now, on the summit, we happened to meet. We were like-minded souls; that was all we needed to know. Once we'd done all the pointing at bikes and giggling, we shared a group hug and went on our separate ways, with a downhill reward for all our hard work.

According to the map, I was *nearly* at Lake Baikal all morning, but the forested hills limited the view until I was upon it. Descending around a corner, the view opened up and there, at last, were the mighty waters of Lake Baikal. Reaching the lake was a huge landmark and not just physically (it is really big!). It was a place on the map I'd looked at so often, imagining myself there – and it signalled that Russia was nearly over and I'd soon turn south and head into Mongolia.

Just one month ago I was at a garden party, saying goodbye to my lifelong friend Mary. We have been friends since our very first days in primary school and remained each other's best and worst influences throughout our teens. We then went on to have our families at the same time and share all those magic moments together. We knew each other inside out and believed in one another's abilities without question. She was in on the Round the World plan from the start and any time I had doubts she would tell me that I must do this, that I was born to do this. She is great and knows how to throw a party. There was a band playing on a makeshift pallet stage and a BBQ cooking up a storm. None of this was actually in my honour – it was the 21st birthday party of her oldest daughter and my goddaughter Rachel – but it was the last time for seeing friends, so you could say I gatecrashed and made it a double whammy.

It was the perfect way to spend the weekend, a release of all the built-up stress, and I was surrounded by faces that I'd known a lifetime. I reeled off the route in a, by then, practised patter: 'Okay, so I'll leave from Berlin, head east through Poland, Lithuania, Latvia. Then get to Russia, ride *allllllllll* the way across it until I hit the big lake! Then I'll swing right and into Mongolia – yeaaah, Mongolia, baby... China, BOOM, end of leg one!' They'd heard it all before, of course, but after a few beers it did sound a lot funnier.

Just one month ago – and so much had happened since. Now here I was, at the big lake. This would be the last good view of the lake as I skirted around its shore, before the road climbed back into the trees and undulated around the southern edge of the shoreline.

The tarmac had been recently relaid and had created a drop of a couple of inches into the verge. This was fairly common; I couldn't remember when I last saw a kerb. I began descending and as I looked down to check my GPS, I slipped off the side of the tarmac. I went to hop back on to the road, but I had underestimated the depth of the tar and caught the edge of my wheel, clattering down on the road. I picked myself up and moved my bike over, buzzing with shock. A lorry came flying around the corner and swept past, zooming over my abandoned sunglasses and squashing them.

It was a sobering moment. I couldn't help but feel like I'd just dodged a bullet. I was so tired, mistakes were easy to make, but I couldn't afford to make them.

Days 29 and 30 • 14–15 July 2018 • Ll'inka to Shaamar, Mongolia • 28 hours 4 minutes • 545 km • ODO : 8348.35 km • Bivvy under a tree and nap in bus shelter

There was a stark change in the scenery since passing Lake Baikal yesterday; it was hilly, almost mountainous, with lots of lakes and rivers. Often the vegetation had been dense in Russia, but today I cycled past rows of silver birch trees and pine, which felt comfortably familiar.

I had gone into a shop in Ulan-Ude to pick up some sunglasses after losing mine in the crash yesterday. The lassie serving me was great fun and kept passing me loads of different pairs to try on before giving me the thumbs up or thumbs down depending on what she thought.

The tarmac road disappeared at one point and I was just on dirt tracks that had enough wind and traffic on them to create a dust storm. I wore my neck scarf right up around my face and I was so glad I had replaced my glasses to protect my eyes.

The long-awaited Mongolian border was only 200 km away. I planned to get just a small nap somewhere tonight and try to roll in quite early as I anticipated there being a long wait when I got there…

🎧 *I knocked on this minibus window and gestured to get in. This couple were sitting in the back and a driver in the front and they were like, 'Yeah yeah yeah, no problem'!*

I took the front wheel off the bike and we put it on top of all their shopping in the boot. Little did I know that was going to be us for the next five hours together. Just to get 2.5 km over the border.

I got into the van and the Mongolian couple were amazing. She spoke pretty alright English, really broken, but we could piece it together. He didn't speak any but you could tell he was very funny by his facial expressions, so we had quite a laugh about Mongolia and Russia. They had been over to Russia to buy their shopping in bulk, and they weren't the only ones doing it. Some items were in limited supply in Mongolia so going to Ulan-Ude was the easiest way for them to stock up; the boot was full of big bags of cashews, tea and sweeties. They drove from mid-Mongolia to the Russian border, then hired a driver to take them over the border because he had a Russian number plate, which made it easier.

We were second in the queue at the border gates when there was a big bang. The car in front's tyre had seemingly just exploded off the rim. There was a bit of a commotion with people gathering to see what was going on. A few minutes later the woman from the car was rolling her wheel over to us. There was some chat in Russian before the woman opened the backdoor, got in with her wheel and, before I knew it, we were out of the queue and driving full speed around the back streets of the border town; we created so much dust it was difficult to see out the windows. The Mongolian couple just gave me reassuring nods when I asked where we were going. We stopped in a yard that had piles of tyres lined up against the outside walls. The woman and the driver got out of the car, returning 10 minutes later with a fixed wheel. We then drove our kamikaze route back. We'd lost our place in the queue and re-joined at the end.

The border was in three parts. First, we went through some gates, which closed behind us. There were about 20 cars and vans in there, and eight Russian guards walking around.

The guards would spend 10 to 15 minutes at each place. Everything had to be removed from the van: clothes, food shopping, Little Pig. They used mirrors to see under the vehicles, and looked through all the luggage. There was no order to how this was done. When the guards looked like they were finishing with one person, a chaotic rabble began trying to bid for their attention. People were calling out in Russian and waving their arms.

After our van was manually inspected, it needed to be taken away for a more thorough check. We sat in the courtyard, vanless, watching the last of the other vehicles leave until it was finally our turn. After the yard we had two passport check stations. Mine was taken off me by eight different people until it was finally stamped. Then it was time to drive across the no man's land that I was forbidden to ride on.

On the other side, I paid the driver then emptied the remainder of my Russian currency. I gave it to my border friends, and we shared big hugs and a wave goodbye.

• • •

My Mongolian route would first take me to the capital, Ulaanbaatar, which sits at 1350 metres, and from there into the Gobi Desert, in a south-easterly direction towards China. That would be 1235 km across this beautiful country.

The first thing I came across in Mongolia was a great big cow resting by a blue stone wall. Behind the wall was a two-storey wooden house with no windows or roof and a huge silver birch in the garden. The word 'rustic' just didn't cut it.

I had romanticised this land before ever setting foot in it. Mongolia already had a place in my heart and secured that position over the next five days, thanks to the people's welcoming, curious and upfront ways of being.

The sky was filled with a dusty haze. I rode under the 'Welcome to Mongolia' sign, spread across the dirt track road. In front of me three men galloped around, herding their 50-plus horses as they crossed the road, before disappearing into the grassy landscape.

Night set in and there was a sudden torrential downpour. Thankfully, the rain was warm, but I was quickly drenched. I pulled into a supermarket to take cover for a bit. Inside, the shop was lined with shelves – all bare except for one aisle containing instant food like noodles, mash, sugary sweets and biscuits. There were no fresh ingredients, much like the petrol stations I'd passed through recently.

There was a little kettle on the side, where I could heat up a pot of noodles. I sat eating them with a cup of tea from the machine on the window sill and I plugged my phone into the charging point. I did this pretty much everywhere I stopped, as there was always something that needed to be charged. No one seemed to mind, although I'd been struggling to get enough energy via the cheap petrol station cables I had bought to replace the broken ones.

The staff were four young women, in their late teens or early twenties. They had a couple of their friends in with them and two preschool kids who were beautifully untamed as they played intensely, running around the aisles, climbing on shelves. Occasionally an adult would jump in to grab a leg as they disappeared head first out the window, but other than that, their free play was mesmerising.

I left the window sill and went back out to my bike when one of the women appeared by my side. She was quieter than the others, maybe a little older too. She handed me her phone, and a woman's voice on the other end said, 'Hello, my friend would like to offer you a bed, with her family, at her home. It isn't far away.' The woman holding the phone smiled deeply. I started explaining that despite the storm, I must continue to cycle. She told me it was a long way to go to the next town. Her friend could drive me to her home and I could sleep.

I couldn't take the chance of any more hold-ups today, though. Even if she lived really close, I could never get up in five hours and just ride away, instead I'd stay longer, chatting, eating and enjoying connection. So I declined, feeling awful, but I had to stay in charge of my own itinerary. I was afraid this might offend the woman when her friend had translated my message to her, but she hugged me and left me to get on my way.

The rain flooded the ground I rode on for another few hours. When it was time to stop for the night, I found some trees at the side of the road and a little muddy path. I followed it to a massive pipe lying under the road.

Peering inside, I saw the bottom of the circular pipe was layered with cow poo. A pretty grim place to be, but dry, so I wheeled my bike in and carefully changed out of my wet kit. I thought about staying inside the pipe, but in the end decided I'd take my chance in the storm instead and lay under the tree with the bivvy bag pulled up over my head, thinking about how different my evening could have been.

Day 31: 16 July 2018 • Shaamar to Bornuur • 11 hours 26 minutes • 205.8 km • ODO: 8554.15 km • Café

By the early morning the storm had made way for a big blue sky. The day started with a steady climb before a drop down to a small roadside village with a handful of houses and a bar, restaurant and shop. I hovered around on the doorstep until a woman came out to see if I was okay.

I asked for food and she mimed that they were closed. I mimed back 'Please'. She smiled. She spoke a little English. 'What do you need?' 'Anything,' I replied. I was needing a good meal. It felt like I'd been eating noodles for weeks now. She welcomed me in, although she seemed really concerned about me leaving my bike outside, so I moved it to in front of the window where I could see it. This felt like the least dodgy place I'd left Little Pig since setting off from Berlin.

The woman heated up a bowl of meat and pepper stew with rice on the side. It was literally the best meal I have ever tasted. Everything was so fresh and homemade. I could have eaten three helpings.

I got some supplies at the adjoining shop and started filling up my packs when her 18-year-old daughter appeared. Clearly, she'd been woken up to speak to me and I appreciated the gesture. She was home for the summer from university in Ulaanbaatar. We sat on the wall outside the shop, swinging our legs as the early morning heat shone down on us.

We talked about her life, about her university, how she missed being at home when she was in the capital, which was so busy in comparison. I understood what she meant, looking at the wilderness around us.

Then she explained why her mum had been so concerned about my bike. A couple of years before, a traveller had been passing through on his bike, which was stolen from the village. This brought great shame on the community and seeded distrust amongst the locals. In such a virtuous culture, theft was an incredibly rare occurrence and this was a crime that had never been solved. I wondered about the rider and what they were doing there. I had no idea what I'd have done if Little Pig had been stolen from such a rural location. We parted ways, and I felt powered on by their food and time.

The landscape was a blanket of green rolling hillsides, the same vivid colour as the feathers of a budgie. The short form of the grass made it look even more appealing, as if someone had been out and mown the thousands of acres that lay before me. This was the Mongolian steppe, an area of grassland that stretches all the way from Hungary to China. The Mongolian people are known for their nomadic lifestyle. Living in *gers* (known as yurts outside Mongolia), they migrate with the change in seasons, moving to find the most suitable pastures for their animals and carrying their collapsible homes with them as they go.

This is an ancient practice and the further I travelled inland, the more *gers* I could see, scattered across the open expanse. Many were obviously temporary, but one or two looked a bit more settled, with a massive satellite dish outside the front door and solar panels. Despite there being many different families using the grazing land, I didn't pass one single fence. Just open wilderness. Sometimes women would be sitting at a table by the side of the road, selling milk from a big clay pot. Hot milk is super-common in Mongolia, because they extract it from all of their animals: cattle, horses, sheep, goats and even camels! I'd read on some blogs about – or, more precisely, been warned about – fermented mare's milk, a traditional nomadic drink known for its rancidness. Over the next few days, I was handed many milky drinks and always enjoyed them. So, I've either got some strange taste buds (quite possible) or I had instead been given a milky sweet tea mix called suutei tsai. Either way, each time I went for my first sip, I was cautious.

That afternoon, as I pulled into a shop, a horse was tied to the post outside. Just then a young Mongolian child, around 10 years old, ran from the shop and leaped on to the fully grown horse with a bag of bread in one hand. He stared at me and we locked eyes, mesmerised by one another's worlds for a split second, before he galloped off down the street, bareback.

Later in the afternoon I passed a little hut set back, just off the road, that looked like it was selling supplies. I had passed a couple of these in the last two days. It had turned warm and humid after the storm, so I pulled over, hiked up to the shack and bought some water from a couple of young kids. Then I was greeted by a smart-looking guard in uniform.

I liked the way people just came over to me. They sat down beside me or stood by my side, with often no language to share. It was primitive. There was no fear of rejection or ego; every interaction was just driven by curiosity.

The guard – I'll call him Charlie – walked back down the hill with me and sat on the bench. He then patted the space next to him. He was sweet. I hadn't managed to stay anywhere indoors for nearly a week – and indoors was the only moment I had for washing my socks, since I didn't have another pair. Combined with the rain of last night and the heat of today, that meant I could smell my feet reeking on every pedal stroke. I must have stunk to high heaven. He didn't seem to mind. We swapped Facebook accounts and he continued sending me pictures of himself in his uniform throughout the trip. Occasionally he FaceTimed, but all we could do was smile and nod at one another so usually I'd just reply with pictures of the road.

Day 32: 17 July 2018 • Bornuur to Ulaanbaatar • 8 hours • 141 km • ODO: 8685.15 km • Posh hotel

🎧 *Hey! I'm sitting in a café now in Batsümber. I stayed here last night. It's a sort of motel/trucker type place, pretty busy. I was just getting ready to leave this morning and this massive thunderstorm has just started. We're quite high up here, about 1000 metres, and it's just belting down, like bouncing off the floor sort of rain, so I came back inside and had another coffee. Things have just got very busy here because people are running inside with plastic bags on their heads. Even the cars have had to stop and water is pouring in the windows. Mongolia, wow! What a place.*

I'd been waiting for the storm to pass for well over an hour and was feeling restless, as I'd already had quite a leisurely breakfast. So, with the rain still lashing down, I decided that maybe I was just overthinking it and I should go outside and try to ride. The roads were rough up here, tarred mostly but weather-beaten and with massive potholes and erosion. After only a few hundred metres, I dived for shelter again. This time I took cover under a restaurant porch as the owner stood in the open window with a bucket, emptying all the water out that had leaked inside.

In another half-hour it stopped and the sun was straight back out, so I continued riding towards Ulaanbaatar. The city was only 100 km away, but I wasn't sure my chain was going to make it. I'd run out of oil about a week ago and the two big storms had left it squeaking like a great big mouse. It had done pretty well, mind you: 6440 km in four weeks. Chains on my other bikes take four months to do this kind of distance, so I was more concerned than normal that I'd overstretched its lifespan. I'd tried drizzling sun cream on it the day before, which didn't help much and may have actually encouraged it to dry out.

I had reached a small village called Bayanchandmani, where, considering its size, there were plenty of people around. The streets were untarmacked and grazing cattle spilled out on to them. Kids were playing and a few young men passed on motor dirt bikes, often with a couple of passengers on board. I found a car garage and made some hand and oil actions towards my chain to the mechanic. He came back with a big tub of gloopy grease that I regretfully turned down with thanks, imagining it getting all mixed in with the dust and causing more issues. I said goodbye, crossed the road to the food store and came back out with a cold can of Fanta and a tin of sardines. I used the sardine oil on my chain instead – an extremely successful bodge! It fixed the squeak and would get me to the city.

When I arrived in Ulaanbaatar by early evening, I instantly began haemorrhaging time. As much as I was hooked on this country and culture, it had been a hard slog to get here. So, when I began recognising chain stores and a way of life that felt so familiar, I was drawn to savour a slice of normality, just for a moment.

I was also conscious I needed to find a bike shop for more chain lube. And a new rear tyre. I'd been picking up a few more punctures recently and it was looking quite worn, so rather than sticking to the ring road, I headed straight into the centre.

Coffee was needed, so I stopped at a hotel and began looking up possible flights for the next leg: Beijing to Perth. Really the most pressing thing to do was getting to a bike shop to see me through to China, but dwindling the time away was easy.

After about an hour, I left with no flights booked. I had, to be fair, taken screen shots of all the possibilities to think about while riding. Back out on the street I called into a small corner shop to pick up snacks, the concept of the clock ticking and time evaporating having now left me altogether. When I eventually made it to the bike shop, it was closed. I googled my other options, but everything was shut.

I thought about stopping for the night but it was only early evening and my mileage for the day was really low. I'd just have to take the chance and carry on without. I reasoned that I could always swap my front and back tyres over. The front one had less wear and usually lasts longer than the rear one anyway because it carries less weight. So, after three hours in the capital, I started to ride away with good intentions until I came across a Pizza Hut sign. 'Well, I've not really eaten yet,' I thought, 'I'll just quickly order something to take away and I can have it later on.'

But when it arrived it smelled so amazing that I just sat in the porch with my helmet still on and ate the whole lot. The boy behind the counter looked on at me, confused as to why I hadn't just taken a seat.

The phone call charges were much more reasonable in Mongolia than they had been in Russia, so I was enjoying being back in more regular contact with home. My friend Fiona was in touch most days. Dropping voicemails, texts and now a whole playlist she'd put together for me, called 'Beijing Bangers'. She filled it with all our favourite tunes from the late '90s and early 2000s. Each song held a memory and I could picture us singing at the tops of our lungs to them. I was lucky to have such a thoughtful friend. I could give so little back in return. My replies were sporadic but the strength I took from knowing they were there for me was immense. I downloaded 'Beijing Bangers' and was finally ready to leave.

The route took me out of the city centre, with another 500 m to climb until I'd reach the highest point, then I'd gradually be descending to the Gobi Desert. But after less than a hour on the road my tyre burst, again. I sat on the dust under a lamppost leaning against a wall, fixing the hole. I kept pumping the air in, only to let it all out and start again as it refused to seat properly in the rims. I could see three big tears on the side wall, and splits all across the rubber. It was in a worse state than I had realised, and the front one wasn't any better.

The sensible decision would have been to backtrack and then pick up a new tyre in the city the next day. As I'd been so reluctant to leave

Ulaanbaatar and deep down, I really wanted a bed and wash, I found the decision-making hard. Was I considering backtracking for the correct reasons, i.e. the new tyre, or was this a moment of weakness that I would regret?

I weighed up the likelihood of a tyre blowing out in the next couple of hundred rough miles and the impact that would have on my timings. As there would be very little, if anything, in the way of bike shops between here and Badaling, nearly 1000 km away, I decided to head back into the city. I found a large Trek workshop that was open at 9am the following morning on the same street as some high-rise hotels, so I booked a room in one of the gorgeous hotels for me and Little Pig. It was the fanciest place I'd probably ever stayed in, but they were so welcoming and, thankfully, allowed my Little P into the room with me. I was feeling frustrated that I had messed up so much throughout the day, but equally enjoyed the luxury for the night.

Day 33: 18 July 2018 • Ulaanbaatar to Choir • 11 hours • 242.68 km • ODO: 8937.83 km • Motel

🎧 *The lassie in the bike shop today was so nice. She'd travelled to England to work and study. She'd even been to Scotland! She spoke really good English. We had a great conversation about the people and the way of life in Mongolia. I told her about how well I'd been received and she wasn't surprised. 'It's in our culture. We are nomads so we understand the basic needs of a traveller,' she told me.*

I got a new tyre. It's a proper touring one with extra tread, so not as quick as I'd like, but that's okay!

I set out again. Mongolian landscapes came in two flavours. I'd left the fertile soil of the steppe behind and the dry arid bedrock heading into the Gobi Desert would be my surroundings for the next few days. This meant long straight roads and huge horizons, with occasional settlements scattered back from the road. It was so remote that I was as fascinating to the people out here as they were to me.

I was still a bit edgy when I first heard a horn beeping, perhaps some trauma left over from Russia, but I soon discovered that the Mongolian beep meant something very different. Nearly every car passing me in the countryside gave me a honk, followed by a big wave or cheer of encouragement. It was so sweet. People handed me bottles of water out of their windows, and some teenagers ran from their parents' cars with biscuits and snacks, and to ask if I was okay.

The most amazing gesture came from a family who passed me in their red car on a climb. By the time I'd reached the top, they had set up a picnic on the boot and within minutes were feeding me and offering me a flask of Mongolian milky chai. Maybe my trip was partly 'supported' after all!

Day 34: 19 July 2018 • Choir to Sainshand • 13 hours 45 minutes • 269.2 km • ODO: 9207.03 km • Pipe under the road

I woke up with a bit of a fright on the motel bed. My legs were dangling off the end and my feet on the floor. My arms lay out to the side with a 90-degree bend in my elbows – and all the battery packs, cables and plugs, which should have been charging, had just fallen from my hands onto the sheets. I was still fully clothed in my cycling bibs, sweaty dust-drenched top, string vest and socks, with my shoes still done up.

This had happened to me a couple of times crossing Siberia. I'd sat down to take my shoes off, lay back and slept hard for five hours. It was a sad moment waking up to realise that nothing was washed or, more importantly, charged.

I was running a SON Dynamo Hub on the front of my bike. As the front wheel rotates, it generates a small amount of electricity that I'd then use to keep on top of my daily charging duties. I needed to keep my GPS, phone, two rear lights and a front light charged daily. I also needed charging cables and battery packs. My cables were so worn that they wobbled free from the packs after a while, and the battery packs themselves started to struggle. I was running 6000mAh battery packs. I had no idea what the m capitalA h stood for, but I had worked out that 6000 was the perfect amount of m capitalA h to take a charge from my dynamo hub. Any bigger, and it would take days to charge; any smaller, and it wouldn't hold enough energy to deal with charging bigger items, like my phone. I relied on using power from the mains during overnight stays and café stops to give my battery packs a 'big charge'. The dyno would just keep things ticking over for a few days.

I showered, changed into fresh bibs and went to collect Little Pig – reception had insisted I leave my bike down there with them, pointing to their CCTV cameras. As usual, I hated leaving her. No one had any concept of what she meant to me.

By midday it was well over 40°C. I was carrying three litres of water in my water cages, and a two-litre bottle strapped under the elastic on my saddle bag. There was nowhere to hide from the heat, and I couldn't afford to run out of water.

A man passed on a green motorbike and I gave a wee wave. He doubled back and pulled in up ahead of me. He had on an orange T-shirt and a great big smile. He was wearing an over-the-shoulder messenger bag – and from it he pulled an ice-cold can of Pepsi Max and handed it to me. No liquid had ever tasted that refreshing before. We shared it, nodding at each other in approval. He told me his name was Batbayar.

Then, just before he drove off again, he lifted his seat up and handed me a milky ice pop. I was bewildered about where he'd found these, or how he kept them cold; there was nothing for miles around. But my goodness, it was delicious.

On I rode, through a landscape mostly unmarked. There were only the long straight tracks of the Trans-Siberian railway in the distance, running parallel to the road. And the 'paper policemen' that stood by the side of the road as a deterrent to speeding drivers.

I paused to take out my phone to send a video home when I spotted some large, out-of-place rocks up ahead. I hadn't seen this kind of boulder in the last couple of days – weird! They were almost enchanting, pulling me in. Then the rocks turned their heads around to look at me as I passed. Woah – it was a camel, hanging out at the side of the road! I'd never seen a wild camel before, just chilling doing his own thing.

I rode until the early morning, then found a pipe under the road to sleep in and looked out across the desert sky. I was feeling the effects of my high-sugar diet: my mouth was full of ulcers and my lips were cut and burnt from the wind and sun. Other than that, my body was bearing up well. I felt strong, both mentally and physically, although I was definitely aware that I'd been riding non-stop for five weeks.

Day 35: 20 July 2018 • Sainshand to east of Zamyn-Üüd • 8 hours 28 minutes • 170.4 km • ODO: 9377.03 km • Hotel

Border day! It was an exciting day. I had just 170 km left in Mongolia, so by that evening I'd be crossing the border and into China, for the very last 645 km of stage 1! My daily average was 267 km, which meant once I added on travel days I was behind on my own 110-day target by three days, but ahead of the record by 31 days. And, importantly, I was on target to make my flight at 5 a.m. on Monday from Beijing, which was two and a half days away. I knew I would be able to push on once I crossed the border into China, so I gave myself an extra hour of sleep in the pipe to start with plenty of energy.

Annoyingly, food supplies were sparse that day. I had breakfast in a *ger*, where the family had chai heating on the stove and some stew, which they happily sold to me. Then that was me until the evening.

As I got really close to the border, the road turned to sand unexpectedly. I slid around before falling on my face in front of a local kid, who was also riding his bike. I dusted myself off and gave a wee wave (so embarrassing). It was 8.10 p.m. when I arrived at the border, 10 minutes after it had closed. I couldn't believe it. When I was planning the trip, I was *sure* it had said this was a 24-hour crossing – if I'd known that I definitely wouldn't have had that extra hour of sleep. With the decision made for me I found a hotel, lots of food and rebooked some flights.

The next morning was a busy affair. I got to the border to find cars lining the streets and people jostling around. The clock was ticking away for the 9 a.m. border opening. However, in order to cross I needed a lift and, with a help of a man who seemed to be haggling on my behalf, I bought a seat for Little Pig and me in a Land Rover driven by a small energetic woman. The whole street was chaos as pedestrians looked to find a way across. I was settling in, my bike lying across me in the back seat, when the same man who had helped me opened the door and, talking urgently in Mongolian, took Little Pig and chucked her up on the roof. The rear of the Land Rover then immediately started filling up with people. Thankfully, we were the first through and compared to getting into the country it was a fairly swift process.

● ● ●

I had managed to change my flight from Beijing on Monday from early morning to the afternoon. This gave me an extra 12 hours to make up for the massive border town delay in Zamyn-Üüd. I had 46 hours to ride the next 652 km... No problem!

I was through the border, into the Chinese region of Inner Mongolia, and a whole lot more desert. There wasn't a great deal to mark the landscape here except for life-size statues of dinosaurs lining the road for miles. Such a strange sight made me laugh. It ended as I cycled under two gigantic brontosauruses, one on either size of the road. Their necks reaching across the tarmac, the two met in the middle and seemed to be kissing one another. I later found out that this dinosaur wonderland celebrated the number of fossils found in the area.

Suddenly, and instantly, I felt lost. All the signing was now written in *hanzi*, or Chinese characters. Although I hadn't been able to read or pronounce the majority of the place names crossing Russia and Mongolia, the alphabet was more or less familiar.

I cycled until well into the night with the road climbing into a grassland area and slept out in a field. When I woke in the morning with nothing but the imminent flight on my mind, I discovered my front wheel had punctured. As I sat by the road mending it, a man appeared, apparently from nowhere, and stood over me, watching but saying nothing. Once my wheel was back on, he smiled and gave me a nod before disappearing into the field once again.

Day 37: 22 July 2018 • Zhurihe, China and Badaling • 22 hours 12 minutes • 427.55 km • ODO: 9602.03 km • No sleep

Even as I rattled off my plans down the phone to Nic, I knew it was big chat. I told her that I'd ride straight through the night; that, despite missing the previous two flights, I'd make this next one. 'It's just 290 km to go. I have 14 hours. If I ride all night, I'll make it.'

I can't remember her reply, but I know it was said with that caring but *this-is-never-going-to-happen* tone in the way only a sibling can do. She told me to take care and that she would check back in with me in the morning.

The truth was it had taken me all day to cover less than that. I was moving so slowly it was as if the road had turned to treacle, hanging on to my tyres just a little longer than needed. Already tired, I was struggling to imagine doing the same again.

My bronzed thighs were no longer a structure of strength. Instead, they would hold my weight momentarily before melting away to mush. I likened them to an art experiment I once did in primary school; the one where you mix cornflour with water until it becomes a paste, but then returns to liquid with just a simple touch. Perhaps I had developed cornflour legs? I was sighing a lot today too. I'd find myself just stopping and then, after a long, deep breath, I'd let out a loud 'Aaawwhhhhh'.

The days upon days in this hot dusty climate, with little or no water to wash my bibs, meant more chafing had appeared on my bottom, so sitting down was painful. This wasn't improved by the start of my period. Before leaving home, I had considered having an injection to stop them throughout the trip, but in the end decided that allowing my body to be free to do as it wanted was the best plan. I had wondered whether the physical strain would mean I'd stop bleeding for a couple of months, but this was not the case for me. My body clearly had just about enough left to produce a period; there was something reassuring in that, albeit annoying.

So, there it was. If I could just find my zone, up my pace, solidify my legs, care for my bum and stay awake all through the night, I stood a very good chance of making my rearranged flight No. 3.

Until this point on the trip I had spent nearly all my time on main roads. Despite these being treacherous in places, finding resupplies had been relatively easy, but in the first part of China the road had turned into a busy motorway, so my route would follow a quieter back road that ran adjacent to the motorway for the rest of the leg. It meant resupply was going to be a bit more difficult due to the rural setting. Another issue I was finding was that services were often indistinguishable from other buildings from the outside. All the buildings had small windows and dusty walls. There were rarely signs outside (not that I'd have been able to read them), so I'd watch for people walking in and out of the building and try to figure out if there might be something behind the door of interest to me. Failing that, I'd get up close and stare in, hoping to see through the darkened, dirty windows.

Earlier that day I had skirted around the city of Ulanqab, where I'd found some buns, sugary snacks and water. I'd sat on the doorstep of the shop eating them and soon had a local woman come sit right beside me. She called over a couple of her friends to join us too. We laughed and smiled as they talked among themselves and I could only imagine what they might be saying. As I was leaving, one of the men returned to the shop and came out with three little bottles of water for me to stuff into my already bulging back pockets. Once I left them, I didn't see anyone else or pass any shops all evening.

I wove my way through back streets late into the evening. By midnight my eyes were beginning to close and my head wobbled. I was desperate to stay awake, but so incredibly tired and hungry, and I hadn't passed anywhere obviously serving food for such a long time.

I had 220 km to ride and just 11 and a half hours in which to do it – doable, but at the speed I was currently travelling only just. I was still up at over 1500 metres, so I was holding out for a huge descent down towards Beijing. I could hear there was a main highway close by and hoped I'd be joining it soon. Maybe I'd be able to find some services there. Ahead, I spotted lights on in a building that had larger-than-normal windows. I wheeled up, cupped my hands around my eyes and peered through the glass.

As I did this I became aware of a man standing at the door. He was slight, wearing a sleeveless vest and holding a baseball bat in his hand. He looked fierce, but was probably just as frightened as me. It was one of those 'You've really not thought this through, Jen' moments, but before either of us could panic, a larger, friendlier female face arrived beside him and we all began talking, in our own languages, at each other. They were quick to usher me inside with my bike. It was difficult to make out exactly what the room was at first glance. There was seating like you'd find in a café, but with the feel of a family living room. In one corner there was a shop, locked behind Perspex glass and piled high with cigarettes and a random selection of food – noodles, crisps, sugary sweets, cans of juice. We stood in the brightly lit shop/café/living area gazing into one another's worlds.

It was only afterwards I could appreciate how bizarre the situation must have been for this family; a white, solo woman, travelling by bike, arriving in their living room/shop, in the middle of the night. I was covered head to toe in dust, my bright red cheeks shining, and frizzy, sun-bleached hair stuck to my sweaty head.

The clock on the wall told me it had just gone midnight. I was acutely aware that the minutes of my ridiculously tight time schedule were ticking away. If I could have walked out of the door I would have, but fear of insulting them along with the hope of coffee kept me there.

I began the usual game of charades, flapping my arms to mime eating and drinking, and saying 'Cooooooffeeee, cooooooffeeee' in that really dodgy foreign accent you use when you can't speak any other languages. I had picked up some key words in Russia, but I hadn't got as far as learning any Mandarin and was sure that if I turned off the airplane mode on my phone it would run completely out of battery.

The man went behind the Perspex glass into the shop and rummaged about. Then he reappeared, holding aloft sachets of Nescafé 3in1 and cheerily waving them at me. In a prior life I had been quite the coffee snob, often fuelled on oat milk flat whites from my favourite coffee roastery, but right now the sight of those Nescafé sachets filled my heart with joy. 'YES!' I frantically nodded with a big thumbs up.

A young boy, maybe 10 years old, had been woken up to say hello to the new arrival. He walked towards me in his blue shorts and white vest, rubbing his sleepy eyes and sharing a shy smile. He sat beside me, slightly embarrassed. He spoke to his mum and then turned to me and said, 'Welcome.' To hear English after days of being alone with my thoughts on the road was wonderful. Nervously he continued, 'This is my mother and this is my father.' I looked up at his parents, who both looked like they were going to burst with pride.

'Oh, pleased to meet you. My name is Jenny. I've come from Scotland.' I beamed back at him. Without thinking, I was about to burst into a conversation relaying all my needs – food, flight and being in an awful hurry. Then the boy smiled again and repeated, 'Welcome, this is my mother and this is my father.'

Ah, of course, there would be no conversation about my needs. This young man had learned a phrase at school, possibly never imagining having to use it, and now here he was, in his very own home, being brought from bed to introduce his family in the room. It was a beautiful moment – and I was disappointed for only a split second.

I was on my second cup of Nescafé now and had been planning my polite departure, realising that food would take too long and aware I needed to get going, but then the mum arrived out from the kitchen carrying three bowls on a small tray. They were filled with rice, vegetables and a curry.

I couldn't believe my luck as I tucked into the delights. I eventually looked up from the food to see the whole family sitting at the table staring back at me, in silence, as I devoured the first good food I had eaten in days.

Soon after a phone arrived and was held to my ear. 'Hello?' a voice said. I smiled; I was now used to this. People were so keen to connect and help that when the language barrier got in the way they usually knew someone who had enough broken English to ask the correct questions. This time it was the mum's nephew in Beijing, who, like the son, had been woken from his sleep to welcome me.

The nephew's English was broken, but the next sentence was easily understood. 'My aunt says you are welcome to her home. You must not leave. It's far too dangerous for a woman on her own. You must stay tonight.' Oh my god, I was actually being kidnapped by kindness. My accent was too difficult for the nephew in Beijing to understand my response, so we developed a four-way system between myself, the woman, the nephew and Google Translate.

I spoke into Google Translate. Google translated it enough for the mum to understand and speak to the nephew. He then gave me the mum's (and his) reaction. This continued for the next 10 minutes as I tried to impress on them that I was in a massive hurry and must leave now. I tried to keep in mind that riding through the night to catch a plane to Australia might have felt perfectly normal to me, especially having ridden alone from Germany over the past month and a half, but it was in fact very much not normal. And certainly not in this part of the world. The people I had met up until this point had talked of staying in their villages all their lives. They had no need to leave and often no means to do so. The choice to travel, so normalised in our Western society, was just not available here. Trying to explain the whole trip, the urgency, etc., was too much of a cultural challenge – most people simply didn't understand.

Hearing myself say it out loud, I had to admit that the scenario was bizarre. Here I was, on my own in the middle of a small village in the middle of the night. I didn't speak the language, I clearly hadn't eaten properly in a while and I looked like I'd been dragged through a hedge backwards. I had a flight to catch, from an airport that wasn't much more than 160 km away, to which I was planning to cycle, in the pitch-black. I could sense this family just wanted to make sure I would be safe and that it was their duty to look after me as a visitor to their homeland. So I lied. I assured them that my friend (who just happened to be a man) was in the next village waiting for me and would be concerned if I didn't arrive. This seemed acceptable and, after what felt like an eternity, the nephew hung up and I began packing. As I stood to gather my belongings, the young boy stood to attention and I realised we were now to take part in a photo shoot. With the last 1% of my phone's battery, the mum snapped a pic of me and her adorable son. Then she got one on her own phone too.

With my midnight guardians waving at the window, I descended into the dark. Down and down the road I went. Up and up my average speed went. I was fixated on it and needed to be – time was tighter than ever. I needed to tick off hard, fast miles as I made my way through the towns and villages.

As the sun came up, I had 120 km to go. These sleepy little mountain towns were soon bustling with life. Tiny vans and cars whizzed around the dusty, dirt-track streets and I weaved in and out of them, avoiding potholes as I went. At one point I rounded a corner as the mist was rising to reveal glimpses of the jaggy mountain side, covered in lush green vegetation. It reminded me of a picture I'd once seen of Brazil. I found my own rhythm within the chaos, letting go and finding the flow that allowed me to float effortlessly through the streets as the early morning sun beat down. If I'd stopped to worry about my position on the road, it wouldn't have worked. Sometimes you've just got to fight crazy with crazy.

With the mounting traffic came more recognisable services and throughout the morning I'd roll into garages for water and to use the toilet. As soon as I stopped, though, I'd have a small gathering of people around me. They would show me to the outhouse as a group, we'd all walk around together, I'd use the facilities and everyone else would wait and welcome me with bowls of warm water for washing when I returned. Then we'd all walk back together to where Little Pig was waiting patiently. I still didn't like leaving her for long, but people were far more interested in me than they were her.

The moment I'd start to speak, I'd have a row of mobile phones in my face recording me. My usual chat to try to explain myself was 'MONGOLIA' pointing back up the road I'd just come from, then 'BEIJING' pointing in the direction I was going. On a roll, I'd then jump into action with my best cycling impersonation before excitedly pointing over at my bike and my helmet in case more explanation was needed. I would repeat until I heard a glimmer of understanding... and then they began chatting loudly, first between themselves and then to me.

I'd guess the next part of the discussion would be 'Where next?' Cue my aeroplane arms with sound effects, followed by 'Auuustrrrraliaaa'. That bit seemed to kill the conversation (I probably just looked unhinged), but the Mongolia–Beijing bit was a winner. I wondered how many group chats in China have shared videos of me prancing about making aeroplane noises. I can only imagine how mortifying they would be to watch now.

On the last occasion I stopped for a wee, my groupies consisted of four women. They were all giggling and speaking to me in Mandarin. I liked it when people just kept talking in their own language. I mean, I clearly had no idea of the content, but they were desperate to connect, which felt nice. One of the women stroked my head. At this point my hair was stuck so tight to my head that I'd have struggled to pull my own fingers through it. She didn't seem to mind. Soon she was squeezing my thighs, mesmerised by the size of them. She reported back to her friend on how they felt. It was fairly good feedback (I think). They were desperate for me to sit and chat some more. I was touched and amazed that they were so delighted to see me. We were so close to Beijing. Surely they saw travellers and Westerners all the time? Well, clearly not ones who looked like me. I promised myself I'd come back here, with more time to give, but with just 30 km to go I *had* to make that flight.

The Guinness World Record rules state that the rider mustn't ride the same line of longitude twice. So rather than riding all the way to Beijing Airport I would stop 80 km short in the town of Badaling. My next leg would start in Perth, Australia, keeping my easterly degrees in order. I had organised the Chinese equivalent of an Uber driver to pick me up at the Great Wall of China, Badaling.

The driver's name was Junfeng. I'd been in contact with him a few times that month, via the Chinese app WeChat, mainly so that he wouldn't forget about me. I knew I would need enough charge in my phone to message him when I was close, but keeping on top of charging had been really difficult in the last few days. I hadn't had a night indoors to get a big charge since the border crossing 50 hours ago and because of the situation with my battered-up cables all my electricals were on their last few per cent of power. I was switching between power banks every 30 minutes just to keep my GPS unit/phone and light working – which meant a lot of faffing at that point in the day. Especially as I couldn't ease the pace.

I dropped off the dust road into the tropical marshlands of Guanting Reservoir. Far from the dry, sandy streets I'd spent the past week on, this was lush and green, and boardwalks skirted around the ponds. I was blown away. I wished so much that I could be filming it.

I'd been riding for the last 36 hours straight by this point. I was exhausted and weather-beaten. I was still unsure if I was going to make my lift – it was so close yet so far away – and everything was on the brink of being empty so I was topping devices up 5% at a time, but in spite of the hectic schedule, I couldn't stop this ridiculous grin spreading across my face, adrenaline running high with the thrill of racing for the plane. I savoured every moment of these magical days and all the memories they held, replaying them in my head, watching the events unfold as if it was a film.

I was now on the outskirts of Badaling, under 2 km away from the finish line of my first leg – at the foot of the Great Wall of China – when everything ran out of charge. I had no GPS, it was seven minutes until I needed to meet my Uber driver and all the street signs were in Chinese.

Nobody around me spoke any English – I tried asking. The only way to get charged was to ride at speed with my electrics plugged in. So, I cycled up and down the empty street, looking for someone to ask for directions while plugging my GPS unit directly into my dyno-charger. If I could just get a couple of percentage charge, I could make it.

And where was this wall? It's one of the greatest man-made wonders in the whole world. It spans over 20,000 km, is visible from space (or maybe it isn't) and I was now less than five minutes away from it, but I hadn't even caught one glimpse.

Then I spotted a young man who looked to be in his early twenties, dressed in soldier's combats, emerging from one of the side streets. I was so relieved to see an official. I thought he'd be helpful and might even speak English. I raced towards him, which in hindsight was probably slightly terrifying for the poor guy. Although I didn't realise it at the time, my face was now black with dirt from the streets and my eyes were wildly bloodshot from being awake for so long. He spoke no English, so I broke into what I felt was the easiest charades conversation I'd had to date. Pointing, then rubbing my hands all over a nearby wall we were both standing by, I said, 'WAAAALLLLL', energetically throwing my arms wide open and adding, 'BIIIIIIIG'. 'Wall Big' felt like a fairly legit request considering we were standing close to the biggest wall on the planet. Up to that point I'd never really considered what the Chinese called the Great Wall of China, but for future reference, it's *Wanly Changcheng*.

The soldier stared blankly back at me, and I sensed my energy (and wild appearance) was not appreciated. The next guy I met had a better imagination and smiled as I flapped my arms: 'Wall! Big! Very Big! Big wall!' He pointed up the hill behind us and I leaped on to Little Pig, riding with urgency and surprising myself that I still had that kind of energy left.

I switched my only-just-charged phone back on as I came to the signs for the car park. With 4% battery a message pinged through, giving the driver's location and car description. I sent him the thumbs up, then cycled another 500 metres, straight past the pickup point, to the foot of the Great Wall for a quick pic and video for Lachlan. 'The Alright Wall of China' has been a standard joke in our house since watching Karl Pilkington's escapades in *An Idiot Abroad*, so now that I was standing there, actually at the foot of the Alright Wall, I couldn't help but do a re-enactment. Which I knew I would find far funnier than Lachlan, but he'd appreciate it all the same.

I rolled back down the busy street to my driver, who looked fairly horrified at the thought of me getting into his clean car. He handed me a pack of baby wipes to clean myself off as he flattened his back seats before lifting my bike in. I'd done it. The air con was on full blast, my phone was charging and I fell sound asleep for the two-hour drive to the airport.

All I had left to do, with one hour until check-in closed, was wheel my bike into oversize baggage, find a shower and eat my own body weight in noodles – easy!

At the check-in desk, however, I was informed that the airline policy of accepting unpackaged bikes didn't apply at Beijing Airport and I would actually need to wrap Little Pig. This was big news as I had nothing in place for this flight. The woman from the airline was super helpful and took me to see a man who boxed up smaller items for people. He was very reluctant to help but the woman's charm worked and he agreed to box up Little Pig, who I'd broken down as much as possible. He wasn't shy in letting me know that he'd rather not be doing it and continued tutting and throwing his arms up in the air – it was a little awkward.

He wanted 600 Chinese yen and I had only 500 on me. I offered him this for now, assuring him that I'd return with the other 100, but he was refusing to give me my bike until he had it. My check-in was nearly closing, so my airport champion again talked him into giving us the bike. We agreed I'd leave him my photo ID (my emergency driver's licence) along with the money I had, as insurance that I would return.

Once Little Pig was checked in, I went to the bank machine and it promptly swallowed my card. I couldn't believe this was happening. I'd taken two with me but didn't want to risk losing the second one. I called the help number on the bank machine and a man on the other end said they would get someone down to me. After five minutes the woman from the airline came and said I'd need to leave it as it would take me 30 minutes to reach my gate: 'You need to go; you'll miss your flight.' So, I walked through the security doors without my ID, and didn't look back. I'm so so sorry, Mr Box Man!

PART III
THE SOUTHERN HEMISPHERE

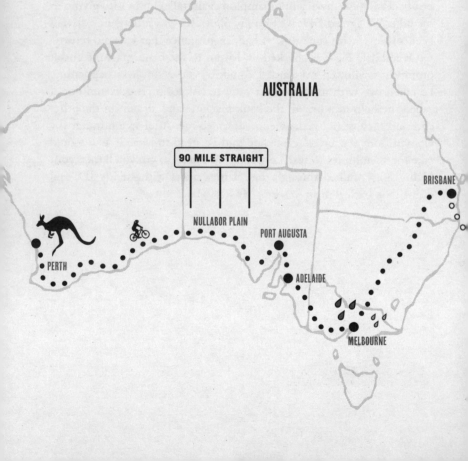

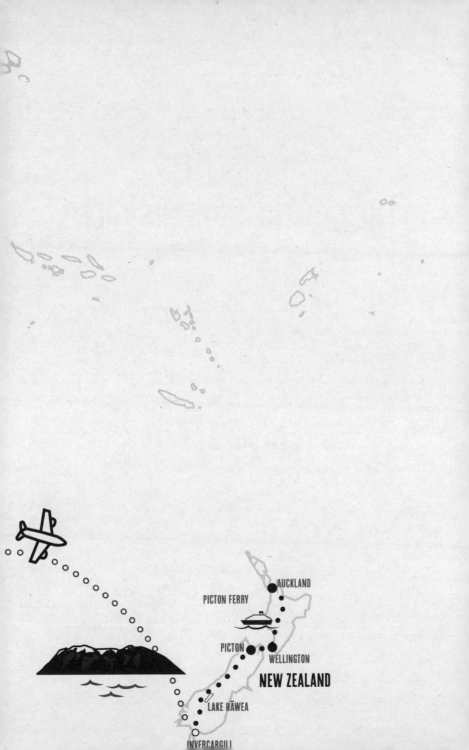

Day 38: 23 July 2018 • Perth, Australia

🎧 *I went to this bike shop in Perth as soon as I arrived and they were the most amazing people in the world. They just welcomed me with open arms, cuddles and coffee, and wheeled my bike off. They were like, 'Okay, what do you need?' So, I started saying: 'New tyres, blah, blah, blah...' but they were, 'No, we've got your bike sorted, what do you need? Do you need a shower? Do you need to charge things? Do you need food?' Just so lovely.*

Dennis Lightfoot bounced his way towards me as I was dragging my battered, stolen cardboard box through the front door and down the long entrance to his shop. He was beaming from ear to ear, with a glow in his cheeks and eyes to match, as he embraced me in a welcoming, broad-shouldered bear hug. It was the best hug I'd had since Melanie on the start line nearly six weeks ago. It felt so homely, like we'd known each other for a really long time.

The self-supported rules that I'd imposed on myself meant that I could receive support from public services, such as bike shops, post offices or hotels along the way, and I'd found Dennis and his bike shop while googling bike shops in Perth before the trip started. As he refilled my coffee, he told me about the move he'd made from England to Australia, his own bike racing career and how he'd supported the GB road team when they passed through Perth a few years before.

Dennis had dedicated his day to looking after me, and I was surprised at how comforting this felt. I hadn't actually realised how alone I'd been feeling until suddenly I wasn't any more. I needed to top up on electrical gadgets, since every new country meant a new charging plug combo. I'd leave my old ones in airports or cafés in the hope someone would pick them up. I'd also need a local SIM card for my new continent and I was looking forward to being back on steady 4G instead of watching my credit fritter away on receiving messages – it would be much easier to keep in touch with people back home as well as to navigate through cities. Finding a SIM on the first leg had been difficult, so I would mostly just use Wi-Fi when I could find it, but that did mean I tended to have longer breaks sorting out admin.

Dennis took me to the store just around the corner that would sell everything I needed and we efficiently whizzed around ticking things off my list. He shared my story with anyone who looked like they could perhaps supply a discount for me and I laughed. It was fun to be with him.

My strategy for the first leg of my trip had been to run my components into the ground. Easier, I thought, than trying to navigate language barriers and find services in Asia. Now Little Pig was overdue to receive a head-to-toe refurb: a whole new chain set, cassette, chainrings, chain, rear mech and tyres, the winter version of the Continental 4000s that I'd been riding with from the start. I'd need something harder-wearing now I was in the southern hemisphere, leaping from summer to winter.

Jeff Brooks, an ex-international racer and former tour leader in the Tour of Thailand, was the shop mechanic and he diligently worked on replacing gear cables, brake pads and discs. I told him about my saddle issue: despite being a super-duper expensive seat post, it couldn't deal with the weight of my rear bag, which was surely a design fault. The attachment point where the saddle and seat post met was a small, curved, fist-like shape. It seemed clear to me that the weight of my saddle bag was making the saddle roll backwards, but he wasn't convinced.

On closer inspection, he noticed that someone (that would be me) had put the support plate on backwards, meaning that the long part was pointing inwards instead of out towards the weight-bearing section. I had to laugh – 10,450 km of adjusting my saddle every day and I had just put the plate on backwards. I didn't even know that was a thing! At least now I could stop balancing on the tip, trying to save it from yet another slide. I had ridden a broken bike without stressing for a really long way and that felt like a positive – I'd just got on with it, after all – but not taking the time to try to work it out meant that I'd gone through all that discomfort for nothing.

The bike was ready to go well before I was. I pottered around barefoot in the back alley of the shop, fixing kit and finding space for some new winter layers. I was avoiding leaving the comfort of what had quickly become my new safe space. I had been away from home for only six weeks, but every night my place of shelter and safety had been a temporary one. It surprised me how attached and connected I could feel to the most basic of shelters – drainpipes, even – and here I was attaching myself to the alleyway at the back of a shop.

In my real home I had comfort and warmth. I had a bed and pyjamas that I missed so much after spending six weeks sleeping in Lycra shorts. I had a loving, fun community, full of both adventurers and old friends. I had roots and a family. I lived with Lachlan – who was currently heading up our home quarters!

He'd burst into this world 19 years ago, with a tactic that he would continue to employ: bum first with a crash and bang. Lachlan was older now than I had been when I sat on the hospital bed as the surgeon explained to me the process of a caesarean section. My little baby was not only a thumper in size, but had also engaged in a breech position, folded in two. I'm not going to get into the details of childbirth, but rather the result. With limited stress during the event, our beautiful baby Lachlan entered the world with the most wonderful complexion, a perfectly rounded head, chubby cheeks and the bluest eyes. I would stare at his perfect form, feeling that, although all parents thought the same about their own babies, ours actually was the most perfectly beautiful being that I, and probably anyone else, had ever set eyes on. This has, of course, been my opinion his entire life as every stage of motherhood has brought out a new part of Lachlan's ever-developing character.

The home we share in Inverness is a ground-floor apartment with two bedrooms, a living room, kitchen and bathroom, front and back gardens. We planted saplings when he was young and watched them grow with him into strong rowan, birch and beech trees. While I had been on the road, Lachlan reported that we had wood pigeons nesting in them – not the most exotic bird perhaps, but exciting nonetheless.

When I began my preparations for Round the World, Lachlan knew only too well what that would look like at home. He had endured the lead-up to many a trip and race, and was no stranger to bike paraphernalia lying scattered around, maps pinned to the walls and me methodically working through to-do lists in the middle of it all. Perhaps it was a coincidence, but not long after I announced my new adventure plans, he announced he was moving out. I was happy for him: he had met a girl who was studying in the Central Belt of Scotland, and wanted to go and hang out there for a bit, and work out what life would look like.

Letting go of a child is perhaps the hardest part of raising them. That perfectly rounded being with the glowing complexion must be trusted to fly, safe in the knowledge he could come home when the time was right. And he did. Two weeks before I was due to leave, he and his girlfriend moved back for the summer. Again, maybe it was just a coincidence.

I loved having Lachlan around. He was great company, and I missed him when he left, but also felt relief. I no longer had to pretend that I could possibly keep all these plates spinning. I was too exhausted at the end of the week to contemplate keeping on top of running a home, fixing stuff or doing the chores. Focusing on preparations, I would just get used to living with broken things. Cooker, worktop, heating, skirting board... As it turned out, not unlike riding through Russia on a wobbly saddle.

Now that I was on the road, it was a relief not having all the broken bits around me anymore. Like so many other things on the road, 'home' had been stripped back. It was no longer a physical place, but rather a self-defined place within me. No longer somewhere I would return to every day, but one I would carry with me, like a tortoise and its shell.

●　●　●

Dennis had asked a customer to give me and Little Pig a lift back to Perth Airport, where I'd begin the next leg. I bought a coffee and a lemon drizzle cake, and stared down at my feet. It was hard not to notice that I seemed to be frittering away the head start Dennis had given me with his efficiency in the shop. I couldn't explain my reluctance to get started, yet it felt so familiar. Time was passing me by. I could almost touch it as if it were grains of sand pouring from the palms of my hands, but still I would just sit and wait. One more minute.

Day 39: 24 July 2018 • Perth to Threeways Roadhouse, Stuart Highway • 5 hours • 95.3 km • ODO: 9697.33 km • Bivvy on the Roadhouse porch

I cycled out of Perth with a couple of hours of daylight left, the low winter sun dropping away behind me as I gained height riding into the Youraling State Forest. I would soon realise how much I'd taken that sun for granted, but for now I couldn't imagine a world without it. Despite the familiar similarities in language and culture, Australia was always going to be a worrisome place for me to be, mainly because of the 140 different species of land-based snakes that call it home.

I've been terrified of the mere thought of snakes my whole life. As a toddler, I had a red and black carpet with squiggly shapes across it in my bedroom. I would wake in the middle of the night and imagine that my floor had turned into a snake pit, and I would have to tiptoe and jump across it as if I was the character on my sister's computer. As an adult, I knew, of course, that this was an irrational fear. I wasn't frightened of the venomous ones, either. Instead, it was the thought of any of them curling up on the bottom of my sleeping bag, like a cat, or worse, slithering into my bivvy bag with me.

On the lead-up to the trip, when I should have been concentrating on all the wildlife I might encounter, snakes were consuming my thoughts so much that everything else I did come across came as a surprise. Kangaroos especially. I'd known they would be there, but thought I knew what to expect. As I climbed high in the twilight, silhouetted forms emerged from the forest. At least twice my size, the gigantic shapes towered over me as I rode low on my tribars. Their features were all out of proportion: tails as long as cars and tiny little arms, not unlike a Tyrannosaurus rex. Their erratic bouncing was made possible by extra-long launch pad feet. They bounced and stumbled across my path, staggering like a drunk on the street. This would have almost been laughable if it weren't for their serious, empty eyes staring through me. Were they cold and calculating or just empty and dumb? I was slightly bewildered by my reaction: here I was, on my first day on the opposite side of the planet, getting all freaked out by the kangaroos. Really hadn't seen that one coming.

I pulled into a roadhouse, which was closed for the night. There was a truck in the car park and a man hovering around it. Normally I would avoid letting people I meet know that I was camping out on my own, but my mind was preoccupied with kangaroo chat. The driver gave me the lowdown and assured me that, although they might jump out in front of me, they were unlikely to attack – although when I kept pressing for more scenarios, he sounded less sure. I decided to stay in the safety of the roadhouse porch for the night. It was still an open space, but it felt safer than lying on the ground and getting trampled on... or worse! With only 97 Aussie kilometres under my belt I nervously spent my first night ever in the southern hemisphere.

Day 40: 25 July 2018 • Threeways Roadhouse, Stuart Highway to Albany • 13 hours 33 minutes • 315 km • ODO: 10,012.33 km • Albany Hotel

The day started on a high, mainly because I had survived my first night in Kangarooland. Plus, because I slept on the roadhouse porch, I didn't have a single pedal stroke to do before filling up with a bucketload of coffee. I sent out a few kanga SOS messages over breakfast, and had mixed replies:

Nic: 'You're right to be worried. Mega sharp claws, if one attacks go into a foetal position to protect your organs.' Delete.

Dennis: 'Kangas have been a real nuisance the last few months, move cautiously.' Delete.

Lachlan: 'The important thing to remember if you find yourself in a kangaroo situation is not to overreact. More people are killed in the UK every year by cows than any Australian wildlife, it's all hype.' Save!

This seemed like an unlikely fact, but I wasn't about to check. Besides, Lach was right: I needed some perspective to get those wheels turning today, especially come mid-morning when the weather changed for the worst. The rain didn't stop for the rest of the day.

🎧 *This is an utter procrastination chat. I've not got a whole lot to say, but I'm hiding out from the rain. I'm somewhere between Perth and my next destination, Albany. I've got a motel there for the night, but it's still 150 km away. It's dark so early and it's pouring down with rain, Scottish style! This café is open and I've just come in. It's 7 p.m. already.*

Stopping on a night like this is a double-edged sword: at some point you have to put your wet kit on and get back outside. Often, I'd rather just keep going without the momentary comfort, but I needed to call the hotel and a sit-down dinner is always a treat. A chirpy chap answered the phone from the hotel in Albany, introducing himself as Jeff. I explained my timings and how there was no way I'd be there for midnight as planned. More like 2 a.m. I suggested I look for somewhere closer, but Chirpy Jeff wouldn't hear of it. 'No, no, you just come on down, that's fine. Phone me when you're outside and I'll open up for you.'

Another seven hours in that storm felt almost unbearable, but I was swept up by Jeff's enthusiasm. Somehow, disappointing him would be worse than facing the rain. I eventually reached Albany at 3 a.m. and was met by a now-sleepy Jeff. Relieved to be indoors at last, I hung all my wet kit around the room, showered and fell sound asleep with the heating cranked up full blast. Bliss.

Day 41: 26 July 2018 • Albany to Jerramungup • 9 hours 30 minutes • 186.16 km • ODO: 10,198.49 km • Campsite sofa

🎧 *Left from Albany this morning and it absolutely pissed it down all day, all night. Didn't really meet anyone, didn't really see anything. Kangaroo sightings zero, which totally suits me! I found a campsite in a place beginning with J – Jeremiah or something – which is a way shorter distance than it was meant to be. I had another 110 km to go, but it was just disgusting weather. My Garmin said it was only 8°C – arghhh. Oh, Jerramungup is the place name.*

Jerramungup, or 'Yarra-mo-up' as it should be pronounced, managed to bring a smile to my now fairly miserable face. Ending a word with 'up' seemed peculiar to me, but I would soon learn that it was common out in these parts. In the coming days I would pass through places like Jacup, Munglinup and Dalyup. *Up* is derived from the ancient Aboriginal language and means 'place of'. *Jarramungup* translates as 'place of the tall yate trees'.

Were it not for the weather, I would have been able to admire these strong native trees sprouting in a messy entanglement of trunks, with rough brown bark and lance-shaped leaves. If only I had managed to lift my head up and look around. Instead, I rode with blinkers on, stuck in my own head. It wasn't just the weather that was getting to me, but the lack of stimulation. Asia had been full of unknowns and magical encounters. There were dust-filled roads and blazing sunshine. Now I just felt a bit empty, wrapped up in my familiar Gore-Tex layers and riding in single-figure temperatures. I felt a little bit heartbroken, like my soul was still making her way down those dusty trails of Asia, while my body was very much stuck here in wet, cold, boring, kangaroo-filled Australia. I worried how I would deal with the next 6450 km if things didn't improve.

A sign for a campsite was too tempting not to stop. It was around 10 p.m. and my total ride time of the day was just nine and a half hours, but I needed to get out of this storm, look after my body and get my head together. No one was around as I cycled down the driveway; darkness had already fallen, four long hours ago. I found the camp kitchen: a basic outdoor set-up that provided shelter for the night. There was a sofa in the dining area, so I lay down and fell asleep, listening to the rain battering off the tin roof.

Australia and I hadn't yet bonded, but I hoped our relationship would improve – and quickly.

Day 42: 27 July 2018 • Jerramungup to Gibson • 13 hours 31 minutes • 308.67 km • ODO: 10,507.16 km • Motel

🎧 *Everyone is like, 'Australia must be really amazing,' but honestly, all it's done is piss it down. It's about 6°C , so no, it's not amazing yet – get me back to Asia! I'm in full-on waterproof winter gear. I'm just about to get started and it's raining again! Rainy, rainy, rainy, hilly, hilly and lots of kangaroos.*

The rest stop hadn't done my mindset much good, but the tailwind following me that day did a lot to help. The road undulated its way along the south coast. I was only a couple of days away from the Nullarbor Plain and it was nice to have a target. I'd ridden that section many times in my head and it felt as though I'd already been there. The daylight didn't last long and soon it was dark. Those long, dark nights were starting to wear on me.

I was so tired that I was actually falling asleep on the bike. I used everything I had to stay awake. I sang, I drank water, I ate. This is what I call the 'Sleepy Monsters' – a term coined by my friend Huw

Oliver during Lejog-manay (a 96-hour cycle from Land's End to John o' Groats over Hogmanay) at New Year. You can postpone them, but nothing stops them, so when I got them I had to change what I was doing, which meant getting off the bike and going to the toilet – except I was a bit scared to get off the bike. Out in the wild, even going for a pee was quite a big deal for me, because there was just so, so much that I was frightened of. Well, dormant snakes and gigantic kangaroos mainly.

Sleepy Monsters' movements float under your hood unnoticed. Calmly they dull your senses. There may be chaos all around you, yet inside your head the softened edges of your thoughts merge into one another before they drift off for good. Sleepy Monsters congregate in your forehead, heavy and dense. The weight of their presence teeters on the edge of your eyelashes, forcing your eyes to blink shut, just for a second, then one more. Whispered thoughts float around you, urging you to close them for Just. One. More. Second... And now they are closed.

I woke from a Sleepy Monster takeover as I drifted on to the other side of the road, still upright and riding my bike, but momentarily asleep. The road was quiet; I'd been lucky. My task for the next 19,000 km would be to manage these little menaces while ensuring safe forward momentum, so I developed a strategy inspired by Albert Einstein. I once read that he took regular power naps on a rocking chair. To ensure he didn't sleep too long, he held a pencil in his hand. As he transitioned into a deep sleep, the muscles in his hand would relax and the pencil would fall to the wooden floor. The noise would wake him up from his semi-conscious state. A genius in more ways than one!

My bike adaptation was fairly simple. I'd move to the side of the road, unclip my pedals and straddle the bike. Folding my arms, I'd rest my head in them and lean on the tribars that stuck out of the front of my bike from the handlebars. As I began to drift off my muscles would relax and I'd feel my bike giving way underneath me. As it did, I'd wake with a start. This gave me just enough of a rest to get rid of the Sleepy Monsters so I could carry on riding safely.

The key to these naps was not to get too comfortable. I did try getting off the bike, lying in bus shelters, doorsteps and against trees, but all of these resulted in me sleeping too long, getting cold and feeling groggy. Remaining on the bike was going to be a key part of these micro naps for the next two months.

Day 43: 28 July 2018 • Gibson to Fraser Range Station, Eyre Highway • 14 hours 46 minutes • 284.9 km • ODO: 10,792.06 km • Caravan park pod

Today was Mum's birthday, so I sent some messages home and tried not to moan about the weather too much. And I most definitely didn't mention having woken up veering on to the wrong side of the road the night before.

I settled into the ride as I turned north, away from the coast and up towards Norseman. I hoped to go further than that tonight and perhaps hit the famous Eyre Highway – a piece of tarmac that would guide me for 1660 km across the Nullarbor Plain from Western Australia to South Australia. As the rain eased, so did the dark mood that had been following me for the last few days. Rolling into Salmon Gums, I met a lovely woman in the garage, who told me that she had previously run a youth hostel. When she retired, she connected with all the young travellers who had worked for her over the years and then went on a three-month tour of Europe, staying with them all along the way. I thought that was brilliant. It was refreshing to be smiling and laughing with someone again, plus she gave me some free cookies to send me on my way.

It was soon dark and this was the first clear night I'd had in Australia. I was treated to the most wonderful sight: as well as being full, the moon was also at its closest point to the earth along its orbit, making it appear to be much larger than normal as it rose over the horizon. On top of this supermoon, the sky was alight with stars. It felt less like I was looking up at them and more like I was riding through a great glittering blanket of space. I had no idea what I was seeing, but it turns out that the Milky Way is a hundred times brighter in the southern hemisphere than the northern, so this really was the starriest night of my life, and it was such a delight to be out riding in it. It's all too easy to enclose ourselves in the comfort of indoors once the sun goes down, but often these are the stolen hours of our lives. The moments when we know that we are indeed living.

🎧 *The moon's an old friend at this point. I suppose it is the one thing that stays the same. Everything is changing constantly around me: the people, the smells, the noise, the quality of roads, the busy-ness and the one thing that stays the same is the sky. Obviously the moon changes, it goes through its cycle, but that predictability in itself is soothing.*

Day 44: 29 July 2018 • Fraser Range Station, Eyre Highway to Caiguna Roadhouse • 13 hours 45 minutes • 271.45 km • ODO: 11,063.51 km • Roadhouse

The previous evening, I could make out silhouettes of huge big boulders and crooked trees, a bit like something from *The Flintstones*. Finally, some character in the landscape; it would be a good day. I just needed to warm up first. I was already shivering as I opened the door on my campsite pod. This basic wooden structure had zero insulation and was colder inside than it was out.

The frost melted as the sun rose and at last it shone brightly. I was riding east again, with the Southern Ocean to my right and the great wilderness of the Nullarbor Plain to my left. The roads were wide and quiet, with the occasional road train passing me with ease. These vehicles are, just as the name suggests, a lorry travelling long haul with two or three trailers attached. They're intimidating in size, but I found the drivers to be cautious, always moving far out into the road to avoid me. They carried heavy grilles on the front to protect the trucks from collisions with kangaroos. That wasn't great news for the kangas and I got used to the smell of death on the road from their decomposing carcases. As the sun went down I reached the Australian landmark I'd thought so much about, the 90 Mile Straight, a long and very straight section of the Eyre Highway.

🎧 *Hey! It's Sunday 29 of July, and I've just passed the very famous 90 Mile Straight sign. Got really excited about it, took loads of pictures and sent video messages home to my mum and Auntie Lorna. I've just started cycling again, the sun's just going down, I'm listening to some good tunes, and yeah, just delighted to be here basically, very, very lucky, I can't get my head round the scale, it's massive like, just wow!*

[3 hours later]

Okay, the reality of this has just hit me. I've got to cycle for 90 miles in a straight line. It's literally 90 miles of one big straight road. There is not one turn or corner in it. There are small dipping hills but nothing to block your view. I am watching vehicle lights coming towards me and timing them: 28 minutes is the furthest away that I have started seeing them. They are just coming and coming towards me, and half an hour later they'll pass me. It's funny, isn't it? (Laughter.) It is probably quite a nice time to ride it actually, it's so quiet. There is traffic coming towards me but hardly any really. There's a big moon and you can just see all the silhouettes of all the trees and shrubs and stuff. Everything's about the same height as me, but it's not dense so you can see for miles…

• • •

'A hideous anomaly, a blot on the face of Nature, the sort of place one gets into in bad dreams,' wrote the novelist Henry Kingsley describing the first European crossing of the Nullarbor Plain in 1841.

I imagined the first men walking through this endless expanse of sameness, the panoramic horizon seemingly never drawing closer. How easy it would be to question if you were making any progress at all, but as courageous as they were, it was the Aboriginal peoples who left me in wonder. Long before any Westerner, these nomads survived on the edges of the plain, hunting on and gathering from little more than shrubland.

Anybody crossing the Eyre Highway today has an entirely different experience. The wilderness has been tamed by the 13 roadhouses scattered unevenly along the 1660-km stretch of tarmac. These are a safe haven for weary travellers like me looking to refuel and hydrate, for the zealous tourist collecting souvenirs and for the road train drivers taking goods from coast to coast.

I had imagined being here many times before, not because I'd been looking forward to it, but because I'd been warned how desolate and monotonous it can feel. As part of my training, if the weather was particularly bad, I'd ride on an indoor bike trainer with a map of Nullarbor hanging on the wall in front of me. I had visualised being here, ticking off the kilometres between each stop. And the truth is, nothing will ever be as monotonous as riding a stationary bike while staring at a brick wall. In comparison, the plain was positively charming.

Day 46: 31 July 2018 • Eucla Roadhouse to west of Yalata • 11 hours 16 minutes • 240 km • ODO: 11,642.34 km • Bivvy by the side of the road

Darcy O'Shea enthusiastically moved from his own table to mine as I tucked into dinner at the Nullarbor Roadhouse. He too was a visitor to the area, making a trip from Darwin to see the whales that had come into calf this winter. It sounded very cool!

'It's only a short detour,' he assured me. Detours, though, were not in my vocabulary on this trip. They were not a choice I'd make over 29,000 km around the globe – unless it was for roadworks, food or emergency. Then and only then would I detour. There were no shortcuts on this route, I needed the kilometres. No sightseeing excursions, I needed the time!

But a pod of up to a hundred orca mums and their young would be spectacular. We continued chatting about our travels as I collected up my numerous belongings, moving cables and electronics from the table where they had been charging into the dry bag ready to redistribute when I got back to my bike. I loved meeting people like Darcy. Adventure meant different things to us, but we shared an inquisitive curiosity for life.

I'd lost an hour and three quarters today after crossing over two time zones since breakfast: one international timeline and one regional Nullarbor timeline. It was 180 km to the next roadhouse and already 8 p.m. I'd planned for a bivvy out in the open tonight for only the second time since my arrival – I'd done well finding accommodation this far. The cool, wet conditions, coupled with my fear of apparently everything, meant at least I was resting well at night indoors and able to avoid my worries, but that wasn't to last.

Before leaving the Nullarbor Roadhouse and entering the wilds, I made my way to the outdoor toilet block for a wash. There I was confronted by a shabby yet graphic poster, an A4 colour print of an angry snake – a warning to tourists. There were frequent sightings of them in the area apparently and this was a reminder to keep doors closed. As snakes are my worst nightmare, I couldn't bear to look at the poster, but I really needed to wee. I used my right hand to block the hostile glare from view and reached far above with my left hand to push the door open. Holding my breath, I hurried inside, closing the door tight behind me. Walking up and down the well-trodden tiles of the bathroom, I shook my hands rapidly, breathing loudly and trying to get my head around what this meant. Would there be snakes where I was going to bivvy?

Standing by the sink I spoke out loud to myself, reassuring the vulnerable reflection staring back at me. 'The print is faded and torn around the edges. Who knows how long it's been there! And it's so cold, Jen! Below zero at nights. Snakes will need to be pretty desperate to want to be out in this.' I tried to keep it light, but inside I was panicking. 'Okay, you have options: you can just stay here and get a bed inside.' I didn't believe that was really an option given the time I still needed to make up, but acknowledging the choice was important. 'Or you can get changed into your jammies now and ride in them until you stop to camp.' This would save me from exposing myself to a snake by getting changed outside. 'Then, we'll camp somewhere nice and cold.'

I often used 'we', as if my conscious self and my physical self were two individuals worthy of distinguishing – one to do the thinking and rationalising, the other to stay awake and ride her bike. Ultimately, they'd look after one and other.

On the road I had already asked many people about snake activity. In fact, probably every day I'd slip it into conversation with at least one local. 'Don't worry, they'll be dormant right now and you're unlikely to come across any' should have been reassuring, but neither 'unlikely' nor 'dormant' was enough commitment for me. Now, by and large, 'dormant' and 'hibernation' have meanings that are extremely similar, but I liked the concrete rules and time frames that came with the term 'hibernation'. Dormant, on the other hand, just felt a bit flaky. Particularly with cold-blooded creatures, 'dormant' might mean they emerged on warm days to go and find some water. And I didn't want to meet them on the way.

I changed and carried on cycling, and soon passed the junction for whale watching. It was three miles down to the cliff edge. You can stand looking out over the ocean, with little between you and Antarctica, while the biggest mammals in the world mother their young. What a magical scene it would have been. I rode past the turn-off with a tiny pang that I was missing out on a once-in-a-lifetime moment. I hadn't truly bonded with Australia and I couldn't imagine wanting to return; maybe I did need to stop the clock for the detour. In daylight, I think and hope that's what would have happened, but it would be dark for the next 11 hours, so it was unlikely I'd even get a glimpse. This was one of only two times when I regretted being in a hurry. The other would come in Canada.

Hours later, I rode up a dirt track to a recreation point into a large open car park. It felt darker tonight than it had been on the trip to date. I rode around until I found a flat, exposed piece of ground free from wood and sticks and anything that could be mistaken for something more sinister, reluctant to put my feet down until I was sure I was safe. Camping out was, as always, a methodical affair. I began thinking about my system before I stopped. Reaching around into my saddle bag, I began pulling out extra layers of clothes, still straddling the bike like a nervous swimmer keeping her grip on the edge of a pool.

I blew up my mat and carefully laid it down. Then I pulled out my sleeping bag and stuffed it directly into the bivvy bag cover, leaving me with only one opening to protect. Now off the bike, I removed one shoe and stepped that foot into the bags, and then the other. Holding the openings up around my waist with one hand to keep it off the ground, I used the other to shake out both shoes and clumsily placed them in a dry bag. These would be my pillow for the night. I pulled the sleeping bag right up over my shoulders and tied the bivvy's mesh hood closed around my head. I lay cocooned in my bag, with so many clothes on I had to work at breathing. 'This will be fine – they'd need to be desperate to be out in this,' I kept reminding myself as I drifted off.

Day 47: 1 August 2018 • West of Yalata to Ceduna • 14 hours 9 minutes • 254.34 km • ODO: 11,896.68 km • Hotel

Waking up in a bivvy bag when you're bursting for a pee can be a harrowing experience. I tugged too hard at the hooded zip, and extra material gathered and jammed it tight. Taking deep and deliberate breaths, I gently but firmly readjusted my body to release some of the material I was sitting on and started again. Holding the flapping hood taut, I gently pulled the zip open and freed my head! Hooray!

But it wasn't over yet. The recent decline of my pelvic floor meant that as soon as I stood up and released the pressure on my bladder, I'd have a matter of seconds before the uncontrollable flow began. Okay! Breaths had become shorter and sharper now, as I carefully pulled down the clothing from the bottom half of my body while still sitting in the bag. Intense. This felt high risk. Lumpishly turning on to all fours, I crawled out of the bag and into a squat. The relief, both physical and mental, was intense. I scanned the ground and held my sleeping bag high in the air to avoid any wrigglers entering.

There was a fairly constant headwind today and the sun shone so brightly it slightly burned the skin across my face. I didn't mind, though; I welcomed the heat.

The days were so short out here in midwinter and I seemed to be spending more time with the moon than the sun. There was immense comfort in watching her light up the horizon as she rose night after night. The moon had waned dramatically from that first evening hitting the Nullarbor. The journey had taken a lot from both of us, but soon she would build again, bringing with her fresh hope that I would too.

During these long nights, my legs spun like it was the only thing they knew to do. I'd lose myself in hours of contentment; my mind empty, feeling utterly at one with my place in the world. Other times I needed some extra stimulation. It might be counting up miles, storytelling, singing songs, listening to podcasts or leaving voice notes for loved ones. Tonight I had something else to keep me engaged: the S.N.A.K.E situation.

I was already feeling less than relaxed about stopping in the dark due to kangaroo worries, and now I was pushing to see if I could eliminate stopping altogether. Could I ride continuously from when the sun went down? I needed to stop for:

- Food and drink;
- Faffing around with my clothes;
- Sorting out my charging cables, lights, headphones, etc;
- Mechanicals;
- Toileting;
- Rest.

If I could organise myself in such a way that the majority of these items could be taken care of, either before it got dark or from my saddle, then everything could be in place. I couldn't do much about mechanicals other than pledge to look at issues in the daylight rather than leaving them to get worse – only time would tell if that would work – but toileting was the stumbling block. I was stopping for a pee three or four times a night at the moment, but was that necessary? Or could I carry out the task while in motion? I had a 'wee' chuckle. That's silly... I would spend the following evenings mastering this skill.

I had a key piece of equipment to make me believe this was possible – Endura Drop Seat bibs. For the cyclist, bibs are similar to cycling shorts except for the integral braces that eliminate the need for a waistband, giving you a more comfortable, tighter fit and, importantly, less chaffing. The issue can be getting those straps down once you've put all your clothes on top of them. My shorts combatted this issue with a clever zip that starts and finishes mid-thigh on either leg. Once opened, the back of the shorts drops down, baring your bum. It's a great design for minimal toileting faff while on the road and this easy access would be crucial to my plan.

I'm an active learner. Often I need to try and then fail before I can get my head around what the task requires, so there was only one way to find out. I unzipped the bum, pulled the bib flap forward, unclipped my left foot from the pedal, leaned far over to the side while pushing my bike out in the opposite direction, so as to avoid my bike bags and gear as I freewheeled along at a good pace, and released. For a split-second things were going well, until my bib flap moved and I began peeing straight into the chamois. Trying to stop my flow was comparable to an HGV lorry putting the brakes on while going downhill – slowly and with great effort! In the meantime, I continued filling up what appeared to be a bib bucket.

I had 32 km to ride in my urine-drenched shorts and ponder what I'd learned:

- Prepare for the aftermath and have wipes, Sudocrem and a plastic bag at the ready.
- Once you've committed, don't take a pedal stroke, so get up to speed before you begin – a gradual downhill is ideal, but flat will also work if you're cruising and uphill will not.
- Note the wind direction (self-explanatory).
- This is only a night-time activity and preferably in a rural setting.
- Most important of all, pull the bib flap forward, hook it on top of the saddle and for goodness' sake, tuck it in before it forms a bucket!

Just passing a vehicle checkpoint at Ceduna quarantine station, I saw the bright lights of a 24-hour petrol station and a hotel, my bed for the night. I was feeling fairly feral by this point. A constant flow of snot had hardened into rockets across my face and in my hair. It was a long time since I'd eaten crisps with my fingers. Instead, I'd buy the family-size packs (cheese puffs were my favourite) and pour them straight into my mouth, until lifting my arms became so tiring that I'd just place my head in the bag and munch, like I was eating from a trough, covering my face in cheese debris. At this point on the journey, I was crawling into ditches, toilet blocks and bus shelters to sleep without thinking twice (when snakes weren't on my mind, that is!). Now, at 3 a.m., I stood in my wee'd-on shorts feeling excited about the hummus and crackers I'd just found in the garage fridge.

Living like this (a pig on the Pig) made the luxury of hotel stops all the more special. Over the last 47 days I had slept indoors on 22 nights. These ranged from the most well-appointed establishments, as in Ulaanbaatar, where I avoided asking the cost, to fairly basic shelters, where I was just grateful to be able to close the door on the outside world. Tonight's was much-needed, a nice contrast to the pee incident, and I lucked out: a great selection of teas and such fluffy pillows!

Day 48: 2 August 2018 • Ceduna to Wudinna • 10 hours 22 minutes • 212 km • ODO: 12,108.68 km • Toilet block

I made full use of the fruit tea selection as I collected up my kit from around the room. It was raining hard and the forecast told me I would cycle into a headwind all day long. The motivation to leave was low, but I coaxed myself out of the door with a deal: if I just made it to the garage, I could sit there for a bit. So off I shuffled, head to toe in Gore-Tex for the foreseeable.

🎧 *I stayed on the bike for 10 and a half hours today after a few stops to warm up. It's been relentless. All. Day. Long! Water thumping on the ground around me. I've just crawled into a tiny little toilet block to bed down for the night. A woman in the petrol station a few hours ago had offered me a room in her house, as she was horrified I was riding – such a sweetheart.*

Day 49: 3 August 2018 • Wudinna to Port Augusta • 12 hours 31 minutes • 260 km • ODO: 12,368.68 km • Motel

🎧 *Everything is breaking! Two zips have burst on my bag. My Garmin is playing up and not switching on this morning. My bike computer battery has run out. Also need a new chain, it's slipping like mad! My mat's burst – again – and annoyingly, my bank card isn't working so well. It's fine in person but not over the phone, so I can't book accommodation with it. Aggggh! I need to call the bank and get that sorted. It might just be because of too many foreign transactions. I did tell them before I left but they said it would be fine.*

By chance that morning I woke up and found a laundromat at the end of the street, right next to a Subway, petrol station and toilets. It was like the perfect bikepacking street to wake up in. Ignoring the washing machines, I went straight to the tumble driers. They both had a piece of paper taped over the top of the coin entry, reading, 'OUT

OF ORDER'. I couldn't believe it. I looked behind the machines. They were unplugged, so, tentatively, I plugged them in, switched the plugs on, removed the advisory sign and put my coins in. I filled one with my sodden kit from yesterday, leaving out only the shorts and down jacket I was wearing. Once I was confident the machine wasn't going to burst into flames I went to the garage for breakfast and arrived back with an arm full of goodies, including a cappuccino. Then I took off my shoes to try to dry them out and began trying to fix my broken things.

Later that night, about 10 p.m. and somewhere north of Kimba, I was a bit creeped out by a car driving really close to me, then backing off again. Finally, it drove past, a woman shouting at me out of the window. I had no idea if this was an angry yell or I was being cheered on, but the car pulled in ahead, two figures got out and I heard, 'Jenny! Jenny! Stop!' Phew. Friendly – always a relief!

I didn't know Jock and his wife Sheila, but Mum was pals with his sister back home. They'd been following my progress the whole way from Berlin and realised I'd be cycling near them that night. They'd been out for the evening, Jock in his tweed suit. Between that and his Highland accent, he was tugging at my heart. They were so much fun, just the loveliest people. Jock was trying to get my bike into his car to sprint me off to their house. I felt bad breaking the news that I couldn't go with them; he looked so disappointed. He insisted that I take 50 bucks to get somewhere to stay that night. We took some selfies for Mum and his sister Maureen, and they gave me a big wave off – definitely the highlight of the day.

Day 50: 4 August 2018 • Port Augusta to Adelaide • 10 hours 30 minutes • 306.3 km • ODO: 12,674.98 km • Hostel

🎧 *A hard start to the day. I was feeling a bit grotty. It took me about 50 km to start feeling good, even though I had a tailwind. I kept stopping just to fidget with stuff, but then in the afternoon I totally got into it and it was a really nice day on the road.*

Despite the slow start, I clocked over 300 km in the end as I swept through the empty suburban streets of Adelaide. I'd been looking forward to arriving here. Being a child of the '80s I was brought up on a healthy dose of *Neighbours*, *Home and Away* and *The Flying Doctors*. Although filmed in Melbourne, *Neighbours* had frequent references to Adelaide. I hadn't watched the series for nearly 30 years, but was flooded with nostalgia.

My favourite internet search to find services as I rolled into a new city was '— near me'. I could fill the blank with anything, but the regulars were coffee, food, toilets and cheap accommodation. A map would appear on my screen with all the options and I'd use it to navigate. But tonight's search for cheap accommodation showed very few options. It was late, gone midnight, as I rolled up to the door of a lit hotel. There was a vacancy sign and through the great big windows that ran down the length of the green lawn I could see a man behind the bar.

He didn't hear my first knock, so I leaned over to the glass panelled window and knocked again. He turned around and I waved as if at an old friend. He must have been in his early thirties with a tanned complexion, whiter-than-white teeth and sleek hair expertly placed (a perfect image that I suspect I was not mirroring). He opened the door and I burst into chat: 'Hello, I'm so glad you're still open. I've just rolled into town and need a bed for the night.' My enthusiasm hit a brick wall, fell dead on the floor and landed right next to the welcome door mat. 'I've already cashed up,' he replied. Deadpan.

'Oh, I can pay with cash or card. I could pay in the morning if it's easier?'

He repeated his previous answer: 'I've already cashed up,' this time with more finality in his voice.

'I'm alone,' I added, hoping to ignite his conscience. There was an uncomfortable moment of silence.

'You can't stay here,' he said. 'I've already closed the tills.'

I felt a rage inside. Unwilling to slump away and free him from the awkwardness, I stayed put. 'You know, I'm a lone traveller visiting your country...' And I was off, off on some rant to guilt-trip this young man into recognising my vulnerability. Even I was surprised by this move. After a lifetime of convincing others I was strong, self-sufficient, capable and independent, I now wanted to be seen as vulnerable? I think I wanted him to care. To worry about my well-being. To put as much value on me having a bed tonight as him getting to his own.

I felt an overwhelming sense of entitlement to that room. I wanted my freedom to roam and sleep rough, to suffer and push through when I chose, but when I decided I needed a rest and to be looked after I expected my wish to be granted. And I was so close.

I was instantly taken back to the families in Asia with no running water, electricity or monetary wealth, and the kindness and warmth they had shown. I despaired to see him, a product of a Western society, now so desensitised that his inconvenience was taking priority over my basic needs. Where was the humanity?

Eventually, I did manage to own it, to recognise that being born into the very society that I was now blasting is what had allowed me the privilege of having my wheels on this soil, but that reflection would come later. Right now he was turning away and locking the door. What. A. Douche!

Day 51: 5 August 2018 • Adelaide to Tintinara • 12 hours 13 minutes • 240 km • ODO: 12,914.98 km • Bivvy beside a BP garage

Adelaide is sandwiched between the Gulf of St Vincent to the west and the Mount Lofty Ranges that rise to the east. I followed one of the many classic climbs out of the city, heading inland, up Greenhill Road. It felt tough early on. The first few hundred metres were at a gradient of over 9%. My legs hadn't had that kind of ascent since climbing up to Frazer Range at the eastern end of the Nullarbor, nearly 2000 km ago.

I was relishing the moment, though, and clinging on to the small amount of momentum I carried. My bike was pivoting with my weighty saddlebag, so I leaned into the bars until the road relaxed into a steady sustained effort.

The clouds gathered dramatically in the sky above, with the threat of a storm only adding to the atmosphere. My surroundings were lush, an array of greens as trees, bushes and grass enclosed the tight passage and then opened out to reveal the ever-expanding metropolis beneath

The startline at the Brandenburg Gate, Berlin. With only moments to go, I was joined by Tom, Mike and some of Berlin's keenest well-wishers.

Mozzie bites. My ever-expanding sausage face as I rode through eastern Europe, crossing into country number three: Lithuania.

Russian guards posing for a picture after a surprisingly warm welcome.

My tribar set-up. Home for the trip.

I was fixing my puncture when a gardener and barman came out with a bucket of water and some cola. East of Novosibirsk, Siberia.

The sun was beginning to rise on a foggy day when I found this pipe underneath the road in Tulun, Russia which provided shelter for Little Pig and me. I was a quarter of the way around the world!

Meeting a family of bike tourers on a road summit before dropping down to Lake Baikal, Russia.

My Mongolian border hosts. They welcomed me into their van to cross from Russia to Mongolia.

Little Pig meets a little goat outside a toilet block, Mongolia.

Midnight, on my final push in China. A friendly family fed me and didn't want me to leave, and their young boy was woken up to welcome me.

My dusty, surprised and elated face as I made it to the end of the first leg. The Great Wall of China, Badaling.

A warm and friendly welcome at Glen Parker Cycles in Perth, Australia by Dennis and the team.

The sun going down as I hit this iconic Australian landmark. 90 miles of straight road.

Foot selfie: Taken in a scabby toilet block in the middle of a storm in Australia. The pain was caused by foot rot due to poor conditions.

The beautiful Lake Hāwea, New Zealand.

Toad River, British Columbia. My view looking upstream from the Iron Bridge on the Alaskan Highway.

My friend Dave Bach riding with me in Wisconsin, bringing with him some light relief after a hard week.

Playpark bivvy. A double slide provided a modest shelter for a few hours of sleep on the outskirts of Québec City.

Filmmaker Thomas Hogben made a surprise visit to the north of Spain for some of the final miles back in Europe.

My reaction captured by
Alan Goldsmith as Lee
tumbled to the ground
behind him.

Me and Mum on
the finish line.
Credit: Stefan
Haehnel.

The finish line with
family, friends and
well-wishers. Credit:
Stefan Haehnel.

me. It was only from up here that the flat plains of Adelaide came into view and I could get a true feel for the city's neatly gridded streets laid out below. The road continued twisting and bending across the hillside, until 20 km later I reached the summit at 622 metres. The road would drop a little before undulating to my planned lunch stop in the small town of Nairne, but just then the floodgates opened and rain poured from the sky.

With not a lot of traffic on the road, it was easy to spot the same man who kept appearing in lay-bys. At one point he was flying his drone and I shouted 'Hi' as I rode past. He didn't look up and I assumed he was doing his own thing, until he appeared again further up the hill – this time literally pointing a camera in my face and still saying nothing. The penny finally dropped. 'Oh, are you here for me?'

'Yes, I'm Jordan. Tom asked me to come along and grab some footage.'

Delighted, I stopped. I remembered filmmaker Tom mentioning a couple of weeks ago that he might have found someone to capture some of Australia, but I didn't recall any of the details. And I was confused that the cameraman had stayed silent. 'Why didn't you say anything?' I asked him.

'Tom told me not to bother you, that you'd just want to have your head down.'

I laughed. 'I would have been okay with a hi!'

I asked him to join me for lunch. It was nice to have some company, until somehow the conversation got on to mass murderers in Australia. I went with it for a while in the way that you watch horror movies for longer than you should before realising that you're walking home alone!

Still, the dark conversation helped me drag myself away from the lovely warm café and get back into the rain, alone again. It battered down hard, but that didn't matter. The joy of being back into the hills was enough. On the Straight, I'd missed having the hard pushes and the reward of free speed when you reach the top.

I rode late into the night until I found a 24-hour café stop in Tintinara. The building was bookended with outdoor toilets and a covered veranda. The rain had continued all night, biblically at points, so I asked the waiter if I could sleep in the outdoor shelter. It had a concrete floor, so it wouldn't be as comfortable as the grass option, but the pull of being undercover was huge. It was 2 a.m., so I assured him I'd be up and out by 7 and he agreed.

I'd just changed from my cycling kit and begun unpacking my sleeping equipment when the manager arrived. He wasn't okay and instead said I could camp on the grass on the other side of the car park. I didn't take this as hard as the night before; knowing I could get up and come straight in for coffee in the morning made the difference. Still, so disappointing and I sat in the bathroom trying to avoid spending any longer than needed in a soggy bivvy bag.

Day 52: 6 August 2018 • Tintinara to Tarpeen • 10 hours 10 minutes • 224.72 km • ODO: 13,159.68 km • Bivvy in bus stop

🎧 *The rain stopped through the night between 3.30 a.m. and 7.30 a.m., and so I got a really nice sleep and managed to get packed up in the dry. Waking up right next to the restaurant is such a buzz. I just got up and came straight in. They've made me a massive double big breakfast and two coffees! That should hopefully make up for the lack of hours asleep.*

Nothing of note happened today other than the miserable weather. It rained and rained and rained some more, but I was making okay progress, considering. I just needed another few hours in the saddle. Around 10 p.m., I pulled up to a bus stop. I was 60 km from where I planned to rest that night and just 20 km from Mount Gambier, the next resupply point, which I needed to hit, because I was currently fuelled by an emergency supply of sugary sweets. I was also struggling with saddle sores. Even with full waterproofs on, I was finding it impossible to stay dry, and the constant rain and grit from the roads was getting into my chamois.

I stopped to apply some barrier cream. I didn't really need to get off my bike, but the shelter looked so inviting – and it was. Sitting on the wide wooden bench felt like a relief. The structure was made from corrugated iron and had a deep arched roof that protected me completely from the elements. It had been so noisy inside my hood for hours, with the rustle of Gore-Tex being beaten about by the wind and rain. Now the world was silent once again, except for the gentle patter of rain hitting the roof before rolling to the ground.

I woke up on the bench, shivering and completely drained, probably due to an almighty sugar crash. My clothes were still wet and I was now cold, so I changed into something dry and stood with my bike, staring at the ground, miserably. I felt reluctant to start riding again.

Mount Gambier was a much shorter distance than I had planned for tonight, but if I could just make it there, I'd get a proper bed and could warm up. Without checking I'd decided that Mount Gambier was an actual mountain, meaning that the 20 km to get there would be hard ones. Depleted of all fight and drive, I had an overriding urge to lay down. I began to pull my sleeping bag from my bike: I was done. I would get up really early, I assured myself. I'd need to, because a big bus stop like this would be busy in the morning!

I was unsettled and had shivering fits throughout the night. My eyes were getting the rest they needed, but my body not so much. I finally woke completely at 7 a.m. The world was already moving. I lay watching. The traffic passing by, people getting on with their day. Groggily sitting up, my face was crumpled and swollen from dehydration and lack of rest. The sun shone brightly and I squinted my eyes to adjust. It lit up my space, but I felt the weight of the darkness still. I battled with demons sitting there on that bench, berating myself for getting everything so wrong. This was chaotic, messy. 'You're not doing this properly, Jen! This isn't how you ride around the world!'

I was annoyed for taking such a long, unproductive stop. My electricals weren't charging so easily out here. Shorter days meant I had my lights on more and, although I could charge through my dyno hub, it was nowhere near as effective.

My riding clothes weren't just damp, they were actually wet from the storm. I was far from rested, and I thought of all the lovely hotels I'd stayed in and rushed away from in the morning. Yet here I was, still sat bundled up in this bus stop, unable to move and overwhelmed by the shame of messing up.

I found the lack of companionship on the road meant it was too easy to get caught up in my own thoughts when I was feeling down. Speaking aloud helped me to process the situation and find more empathy towards myself, but I couldn't face talking to a real person. I didn't want to be comforted and reassured. I needed straight talk and to acknowledge the fuck-ups. So, I began a video diary. I guess it was my roadside therapy session covered up by the pretence of making a film…

🎧 *It's 8 a.m. and I've stopped for nearly 10 hours and I haven't even got a proper rest. I've not dried off any of my stuff or charged anything. I'm a bit annoyed with myself. I'm not sure what happened, but mentally I was just like 'Boom! That's enough!' Really annoying. What a waste of time. Awww – and I'm still here! Getting going is my problem. Once I'm going, I'm fine, but getting going is a real pain.*

Actually, this is the time I need to be really nice to myself, when I'm feeling like this. I need to start today afresh. That's all I can do, just keep on keeping on!

Oh, and also just got word from my pal Dave, who is in Melbourne. He reckons that I am 320 km away from where he is going to jump on and ride with me, so that's great. It'll be so nice to see him. So nice to see anyone, to be honest with you. I didn't say that to him (laughter). 'Can't wait to see you. Can't wait to see anyone!' Hey, hey, okay, bye, bye.

Day 53: 7 August 2018 • Tarpeen to Camperdown • 13 hours 50 minutes • 275.5 km • ODO: 13,435.18 km • Bivvy in minging toilet

I'd been promised the most stunning section of road as I hugged the coast before cutting inland towards Melbourne along the Prince's Highway. However, the sleet coming in sideways from the ocean, battering into my face, made me doubt that I'd be seeing any sort of beauty today.

My summer shoes, now protected with winter covers, had a small crack in each of the soles, exposing my feet to water from the road. My two-season Gore-Tex jacket struggled to keep out the winter conditions that today had delivered.

My three rear lights shone bright. Two flashed rapidly and the other remained a solid glow. I was as visible as I could be, but still. I imagined the speed of the wipers on a windscreen behind me and wondered how much notice a driver would have to see me. Would they be expecting me at all? I was thankful for the lack of traffic on the road. After a while I put my headphones in, just as a distraction from the reality of the next 10 hours.

I was soon lost in Lee Craigie's *Life Cycle* podcast. It was a programme in which she was discussing the subject of death with her mum, Lesley; an honest and heartfelt conversation about letting your parents go, allowing them to grow in the same way they allow you to grow, except their growth might entail slowing down. It was about accepting the fact that they, and we, are all ageing and ultimately will die.

The tears were soon rolling down my cheeks as my heart ached, thinking about my own mum. The depth of our love felt like physical pain right now. As if my chest had been ripped open, exposing my beating heart. How monumental a part she plays in my life. We are connected on a level almost impossible to describe in words, yet I felt it in every inch of my being.

The faith she had put in me was incredible. The unspoken belief and trust that I'd work it out and get the job done, whatever it might be. Which is remarkable, as she is the one person in the world to consistently be there when things inevitably don't go right. Any life topic I can think of is accompanied by a long list of Mum bailouts – especially travel. I like to put this down to being born an optimist as opposed to being highly disorganised. It just rarely crosses my mind that things might not go to plan or not fall in my favour. This has resulted in me sitting in airports bewildered as my flight takes off without me, waking up on trains at the wrong station, sitting in cars that have just run out of fuel, and shivering in bus stops or phone boxes on an adventure when I've bitten off more than I can chew. Mum has always been available on speed dial, consoling me, transferring cash or even heading out on emergency pickups.

'Oh, don't worry, pet! Donald [my mum's equally incredibly supporting and loving husband, who seamlessly slotted into our family ways and has supported Mum and us on any crazy mission] will come with me. It'll be nice to get the run,' she'd assure me as they packed the car with a picnic, filled a flask, threw in a bag of dry clothes and raced to any far-flung corner of Scotland to pick me up. Instead of holding a long list of failures up in front of me, she has remained my cheerleader, encouraging me across any finish line. She of all the people in the world could write a book of the reasons why I probably shouldn't leave the house, let alone ride around the planet. But she doesn't, it's not where her mind goes. She sees the growth, the learning, and she oozes loving patience.

Mum is fit, healthy, with an infectious spark for life. She has the ability to drop everything in the promise of a new ending to the day; she's such an adventurous soul. She was in her late sixties when I left and had been looking at afterlife admin, and it was here I wished I could show her the same patience that she's shown me for all these years.

As Mum talked of funeral arrangements or what she had in place, I'd feel my chin begin to wobble. My heart would well up, as if it might explode in response to the enormity of thinking about a time I wouldn't have her. 'Jen, it's better we talk about this,' she would say and console me, calmly. This poor woman – thinking practically about her own mortality while having to deal with the anxiety of my grief to come. We've always had an open flow of communication, but now at this stage I couldn't bear to listen.

Hearing Lee and Lesley, I understood that this was the conversation my mum wanted us to have. I had been too scared to let her. I needed her to be strong, keeping the dynamic the same, resistant to the change slowly creeping in. I felt raw all afternoon following the podcast. I sat with it for a while, processing. Then I pulled into a lay-by, bending over to protect my screen from the rain and sent two messages, one to Lee, thanking her for such a powerful conversation, and one to Mum, letting her know I was thinking about her.

The depth of my emotion was short-lived. As I stood up to put my phone away, I let out more than a little bit of a tinkle. My bladder. It had been weakening over the past few weeks; I'd probably picked up a UTI, perhaps worsened by the freezing conditions. All I knew for now was that my pelvic floor could no longer be trusted. It's hard not to fall into catastrophic thinking out on the road: 'It's not my mum I need to worry about ageing – it's me! Maybe this is it, the onset of incontinence?' Of all the physical side effects I'd expected from this trip, this wasn't one of them.

Thankfully the problem did pass, but for a couple of weeks to come I would need to plan for emergency pees before I arrived at built-up areas. It only ever happened when I sat up and released my bladder from the hunched-over position. So, if I was planning getting off the bike in the town, I'd need to pre-plan. When I rode towards built-up areas, I would have to go at the side of the road; I knew I wouldn't have time to make it into a building and find the bathroom otherwise.

It's this level of humility and vulnerability on the road that helps you stay in the moment. Stops you mulling over the big picture stuff and brings you right back into the here and now, and the immediacy of dealing with the simplest of tasks.

● ● ●

By now I couldn't remember life before this storm. In the 274 km I rode that day, the only view I had was through the tunnel of my hooded jacket, out to the immediate road in front. It's bizarre spending that much time riding somewhere, but having no idea of the surroundings.

It was 3 a.m. as I arrived in Camperdown. I passed the no vacancy signs at the town's two motels and pulled up to a red-brick toilet block by the side of the road. Toilet blocks aren't the most obvious place to sleep, but once you delve into the world of ultra-endurance riding, you soon develop an appreciation for how much they have to offer.

An inside space, hand dryer, washing facilities, space for Little Pig and a locked door are all welcome comforts in the right circumstances. But even for a connoisseur like me, tonight's accommodation was pushing the boundaries of what's okay and what's really not!

The cold cubicle was covered in off-white tiles and drainage lay around the edges, filled with water and debris from outside. It was a damp space with a wet floor. The toilet pan had faeces at the back of it and a little on the wall. I shuddered at the thought of spending the next few hours in there, but the rain was coming down so hard I was grateful for having at least this space for me and Little Pig, out of the storm.

This would now be my third night sleeping out, unable to dry off clothes and warm up properly – and at this stage in the ride it only accelerated the deterioration of my body. Tonight, the underside of my feet ached so badly, with every bump in the road causing sharp pains on the soles of my feet, as though they were resting on a bed of broken glass. Needing to examine them, I covered the toilet pan with the lid and balanced my bum on the edge, avoiding leaning back into anything awful. I'd taken my shoes and soaking-wet socks off, and my legs felt stiff and heavy, so I was unable to lift them up far enough to get a proper look. Instead, I placed my phone on the floor, resting it against a bag with the screen pointing back towards me. I set a timer on the camera and stuck my legs out in front of me, waiting for the flash to go. The picture was funny. A great angle with my feet taking centre stage. It made me laugh despite what I was seeing and I knew I would spend a bit more time dialling in the shot to send to a group WhatsApp chat, knowing it would gross out my friends back home as they ate their lunch.

In the meantime, though, what it revealed wasn't great. Deep crevices splintered the base of my feet. The skin was pure bright white with extreme wrinkles cracking across them from edge to edge. The flesh on the bottom of my toes had been rubbed off and the cuts throbbed to their own pulse. Three of my toes had grazes on the knuckles too, grazes that covered nearly their whole dumpy length. Bottom line: I had foot rot. Tissue damage caused by prolonged exposure to damp, wet conditions. I'd had this before, but never to this degree – I'd need to dry them out soon for them to recover.

I mopped up a space on the floor and hesitantly made my bed. The cleaners arrived only a couple of hours later and, embarrassed, I made my way out of the cubicle, carrying Little Pig over the floor they had just mopped. I had panicked initially, assuming that they'd be cross with me. Instead, they looked dumbfounded that anyone would have slept in there. I stuttered an apology and assured them the mess hadn't been created by me.

Day 54: 8 August 2018 • Camperdown to Melbourne • 10 hours 39 minutes • 214.12 km • ODO: 13,649.3 km • Hotel

A 24-hour garage supplied me with two plates of cooked breakfast, gallons of coffee and a free shower. Just as I was leaving town, a dot watcher arrived in his car, all suited and booted for a day in the office. We struck up a conversation.

Our lives couldn't have been more different that morning, and I was struggling to describe how I was feeling to someone so clean and well rested, especially when he was talking like I was doing something heroic yet I knew the reality: a night spent in a shitty toilet block. He gave me his card and told me to call if I needed anything. Very sweet!

The next 200 km into Melbourne were a drag; nothing but relentless suburban roads grinding me down. I was lethargic, sore and tired. I wanted to be there so badly, but it was difficult being the only person in control of making that happen. I stopped twice to charge my electrics and hovered around longer than needed both times.

From the city of Geelong I could see the glow of Melbourne across the bay and would continue with it in my sights for the rest of the night. The lights were shining bright, but they never got any closer as I skirted the city rather than entering it. It was 2 a.m. by the time I hobbled around the apartment at the Marriott Airport Hotel with my washed hair wrapped in a towel. My face was puffed out and shiny, now freshly covered with Vaseline. Music was playing loudly from my phone and I was drinking an endless amount of tea. The apartment had a washing machine and tumble drier, so for the first time in nearly two months I had washed my clothes. My shoes were laid out on the radiator and once they had dried, I lined them with duct tape to help keep the water from penetrating through the cracked soles. Such a satisfying ending to the day – and a massive relief to have the chance that night to reset.

Day 55: 9 August 2018 • Melbourne to Shepparton • 10 hours 17 minutes • 177 km • ODO: 13,826.3 km • Bivvy in a field

Dave Moore. I first met Dave on my mountain leaders training course, back home in 2012. Years later, he reappeared in my life on two wheels at our local mountain bike group. His most recent adventure had found him on a tour of Australia, on which he bought an old banger of a car in Perth and drove it east, basically along the same route as me, until he reached Melbourne. There he went to a party, met a local lassie, fell in love, packed up his life in the Highlands and he had moved to Melbourne just a couple of weeks before. When he saw I'd be coming through, in true Dave form he bought a second-hand road bike for a hundred bucks and was giving it its first outing on some miles with me that day. I just loved his adventurous attitude.

Dave and I met up mid-morning and, for perhaps the most uninspiring 160 km section of tarmac ever, he joined me on the road. We hugged the hard shoulder climbing north on the busy Hume Freeway, a stonking headwind adding to the already gloomy day.

Despite our history we hadn't spent any one-to-one time together, but his presence was a comfort and so easy. A little nugget of home! And I appreciated his time and effort greatly – giving me some company on the road was such a lovely thing to do. It was the first time anyone had joined me for more than a few miles since that very first day leaving Berlin. A few hours later, though, in a town called Seymour, Dave had to head off to find a train and head back to Melbourne. Just like that, it was dark and I was alone again…

Before he left I had given him some fairly big chat about the distance I was hoping to get in tonight, but about 30 km later I got a puncture – my first of three. As always, the puncture took only minutes to fix; it was the seating of the tyre which left me a hot, sweaty, sweary mess and it took close to an hour. One hour to fix one puncture! I was annoyed, but still optimistic – until the next one. This time, the tyre seated more easily, but every time I unscrewed my pump it took with it the core valve of the inner tube, resulting in all the air coming straight back out. This was 'operator error' all three times, but still left me in the same sweaty, sweary mess. The evening was frittering away before my eyes and at 2 a.m. a third puncture pushed me over the edge. That was me for the night and I lay down in a field next to the road with my burst tyre by my side.

Day 56: 10 August 2018 • Shepparton to Jerilderie • 9 hours 7 minutes • 146 km • ODO: 13,972.3 km • Motel

Sitting on a picnic bench next to where I had called it a day last night, I fixed the remaining punctures. Each wheel had an inner tube and I was carrying two spares as well, but now three out of four had holes in them. Each was caused by tiny shards of metal on the road – the same as all my other punctures up to this point (now a total of 18).

I wrinkled my forehead up in annoyance while keeping pressure on my final patch, glue oozing out of the edges. I was so annoyed with myself – for having stupid tubes, for not riding fast enough, for sleeping in that bus stop four nights ago, meaning a stream of shorter days ever since, for still sitting here on this bench, not riding! I was falling behind drastically. For two days in a row I had managed little more than 200 km a day (despite being up for over 19 hours).

I can't overemphasise the power of coffee in these situations. Not just the effects of the caffeine, but the comforting crutch it supplies. It had become the stepping stone to getting on with the day and it was good to know I was a short pedal from it this morning. By this point in the journey, the days I woke without it in my sights were genuinely distressing.

I had a 56 km/h headwind for the whole day. The news had blasted it out over breakfast, but I didn't need the telly telling me; the trees lining the streets told that story. They weren't so much swaying as buckling. Bent in two, not fighting the force, but just about holding their own. I lingered for too long, both pondering and avoiding life at the same time. Trees just get on with it, using the wind as an opportunity to strengthen their roots and develop; following the path of least resistance, but staying strong, ready to spring back up into form the moment they are able to. Note to self: be more tree.

By late afternoon I'd only ridden 66 km due to a late start and an incredibly slow, but tough, pace. There was one and a half hours of daylight left. Days like this were frustrating and a little soul-destroying, but knowing that the wind was due to die down tonight kept me going…

Day 57: 11 August 2018 • Jerilderie to Wyalong • 11 hours 40 minutes • 256 km • ODO: 14,228.3 km • Motel

🎧 *Today was so good! It sort of rained biblically for most of it, but I had a little tailwind behind me, and Matt and Kerrie came out. Matt rode the first 110 km with me. Kerry jumped on the bike and Matt drove. She was on the bike for about 60 km till it got dark. Then they were off in the van. They've got a camper van and a wee doggie, and are going to meet up with me again tomorrow, which is so cool.*

Matt Kemp is a fellow bikepacker and we'd met two years before at the Highland Trail 550, the classic route across the Highlands. We had friends in common, so the hours flew by as he told me stories about his adventures from all over Australia. Matt was originally from England and had moved with his wife Kerrie to set up home in Melbourne. I was pleased to have their company for a few hours.

The sun was setting at around 8.30 p.m. now, quite a difference from arriving in Perth three weeks ago, but the days were still gloomy and wet, so it felt dark much earlier than that. I rode through to 11.30 p.m. and pulled in at a stop to grab some tea and snacks.

A truck driver came into the garage. He was driving a two-carriage road train across the Nullarbor, heading for Sydney, and told me he'd been looking out for me for hours. The drivers were all on a radio system telling one another about road conditions, etc. and I had been flagged up this afternoon. They couldn't believe I was riding through this storm. I gave him the Round the World chat. He got so excited and insisted on buying all my shopping for me. People's reactions always took me by surprise.

The genuine excitement of complete strangers was always welcome. At this stage of the trip I was too busy obsessing about getting the pedal strokes in, dealing with the admin and focusing on the kilometres I *wasn't* doing – and it was easy to lose touch with the strokes I had ridden, the scale of the journey and how much I had already achieved. Strangers could see the bigger picture.

Whether they shared some kilometres, bought me dinner, wrote me a message, took a picture or shared a hug, they all had their own story and reason for connecting. Of course, the majority of people couldn't care less, and rightly so. It was only a bike ride, but those who did care nourished me for the hours and days to follow.

I stayed in the town for the evening. It was earlier than I'd have liked, but the next accommodation was 110 km away and the weather was still wild, so I cycled back up the street to a motel and woke up the owner, who happily gave me a bed for the night. It had been a miserable day and though I had ridden myself into a good mood – as I so often did – I was aware of the need to look after myself. I'd been low the past couple of days and my feet had really suffered with the wet weather. It wouldn't have taken much to find myself with trench foot again.

Day 58: 12 August 2018 • Wyalong to Dubbo • 11 hours 43 minutes • 255.5 km • ODO: 14,483.8 km • Motel

Kerrie and Matt joined me by mid-morning for another pedal and we all had lunch together in a diner near Narrandera before they drove back to Melbourne and I carried on north towards Dubbo.

Today I had the wind on my back and, although it was bitterly cold, the sun shone bright – a real boost after last night's crazy weather. Waving my new friends off after lunch, I rode only 300 metres up the road when the digits I'd been waiting for appeared on the small screen of my bike computer: 14,500 km or 9000 miles. I was *halfway* around the world! *HALFWAY* around the planet in 57 days. That works out as a daily average of 255.8 km. The current record holder averaged 201 km per day, so I was well on record target; although my aim of cycling 280 km daily to finish in 110 days had begun slipping away. If I continued at the same pace I would now be looking at a 117-day finish, including my upcoming flights. The halfway landmark was such a boost after an emotionally tough week.

Excited, I turned to ride back and share the moment, but was faced by a wall of wind. I rode into it fleetingly, but the extra effort was so considerable I decided to message them later instead, even though in the distance I could still see them fiddling with their bike to get it on to the van. Ha! I'd made it *halfway* around the world!

My mood was high – from the favourable wind direction, the flat landscape and the halfway point being hit. I hadn't felt this strong on Little Pig since Adelaide, so I allowed myself to make some big plans. Reaching 320 km tonight would keep me on track for my Wednesday flight from Brisbane. I made a conscious effort to be the most efficient I could be at stops – and stuck to it. When you're that focused, this is easy, but also drains you and the rest points throughout the day are valuable.

Past 11.30 p.m., I found myself standing outside a motel apartment block in Dubbo. A chill had taken over my whole body. I wrapped my arms around my front, with my hands stuck deep into my armpits. My shoulders were tense and tremoring, quickly and involuntarily. My teeth were chattering relentlessly. I felt faint and nauseous, but questioned if the sudden extreme reaction was to the thought of having to bivvy out in freezing conditions tonight. Surely I couldn't be fake shivering? It's disconcerting not knowing whether you can trust yourself. Is your tired brain taking over or is your health actually at risk? My well-being was balancing on a knife edge right now. When I felt good, I glided with ease; but when I didn't, I'd fall fast. There was no middle ground: all or nothing.

I was at a daily total of 260 km – 60 km shorter than I wanted to be and 70 km between here and the next motel. In the end I listened to my quivering bones. The guy on reception couldn't have been nicer: with no budget rooms left, he gave me a free upgrade. I just needed to carry my bike up to the first floor of the apartments and wheel it along the outside corridor.

In the room, a white jacuzzi bath stood against the far-off wall. I sat on the king-size bed and carefully removed my shoes and socks, trying to leave as much skin intact as I could. The smell of rotting flesh was potent. I switched on the electric blanket, cranked the heating up to 28°C and left both on all night. I sink-washed the basics, my bibs and socks, then hung all my damp kit around the room. I filled the bath with water too hot for my cut feet to step into and lay in it with my legs hanging over the edge, the heat relaxing my aching muscles. I dozed.

The bed felt luxurious, with pillows that I melted into. I slept for six and a half hours, and woke tired and dehydrated from the warmth in the room, but now in a much healthier state.

Day 59: 13 August 2018 • Dubbo to Narrabri • 12 hours 31 minutes • 234 km • ODO: 14,717.8 km • Bivvy in toilet

🎧 *Cycle was very hilly. Headwind. Mega cold! Stopped about 1.30 a.m. at a public toilet at truck drop. Was minus 3 degrees, so cold. Roll matt is too lightweight. No hood on sleeping bag... Bivvy bag too thin. It is FREEEEZING! Shivered to sleep and shivered myself awake again. Rubbish mileage – never going to make plane.*

• • •

For the past 10 days, trip logistics had kept me busy. Thoughts of flight times, bike boxes, bike bag replacements and airport transfers were all-consuming. As I've said, the Guinness World Record Association did not recognise the difference between supported and unsupported record attempts, but for me it was deeply important to the integrity of my own ride, so I had added the ethos of basic self-supported rules to the trip. I wanted to be as pure as possible, but there were grey areas. Just like anyone who bends the rules to suit their needs, I had extremely plausible reasons for doing so. I'm not sure these will matter to anyone, but for total transparency, here they are.

Flight/bike box: I booked and paid for all my own flights, and called to change when I realised I would miss them. I got in touch with bike shops and organised the flight boxes, etc. The grey area was the information my sister Nic was sharing with me. Nic and her wonderful spreadsheet had all the answers. She knew my average pace over days, weeks or months. She knew distances to airports and the speed I'd need to ride at to make the flights. This was info that was invaluable.

Since that time in Russia when she'd told me about a nearby bike shop, she had got better at withholding info until asked, but we slipped into three casual ways of sharing:

- Nic would drop in the odd stat, like 'Yay, 260 avrg pace this week!'
- I'd send her my flight plans followed by '??', knowing she couldn't resist giving her approval or making suggestions.
- While discussing whether I could put in the effort needed to reach the airport on time, I'd ask her outright what was the best flight to catch.

We'd flit constantly between the three modes. Sometimes I'd push back from the help, other days I'd soak it up, grateful to feel we were in this together.

Branded kit replacement: One of the classic rules for self-supported bikepacking is to use only commercial services that are available to all challengers, so no private resupply or lodging.

I'd never had any money from brand sponsorship before this trip, so didn't quite know how best to honour the partnership while on the road. Inevitably I had to replace pieces of kit as I went and it was difficult to stay 'on brand' so, mid-ride, I made a new rule: I would accept a new piece of kit from private sources to keep me 'on brand', firstly as long as I could find a store which sold the item I needed (even though it was 'off brand') and secondly I could prove (to myself) that I had the money to buy it.

While I was passing through Adelaide, I stopped at the Bike Society to replace a chain and grab a seat bolt before climbing into the hills. I also needed replacement bags for the frame and top tube. Both zips had burst wide open, because I'd been over-filling them, and they were currently closed over with zip ties. The shop did have bag replacements available, but these weren't made by Apidura – and the lovely folk at Apidura had agreed to send me out what I needed.

Dennis from Glenpark Cycles in Perth put me in touch with a woman in Brisbane called Rosemary, so I could get the kit and a new bank card sent to her. Somewhere along the line I'd got muddled up and thought she owned a bike shop in Brisbane and was part of the Warm Showers network (a website for touring cyclists). Once the kit had been arranged and sent, though, I found out she was in fact just a friend of Dennis's. This played on my conscience, as it felt like accepting favours from mates, so in the final days of Oz I decided that I could no longer accept her help, but instead found a hotel in New Zealand where she could send on the Apidura kit (the card never arrived). This made her a link in the chain whether I liked it or not, but not physically meeting with her made me feel slightly better.

These were my personal tweaks, but not every ultra-distance rider claiming a self-supported title would choose the same rules. Mine were possibly a bit pedantic and not the most efficient. They definitely slowed me down, but they enabled me to maintain my integrity and the integrity of my ride, and they motivated me.

Every day I was aware of the Round the World clock ticking. Whether I was counting up my ride time, trying to hit the golden 15 hours a day in the saddle, peeling myself away from cafés or pushing on through the dark, long after I wanted to stop, it was that clock motivating me, but when I have a flight to catch my whole world ramps up a notch. From about three days out my focus begins to tune in. How was I moving? What effort did I need to put in to make it?

It was never a conscious decision, but if there were two flights – one I'd need to ride continually towards for 30+ hours and one half a day later that I could ride to comfortably – without exception I would choose the one that meant cutting it fine. The thought of having 'time to spare' at my end point didn't motivate me. Of course, I could have spent it fixing my bike, eating or sleeping, but I learnt that the added stress it brought drove me forward and even after all that time on the road I got an adrenaline boost from it.

The flight I was going to catch on Wednesday morning was now unachievable, so I rebooked for Thursday morning, although that hadn't yet been confirmed by the airline, giving me 46 hours to ride the 625 km into Brisbane. And just like that the 'airport smash' was on.

Day 60: 14 August 2018 • Hours to flight transfer: 46 • Distance to ride: 625.33 km • Time: 8 a.m.

- Laith from Crankbrother Bike Services in Brisbane reached out, offering me an airport transfer, bike service and bike box. He's a public service – and my hero! – and I said absolutely yes, please. I'm meeting him at 6 a.m. on Thursday morning by the river in Brisbane. Whoop!
- Qantas Airlines is still not answering email or phone calls – stressful! – so no flight confirmation yet.

Hours to flight transfer: 34 • Distance to ride: 473.33 km • Time: 8 p.m.

- Flight confirmation for Thursday has arrived! Yahoo!
- Messaged Rosemary and ask her to drop the bags at Laith's shop instead of posting them to New Zealand. She is brilliant!
- Super-flat all day!

Day 61: 15 August 2018 • Hours to flight transfer: 26 • Distance to ride: 362 km • Time: 4 a.m.

- Found a motel for a quick nap in Boggabilla (great name!). I'm so glad.
- About to cross into Queensland, which is my fifth state.
- It's so cold this morning, I'm shivering. Temperature has dropped to -2°C.

Hours to flight transfer: 22 • Distance to ride: 362 km • Time: 8 a.m.

- Managed three and a half hours' sleep.
- The bearings on my right pedal have deteriorated so badly it's wobbling like crazy and I'm worried it will fall off. Hopefully, Laith can get me new ones.

Hours to flight transfer: 15 • **Distance to ride: 231 km** •
Time: 3 p.m.

- Nipped into a BP garage in Millmerran for a quick lunch.
- I can't wait to sleep on the flight.
- The weather is cloudy but much warmer now – 13°C!

Hours to flight transfer: 8 • **Distance to ride: 125 km** •
Time: 10 p.m.

- Message from Nic: 'Hey Jen are you riding through the night?'
  Me: 'Yes, if I push on I should make it!'
  Nic: 'This is so Jenny! You can do it! If you have time, call Mum,
  she's worried…'
- Voice note to Mum: 'Hey Mum, I'm all good, feeling great,
  just going to ride to plane. Should arrive by the time you're
  going to sleep. X'
- A lot of climbing today, then hopefully downhill to the
  coast.
- I can't eat enough today. Freedom Pitstop at Toowoomba.
  Stopped at 24-hour garage for sugary tea. I don't need any
  more sugar. I'm rattling!

Day 62: 16 August 2018 • **Hours to flight transfer: 3** • **Distance to
ride: 55 km** • **Time: 3 a.m.**

- Lots of downhill. Yeaaah!
- Really sleepy. Hope I can stay awake.
- Left message for pal Mary, telling her the plan. Nervous about
  missing flight if I need a nap.

Hours to flight transfer: 2 • **Distance to ride: 35 km** •
Time: 4 a.m.

- Stopped for toilet.
- Facebook tag from Mary repeating all the messages I'd sent her
  in a social media post. I messaged her, all hurt and annoyed:

'Take it down. That was just for you, not all your FB friends, FFS!'
Mary: 'We all just love you, Jen, and everyone is cheering you to the plane!'
Me: 'Take it down!'

Now I wince at the thought of being such a diva, but I was feeling the time pressure and the desperate need to finish with Australia, and Mary assures me she holds no grudge. She's used to me!

Hours to flight transfer: 1 • Distance to ride: 20 km • Time: 5 a.m.

- Unbelievably sleepy.
- Nearly there!

Hours to flight: 2 hours 15 minutes • Distance to ride: 0 km • Time: 6 a.m.

BRISBANE! Yes! I stood by the river watching the sun come up before Laith arrived.

- Laith insisted on dropping me at his house to have a shower and his wife Eloise made me coffee as she got the kids ready for school. He took my bike to his shop to give it a service and new pedals. I was really nervous about leaving it with him, but the shower was great!
- Laith collected me with my bike all packaged up in the boot, but we were cutting it fine with time...

Hours to flight: 1 • Time: 7.15 a.m.

- Less than an hour to flight time and stressed we'd miss it. Luckily, traffic was quiet and we made it in 10 minutes.
- Checked in. Yaaas!

Australia – completed it, mate!

• • •

My bias towards the land where my roots lie is always present. I'm surprised when places that aren't the Scottish Highlands show me outstanding beauty. I compare mountains, landscapes, people and culture with Scotland, and it always comes out top. I even find myself being competitive about the bad stuff too... When I was told that winter in Australia could be really rough, I'd find myself replying, 'Aw yeah, you should try the Scottish Highlands if you want to know about winters.' Or told that it can rain a lot in New Zealand during those months, I'd say, 'Ha, yeah, practically rains every day in Scotland, I'm so used to it!'

Turns out that wasn't a helpful mindset, because it meant I'd *completely* underestimated the southern hemisphere. The harsh weather and minimal nights spent indoors meant I was now entering New Zealand with very little left in the tank. Both my body and mind had taken a beating. I'd need to manage things better out here. My ambitious aim was to finish New Zealand in six days, as long as I could seek out indoor shelter each night.

I flew into Invercargill via Christchurch, the journey taking six and a half hours with an hour and a half layover, landing the previous evening. The atmosphere in the airport was friendly and welcoming, with local travellers and security guards making jokes and encouraging me on my way. I instantly felt at home, because of course this is the kind of welcome you'd receive landing in Scotland, right?

The mountainous landscape would keep me mentally stimulated and give me a challenge. I felt comfortable in the hills. It was dark as I set off on an 80-km ride out from the airport up to Lumsden, where I'd booked a motel for the night, but the race to the airport had now caught up with me. I limped my way through those final miles before pouring into the small room and cranking up the heating. Barely able to undo the zip on my jacket, I spoke briefly to my audio diary, but was drifting in and out of consciousness. This was utter exhaustion.

Day 63: 17 August 2018 • Lumsden, New Zealand to Lake Hāwea • 11 hours 22 minutes • 217 km • ODO: 15,643.24 km • Hostel

I was three coffees in and it was only 10 a.m. I was battling with the now familiar conflict of excitement to be pedalling over new lands and a blanket of lethargy that threatened to prevent me from leaving the warmth and comfort of the café for the grey day ahead. My internal battle was broken by the warmest smile as Hamish Murie walked through the door. He had been heading north to go skiing when he noticed on social media that I was in town and decided instead to hunt me down. The previous year, he had supported Mark Beaumont's team as they passed through with a bike build and a signing of the witness book. Which was a great reminder of my own witness book. 'Oh yes! You must sign mine too,' I said to him. I was getting worse at remembering to collect signatures.

As part of the Guinness World Record rules you need to collect the signatures of the people you meet, confirming that they have seen you and giving a location, date, time, address and any comments. Some people were very excited about this and it was a lovely way for them to be part of the ride, although it was yet another admin task for me to manage. I'd taken two little pads and a pen in the document pocket of my frame bag, and so far had lost the one from the start of the trip, having left it in the bike shop in Mongolia. The woman I met there, Khaliun, got in touch when she found it and posted it to me on my return. The one I was left with was in surprisingly good shape considering the number of times it had been squashed back into that pocket. It was never the thing I thought of doing first, though, as we would go straight to swapping social media accounts, and often I'd be cycling away before I'd remember and have to hastily backtrack for a signature.

Hamish handed me 50 bucks to buy myself dinner. I got embarrassed and tried to return the money, but he insisted. 'This stuff's expensive!' he said. 'Please, have a dinner on me.' It meant a lot and undoubtedly gave me a boost to carry on. It amazed me when people took time out of their lives to just come and say hi, and share some kindness for the day. In the glow of his warmth and enthusiasm, I packed up. It was already midday as I mounted Little Pig and carried on north towards Queenstown and beyond to Lake Hāwea.

With its glaciated glens, rocky outcrops and hills that rose up from the lakeside I could see why this land was so often compared to Scotland. And there was the rain. Yup, let's not forget the rain. That was very Scottish.

🎧 *I booked a hostel tonight. There were only shared rooms, so I was a little bit dubious because of the energy it takes to speak to people. There were three guys, medical students, playing cards when I arrived at 2 a.m. They were so excited! All getting selfies and tagging me on Facebook. It was really cute. I wanted to go to bed so badly, but obviously you can't be rude, so I chatted to them a bit.*

Then I went into the room, trying to be really quiet, and I woke the lassie up. Ping, her name was. She went to the toilet and she came back and asked, 'Are you by bicycle and by yourself?' I was lying slevering on my pillow with exhaustion and this young lassie was chat, chat, chat. It was three in the morning now. She was so adorable. She was from China and I wished I had more energy for her. She appeared to be really quite young and anything I said, she was like, 'Oh, wow! That's cool!' Just so lovely. But anyway, in the end she said, 'I must shut up and let you sleep!' Yes, Ping, yes, you must, ha-ha!

Day 64 : 18 August 2018 • Lake Hāwea to Fox Glacier • 14 hours 37 minutes • 249.55 km • ODO: 15,892.79 km • Hotel

I woke to a blue sky day, the sun bouncing off the snow-capped mountains that lined the horizon. The road followed the ancient turquoise waters of Lake Hāwea as it climbed to a thin strip of land known as the Neck. From there you could see the equally impressive Lake Wānaka lying adjacent to Hāwea, just a kilometre away.

I continued over the Haast Pass, taking pictures for the first time since crossing the Nullarbor. After the drizzle and grey of the rest of Australia, it was so lovely to have an inspiring view again.

The Haast is one of three road passes going over the Southern Alps. The high point sits at just over 500 metres, but meanders around before dropping to the Atlantic Ocean. It's a remote area with no obvious settlements, but plenty of rivers, waterfalls and beech trees, with the Mount Cook range dominating the backdrop.

I'd been struggling over the last two days to deal with some of the changes that Laith had made to my bike in Brisbane, particularly with the bar tape. The handlebars are a critical contact point on the bike. The tape wrapped around them acts as a shock absorber from the vibration of the road, as well as providing grip and comfort. On the lead-up to Round the World I had tried many different brands of tape and most would work on day rides, but the extreme vibration going through your wrists day after day can damage your nerves and leave you with 'claw hand': you lose the ability to grip or pull with your fingers, which makes braking and gear changing extra hard.

I'd found Lizard skin tape gave me the best results and fixed it to my bike just days before I left. Although fairly straightforward to apply, it had started to unravel about a week into Russia, so I wrapped a ton of duct tape around the end to keep it in place and give me extra cushioning, which really helped on some of those Russian roads. I continued adding to the bars along the way and by the time I got to Brisbane I had the perfect comfort and protection for my weary wrists. But this highly functional bodge looked an absolute mess to an untrained eye, let alone the eye of a meticulous mechanic. I made the mistake of letting Laith take my bike away to make the changes we had agreed on, but in his enthusiasm he'd gone off-piste and 'fixed' things he assumed I would be grateful for.

I was not grateful. As soon as I started riding the vibration came straight up and through my wrists. It wasn't just painful, but really annoying. I couldn't believe he'd changed my perfect tape for this cheap, thin version that couldn't protect me on even the flattest of roads. I stopped and wrapped what duct tape I had left around the bars in the hope that it would give me some protection.

He had also removed my joystick light holder, which sat in between my stem and feedbags. Now I never actually used it with the light on; instead it was a place to put my Link Exposure bike light during the day, so as to give my neck a little rest from keeping it on my helmet.

I was riding along not only with the extra physical stress, but I was getting angry that he had taken such liberties. I was angry with myself too. I should have known better! Very few people you meet would understand the dramatic difference these subtle changes would make.

My saving grace today was the heat from the sun and the mountainous views. Every corner I turned gave me fresh perspective on the situation. I replenished my soul while riding through landscapes like these and forgave the overly helpful mechanics in my life.

• • •

The sun had been down for hours by the time I reached my next stop en route and I was concerned I'd missed dinner, but the Heartland Hotel in Haast was still serving food, so I got tucked in and made an evening plan. The next available accommodation would be in Fox Glacier, 119 km away. It was an ambitious evening considering it had taken me all day to ride just 130 km to this point, but I told myself that the thought of sleeping indoors would keep me going.

But the Sleepy Monsters were coming on strong. I was aware that my legs were turning, but I had no grip on what speed I was going as I undulated around the coastline in a dream-like state... until suddenly I let out a loud scream. What the hell was that?! A big, chunky black cat was walking right beside me. Surely I had dreamt it? It woke me up, though, all the way to the cabin. I rolled in at 5 a.m. and finally I could shower, wash clothes, charge equipment and make a cup of tea! It wasn't carried out as methodically as that list makes it sound, though. Instead the kettle went on, clothes hung off me and I found myself washing my bibs with helmet still on...

Day 65: 19 August 2018 • Fox Glacier to Kumara Junction • 11 hours 54 minutes • 192 km • ODO: 16,084.79 km • Bivvy at bus stop

I was on the road by 10 a.m. It was great to get moving, but after only a few hours of sleep it felt harsh. However, there was an endless choice of coffee and breakfast in this little mountain town, so that was a positive.

Eggs Benedict had become my Round the World breakfast of choice. I was, and still am, unable to resist the thick creamy hollandaise sauce with runny egg yolk pouring over my toast. The waitress confirmed my cat sighting last night as an actual possum. Huh? The bad news was that I had lost my neckwarmer somewhere between here and Brisbane. To date, my lost property list was:

- x2 sunglasses (one pair lost, one smashed in a fall)
- x1 outer mitt that had come flying off the hood of my handlebar in Australia
- x3 water bottles
- x1 spare tyre
- x1 jacket in Asia, for which I did a 30-km detour only to discover it was right at the top of my saddle bag, where it should be.

And now my neckwarmer. I had really missed it on the descent the night before, as normally I'd have it up over my mouth and covering my nose to keep me warm. Luckily, Fox Glacier was just the place to replenish stuff. There wasn't a whole lot here except for coffee and outdoor equipment, which was kind of perfect. My new neckwarmer was made with a merino wool mix and had been doubled over and sewn down the middle to make a tubular shape. It was dark grey with black snowflakes scattered across it. This simple item would become the best buy of the whole trip and I'd wear this cosy gem for the remainder of the ride.

The little tourist town being so well equipped lulled me into a false sense of security. I assumed all the villages along the coast would be open too. Having already spent so much time in Fox, I decided to resupply with food later, sure I'd have enough time to make it to dinner that night.

A hundred miles on I was riding through yet another coastal ghost town as the streets lay empty and the promise of a pub meal dwindled. Why on earth had I not resupplied earlier when I had the chance? Now there was no edible food in my pouches, just the odd mouldy, damp nut and a handful of chewy sweets.

Somewhere after Hokitika I passed a village hall with people and music pouring from its doors. The cheesy disco classics were almost drowned out by the sea of loud, excited voices. It was nice to be in among so many good vibes, although everyone was so drunk they didn't even notice me peering through the door. I was holding out for a buffet, but instead left with three packets of crisps picked up from the bar. Luckily the 21st birthday excitement was more nutritious than dinner for the evening and I left happy, smiling at the silliness. I missed my people. I missed long conversations into the night and the intensity of having so much to talk and laugh about.

There wasn't too much time to get lost in that, though. My next task was finding where to sleep that night. My Google search was telling me no accommodation for another 64 km. It was a campsite, so I called and the kind woman on the other end of the phone told me the laundrette would be the cosiest place to sleep that night. The warmth of the tumble drier – I could feel it already. She told me to help myself to the washing machines too, but I had no interest in washing these clothes. I'd already washed them back in Melbourne so I felt fairly clean. Those kilometres would be a stretch, but the thought of staying out in the frosty conditions was even less appealing, so I leaned on to my tribars and settled in for the night.

I was going well until I came to the one and only major junction since leaving Fox that morning: a large, empty roundabout. I needed to stay on the coastal road heading for Greyhound, but instead turned right and began climbing up Arthur's Pass. I was so busy zooming into my GPS unit that I'd missed the gigantic road sign telling me this. I climbed and climbed away from the sea, questioning nothing. My eyes creeped closed like so many nights before. 'Come on, Jen! Get to the laundrette!' I urged myself.

The road was wide and a long deep ditch ran alongside it, built up with stone and rubble. It was this ditch I was heading for as I woke up startled, slamming my brakes on. Fuck, fuck, fuck! That was too close. I laid my head down and napped on my tribars until it was too cold to stay still any longer. Then I remounted the bike and continued, still riding in the wrong direction, further up the hill and now at a crawling pace. My head was fuzzy around the edges and I was drifting in and out of consciousness. I looked at my GPS. It had taken me one hour to go just 5 km up this road. I swiped the screen to look at the map and finally saw my mistake. 'I'm such a tube!' I shouted out to no one as I turned and freewheeled back down to the roundabout.

Just a hundred metres along the coast road stood a bus stop. The shelter was deep enough that I could fit my bike in with just a half wheel sticking out from the side. Sheets of woodchip held together with battens of wood made for excellent shelving in the inside. The outer was covered in corrugated iron, and a long bench the width of my body spanned across the rear. By now it was around 3°C and the rain began to batter down hard on the tin roof. Knowing the laundrette was waiting for me some miles up the road felt like knowing a five-star hotel was empty for the night and I was sleeping in the garden. I imagined how luxurious the laundrette would have felt tonight, but reminded myself how horrific no shelter at all would be. The fact that I had found not only a comfortable bench, but a cover with total protection, was extremely satisfying. It's funny how quickly your mindset can change when your basic needs are at risk of not being met. I used the wooden shelves to hold my light and spoke into my phone as I began the process of getting warm for the night.

I undid my winter booties and pulled off my shoes. I unclipped the worn bumbag that I trusted with my most important documents and tucked it down my front, as I did every night. I started on the long task of pulling on and zipping up all seven layers before climbing into my sleeping and bivvy bags. Lying on the bench, I pulled my bike around in front of me to keep it safe... like anyone was going to steal it.

Day 66: 20 August 2018 • Kumara Junction to Murchison • 10 hours 4 minutes • 180 km • ODO: 16,264.79 km • Cabin in the woods

The Junction Honey Café sat directly across the road from my bus stop bivvy spot. I walked over for a hearty breakfast after yesterday's lack of calories and smiled at the sign on the door, which read: 'Today's weather: It's raining! So... before you get depressed or complain about today's weather, consider this: you are in a RAINFOREST! It requires rain even if you don't. It's lovely and green and scenic, which we are sure you appreciate. We didn't plan your holiday YOU DID! You are on the Wild West Coast. ENJOY our wild weather.'

It went on to make some digs at tourists for continually asking staff weather-related questions, but the general messaging was fab and apt, as it would rain continually for the whole day and all I could do was be grateful that the trees, at least, were happy about that!

I was now in the Westland temperate rainforests, lush and jungle-like with giant ferns and big broadleaves dangling over the road as I climbed away from the Tasman Sea, cutting inland towards the north coast of the South Island, home to the ferry port, Picton, which I should reach by tomorrow. From there I'd sail on to the North Island via a short, yet jaw-dropping crossing.

I'd been riding in torrential rain for around seven hours when I stopped for dinner in the Dawson Hotel in Reefton and stared out into the dark, watching the water streaming down the windows. In Scotland we have a ton of words to describe the rain, each picking apart the subtleties of the type of rain falling and how wet it might leave you. Drizzle, mizzle, smirr, yillin, dreich and drookit are just a few of my favourites, but tonight it was stoating – pouring down so heavily that the huge drops of rain bounced off the ground.

There wasn't a single patch of dry clothing on me. I made myself at home in the hotel restaurant and hung my clothes all around my table, hoping the heat from the roaring fire would find its way over to them. The room was filled with the hearty laughs of family and friends sharing the night together. It wasn't the type of night I was rushing to get back out into, but I had booked accommodation another 85 km away in Murchison. Once I finished dinner I contemplated trying to get a room in the hotel, but knew it would be far too short a day distance-wise to keep on track – I needed to continue making progress.

The physical benefits of training are easy to measure, but it's only in times of resistance that you will see the resilience you have built up mentally to adverse situations. Earlier that year I had a big ride on the west coast of Scotland. I was aiming for a 200-mile loop passing through Torridon, Applecross, Plockton, Dorney and back home to

Inverness. Halfway around the route I passed the front door of some old friends. The west coast villages are remote and people aren't often just 'passing by', so when you do it's practically illegal not to pop your head in and say hi. It was late Sunday afternoon when I tapped on Lynda and Mike's living room window.

Their dog Duke was lying in front of the fire and the house was full of family and chat. A roast was sitting out cooling and red wine was about to start flowing. 'Stay,' Lynda enthusiastically encouraged me. I battled with myself over two cups of tea and a handful of biscuits. 'I'd love to, but I really need these miles,' I said, trying to convince myself as much as my friends. I hadn't seen them in such a long time and this was looking to be a really special evening, but I found the willpower from somewhere and made myself leave that cosy country scene to head out into what would become a blizzard.

I would find myself walking up a remote glen at 2 a.m. when the snow became too deep to ride in. I found an open door on the side of a closed hotel, wore all the clothes I had with me and sat in the hallway floor hugging my knees in close for warmth until it got bright again, imagining the night it could have been over at Lynda and Mike's and telling myself that at some point during my Round the World trip I would feel the benefit of the hard (and now questionable) decision to leave.

Now, here I was, on the other side of the planet, surrounded by the same feelgood vibes as that night, torn between leaving or staying, and all that came to mind was, 'Well, if you left Lynda and Mike's, you can leave here too!' Somehow it made putting my wet kit back on easier, knowing I was now making that decision count.

Four soggy hours later I arrived at a cabin in the woods, where the host had cranked up the heating for my arrival. I warmed up the bed with the electric blanket. I'd been shivering a lot lately, so I hung up all my wet clothes then wore anything that was still dry, including my down jacket, and climbed into bed with the blanket still on full. I woke up five hours later stuck to the bed and struggling to breathe in the stuffy air, but utterly content that my bones felt warm again at last.

Day 67: 21 August 2018 • Murchison to Picton Ferry • 10 hours 9 minutes • 191.46 km • ODO: 16,456.25 km • Motel

This morning I met a beautiful family with Scottish ancestry, and as the very cute, red-haired, rosy-cheeked little boy climbed all over Little Pig and me, I laughed with his mum and we shared stories of Scotland. It was only when I went to leave that the mum uttered these words that filled me with dread: 'That's weird he's so sprightly. He was up all night with a high temperature and was really sick.' On that note I cycled away, carrying all his germs with me.

There was 200 km and 1000 metres of climbing between me and the ferry port in Picton, and I'd need to get there within 10 hours if I was to make the last sailing of the day. Yesterday's storm and the cold weather days were catching up with me. I felt worn down. Being able to ride the distance was a given, but any 'efforts' were hard to imagine.

I was also looking at flights to leave Auckland and fly up to Alaska. This would be the longest flight of the whole trip and held potential for a good rest, but there was a range of types of flight available, all with different stopovers, transit times and prices.

A good flight would have only one stopover with a minimal transfer time and would be within budget. The next one I could catch would be on Friday evening, giving me a total of 72 hours to make the distance. Which was more than enough time I felt, so I began to wonder whether I needed to make the ferry tonight at all.

I now had this extra time, so I could have a leisurely 200 km, get the first ferry tomorrow morning and then on the north island it would be one big push for the flight. The answer should have been, 'Get the ferry! Rest on the other side!' and I knew in my heart I should go for it today. In that moment, though, I backed off and chose the 200 km to be more of a restful day.

However, with no deadline to chase I mentally switched off. After all the excitement of the coastal and mountain passes of the last few days I was now on a bit of a dull gradual assent, with a gentle headwind, slightly rough tarmac and drizzly rain. There was no big heroic effort, just a combination of subtle resistances. This would grind me down more than any storm I'd passed through. The most exciting thing to happen was a bird shitting on my face – it ran all the way down my right cheek.

Days 68 and 69 • 22–23 August 2018 • Wellington to Sanson and Flathills Campsite • 12 hours 13 minutes • 213 km • ODO: 16,670 km • Motel and camping pod

Glaciated valleys left semi-submerged formed the scattered coastline as the ferry made its way north from Picton through the Marlborough Sounds and into the Cook Strait. The striking forest-clad ridges shot up from the sea with a blanket of green hugging the hidden bays and inlets floating in the turquoise waters. It was a relief to be making progress again.

Wellington was my first antipodal point on the trip. The Guinness rules allow you to pick your own opposite points on the planet and you must ride through both of them. There's a fun website called Antipodes Map that has an animated person sticking their head through any point on the planet and surprising you with where it appears on the other side. My opposite point would be Madrid in Spain.

Now I was in Wellington I was struggling to fathom why I hadn't aimed for here last night. I could have been riding ages ago. I felt my anxiety about the poor choice rising again. These are such easy thoughts to get caught up in, especially when you have all that time in your own head. 'Come on, Jen, let it go, you're doing okay.' Sometimes these words were just thoughts and other times I needed to say them out loud.

Climbing out of the city, I was waved down by another cyclist – a local man and another Graham – no connection that we could work out, but Tony and I had plenty to talk about as we shared some miles. He had been to Scotland and even to the Shand Cycles workshop where my bike was built. He was a really interesting guy, and shared stories of his track racing career and taking part in the Olympics, and the Commonwealth and World Championships, for New Zealand. An enthusiast, to say the least, and I could see he was desperate to help with the headwind we were riding into and kept skipping in front of me. On narrower roads this meant I'd need to slow down so there was enough space between us to ensure that I wasn't drafting (gaining an advantage from slipstreaming is against the Guinness rules). I felt bad having to keep telling him to get behind me and it must be hard not to be able to help when it's your natural instinct. He laughed, though, telling me I was staunch for not accepting any outside assistance – quite the compliment, I felt.

After the dark rainy nights on the South Island, I needed a vest larger and more visible than the one I was carrying, so that it could go over my jacket. I'd thought about this towards the end of Australia, but the roads there seemed to be wider and less winding. Tony told me we'd be passing an outdoor store in Porirua, so we went in and he proudly announced my mission and coaxed the store manager into giving me a massive discount on a Proviz vest with a bright yellow lining. This vest lights up like a reflective road sign as soon as headlights fall on to it. It felt as though I'd just put on a shield of armour. There was no way I wouldn't be seen in this!

Tony and I said our goodbyes outside a petrol station where I had filled up with a late lunch. Part of the petrol station grab was a warm macaroni pie that had been sitting out for far too long. I ate it knowing that I probably shouldn't, because it was pretty greasy, but cheesy pasta in a pie was too good to turn down. I thought you only got these little wonders in Scotland.

I'd felt really good up until that exact point, but over the next two hours my energy began to drop. The grim taste at the back of my mouth made me regret the pie. Riding up the dark highway, I felt my head spin. My mouth was filling up with saliva. I spat large gloops out every minute or so as it kept gathering in my mouth. All day the temperature had been just hovering around zero, but now I was heating up. I dismounted and sat on the gravel at the side of the road, unzipping my top layers to get some air in, and then hurled up the burned cheesy grease. I layered back up and began riding again, still with not very much oomph, but feeling like it had probably passed over. Ten minutes later came the same familiar feeling of my mouth watering with an unusually large amount of saliva. Was I actually sick? Surely not. Perhaps just a bit tired? Things escalated quickly and I was soon back on the gravel bank with my head between my knees, retching up everything I had left in me. And then, in quick succession, it happened a third time.

I was walking with my bike now as the motion of riding was making me dizzy, still not 100% sure if I was actually sick or did I just need an early night? A motorist pulled over to see if she could give me a lift to the next town. I politely turned her down, but she was able to tell me there was accommodation just 10 km away.

I mounted and dismounted and remounted the bike. Zipped off my layers, all back up again and then down again. I knocked on the motel door about 8.30 p.m. The woman opened the door, and I began speaking, asking for a room.

'Goodness, are you okay?'

'Yeah, yeah, I'm not feeling so well. I just need to sleep it off,' I tried to assure her.

'Are you sure? I can take you to the doctor if you want?'

I didn't want to get into the macaroni pie story in case it set me off again. She gave me her card and told me to call if it got worse. She also said not to rush out in the morning and she could extend the checkout.

'I won't need it as I'll be riding early, but thanks.' This stop was 60 km shorter than I had planned for tonight and I was already on a fairly tight schedule to catch my plane.

My reflection in the bathroom mirror was ghostly – pasty skin with beads of sweat gathering around my hollow eyes. I had nothing left to be sick with, but continued retching into the toilet bowl. The floor tiles felt cool next to my hot skin as I lay on them. I'd begun to shiver as my temperature plummeted before rising sharply again in the next few minutes.

I used two hands to get enough strength to undo my helmet clip and then I dragged myself into bed. I lay in all my cycling kit, my thoughts moving back and forth between the pie and the snotty kid I'd met the other day. Ahhh, it had to be from him, surely? His mum said he had recovered really quickly. I'd already been sick for a few hours now. I set my alarm, imagining that if I could just get a quick nap I could start riding again at midnight.

Come midnight, though, I still couldn't take my shoes off.

There were tablets in my saddlebag which I'd managed to wangle from the doctor in case of emergency. Like now. Eventually, staggering, I made my way to the bike on the other side of the room. Leaning into the wall, I used it to keep me upright and attempted to unclip the buckles on my saddlebag. My fingers were so weak. I dipped in and out of this bag multiple times a day without even thinking about it, but now the pressure of trying and standing up was too much. I slumped back on the bed, defeated. My head was spinning around and around. The light switch was too far away to reach at this point, so I placed the pillow over my head for some darkness.

I drifted in and out of sleep through the night, waking myself up shivering despite the heating being on full. I really wanted a shower for warmth, but the thought of the water hitting off my naked body made me wince, as if the force would rip my skin wide open. This, I decided, would be my gauge. Once I felt I could deal with the flow of water on me I'd be well enough to ride again. This took until lunchtime. A huge step forward for sure, but not enough to make my Friday evening flight.

There were still 512 km to ride to the airport and I had just 30 hours to do it in. I reluctantly called the airline and transferred my flight to Saturday evening, which gave me another 20 hours to recover and do the distance. Ideally I would have given myself at least a full day to recover, then two riding days to make the flight, but this wasn't an option. The pull to leave this cold and wet continent was huge. Forward progress was my only focus; if I could just make it to the airport I could recover there.

I thought about emailing Gerry McPartlin. Gerry was the doctor in the Torridon Mountain Rescue team back in Scotland and he had been very generous with his time before I left. He'd talked me through all the medicines I might need for situations out on the road. I wanted to know if I should start taking any of the tablets he'd recommended.

I went to start typing, then stopped myself, deciding that I might be making a big deal out of nothing. Sitting writing this and replaying the story, I can see that of course I was sick, but sitting there in New Zealand, alone in the motel room, I couldn't be sure just how sick I was.

I was already running on empty. I was constantly exhausted and had been shivering myself to sleep for weeks, and this was just a little bit more. This was just the added effects of being sick, having a sore head and hurty bones. It was nine out of 10 bad throughout the night, but given that I'd probably been operating daily at around six out of 10 it wasn't a huge jump. So I never sent Gerry the message, and I never took the antibiotics either. I would come to regret both.

I packed up my kit and slowly made my way out of town. It was a good sign, I thought, that I felt hungry but didn't want to risk anything too heavy, so I stopped at a sign advertising miso soup. Miso with its fairly light, even tasteless, flavour was about all I could imagine keeping down, so I got some to take away and sipped it while riding along the road. The surface was bumpier than I'd have liked. Long concrete slabs with abrupt edges would rattle my brain every time I went over one. I would hold my head with one hand to soak up some of the vibration.

The camping pod I'd booked to sleep in the previous day kindly moved my booking free of charge and I arrived six hours later. I cranked up the heating and ate the ready meal dinner of lasagne and garlic bread they had left out for me. Just one more night of sleep and I was sure I'd be back on form. I was feeling pretty dehydrated by now, so loaded up with water and painkillers and slept for 10 hours straight.

Days 70 and 71: 24–25 August 2018 • Flathills Campsite to Lichfield • 9 hours and 28 minutes • 450 km • ODO: 17,120.05 km • 40-minute doorway bivvy

Well rested, I woke up in much better spirits. I was still weak, but not sore in the way I had been. The rest was inevitable. It had to be done, but it now meant that I had 36 hours to ride the remaining distance of 450 km to the airport. It would mean staying up through the night, which wasn't ideal recovery, but leaving this continent was a big driver.

I stopped in Taihape for a quick breakfast and some fried eggs on toast went down well, which assured me that I'd flushed the worst of the nasty bug out of my system, although my brain was still a bit rattly, so I continued to support it with my hands when the ground got rough.

I climbed and climbed up Highway 1. The road itself rose to well above 1000 metres. My hood was pulled snug around my head, its peak poking proudly over my helmet, which was pulled down to the top of my eyebrows to protect my forehead. My neck scarf sat right over my nose and hugged my cheek bones, then curved around over my ears, while my sunglasses stopped the snow pellets from hitting my eyeballs. If it hadn't been for the snowstorm I was now riding through, I'd have seen the three peaks of Mount Ruapehu, the largest active volcano on the island.

I didn't care much about the views I might be missing, though, as I had found the perfect audiobook for my situation: *The Worst Journey in the World* by Apsley Cherry-Garrard. Published in 1922, it's a memoir describing Robert Falcon Scott's Terra Nova Expedition to the South Pole. The book recalls a Special Scientific Winter Expedition where three men, including Cherry-Garrard, made their way 60 miles across the Antarctic Ice in a bid to collect an egg from an emperor penguin colony. The trio took a harrowing 19 days in ludicrously inhospitable weather conditions. Weeks of darkness, temperatures dropping to -70°C, frozen eyeballs, shattered teeth, sleeping bags and clothes frozen solid like blocks of concrete – at times, death would no doubt have been welcome. Their tent was blown away, their igloo destroyed in a blizzard and they lay for days with no food, waiting to die. Their suffering was immense.

There's nothing like a bit of perspective. Hearing these tales described so matter-of-factly didn't suddenly take my own discomfort away. Those were all very real feels! But my mind had shifted. It's easy to catastrophise when you're feeling low and fearful that you'd struggle to dig much deeper. I was no longer suffering more than anyone else I knew right now; instead, I had a new benchmark and in comparison my life was looking pretty peachy. Within a few hours I would have ridden my way to a hotel with a lovely bed for the night, a top-quality restaurant and an airport. I would be able to call my family, buy warmer clothes and be sitting in a cosy coffee shop. It made me smile at the choices I had in life and reminded me that I was choosing to push, to suffer, to be that little bit more miserable than I needed to be. I was in it for the long game, the final time, the self-satisfaction, the glory of the homecoming. This wasn't the first trip on which I used the frozen eyeballs as a benchmark – and I'm sure it won't be the last. In fact, I hope I'm never in a position to win that game of top trumps.

My feet had got wet during the storm that day and now the temperature had dropped to -2°C I was struggling to keep the blood circulating. It was 1 a.m. as I pushed my bike up the hill, stomping my feet hard, trying to warm them up. I pulled into a B&B parking lot to grab the final layer out of my bag.

A vacancy sign flashed in three different colours: red, blue and yellow. Vacancy, vacancy, vacancy! I longed to knock on the door and climb into a warm bed. I was freezing, but the thought of having that comfort and being disciplined enough to leave it again in only one hour's time was worse than just staying out.

I spoke into my phone as a film diary and had a wee moan about the snotty kid, and the temperature and the sickness he'd given me, secretly hoping someone would hear and come out to insist I take a bed for the night. They did not! So, slowly and reluctantly, I cycled off.

I hadn't eaten since breakfast that morning, now 20 hours ago. I did feel much better, but as soon as food went near my mouth it welled up again and my stomach muscles tensed as if they couldn't take any more retching. I kept myself going on sugary tea from petrol stations, but if I was going to make the next 190 km in the time needed, I'd have to have a quick nap. I stopped by a shop doorway on the outskirts of Lichfield and climbed into my bivvy bag. I had exactly 45 minutes to spare if I carried on riding at 20 km/h. I set an alarm and woke up unsure if I actually slept. There was no issue in getting up as I was shivering so hard it hurt to lie on the ground. I stuffed everything back into my saddle bag and rode off. It worked, though! An early morning café supplied a breakfast roll and coffee, and I was on my way, feeling revived enough to keep going.

At some point in the last 48 hours, my rear gears had stopped working. I assumed it was a cable, but riding without it was more appealing than losing time by stopping to fix it. I wasn't even sure I still had the spare, as I'd not set eyes on it since Berlin. The day before, I'd called ahead to a bike shop in Auckland, feeling optimistic about reaching it in time to have the cable fixed and bike boxed up. That wouldn't happen now; the spare minutes were frittering away.

But the good news was a message via the Adventure Syndicate from a local endurance rider, Nathan Mawkes. He offered to meet me at the airport with a cardboard box and tape. I was quick to reply.

Me: 'Hey Nathan, thanks for your lovely message! If it's not too late I'd love to take you up on the offer. I just need to double-check because of self-supported rules. Are you on Warm Showers, CouchSurfing or any other forums that would allow other folk access to your support?'

Nathan: 'Hi. I fully understand the self-supported ethos and, yes, I've been a member of Warm Showers since 2014. I admire anyone embarking on a challenge like yours and would offer it to anyone in the same situation. A random act of kindness. And unsolicited.'

Me: 'Music to my ears. I'll be there between 5 and 6 p.m.!'

And with that the next seven hours passed on busy suburban roads and under grey skies. All I cared about was the numbers on my computer and every hour I focused on just making it one km/h faster.

On the edge of Auckland, I was flying down the dual carriageway when a tyre blew out. *Shiiiiiit!* There followed what was without a doubt the slickest tyre change of my life, followed by a 25-minute time trial to the airport. I came skidding into the car park sideways to meet Nathan standing there with my giant cardboard box.

I began stripping down my bike and soon had my kit sprawled across the pavement and two benches. I was trying to keep the conversation going as a way of letting Nathan know how much I appreciated his efforts, but my head was busy organising kit and thinking about the next steps.

Anyone who has flown with a bike before will know all the meticulous packing required to ensure no damage is done to the components. That was not the sight Nathan witnessed: I flung in wheels and stuffed my sleeping bag roughly where the rear mech would be. In between this bad packing and scrappy conversation efforts, I was downloading the visa webpage for my American visa ESTA, so that I'd be allowed entry into the country.

This had been on my to-do list for some time. 'Just need to check in as well,' I said, trying not to panic with only 25 minutes left until my flight closed. I wrapped my life, shut tight with the tape.

'I thought you'd be a slick machine by now.' It was an innocent comment from a bemused Nathan, but other people's disappointment is a heavy weight to carry. It had taken me nine and a half days to make my way up the 1726 km of New Zealand – one and a half days longer than planned – and I was now teetering on the edge of missing my third flight. I couldn't yet recognise what I'd fought through to get here or give myself any praise; I saw only all the things I could have done better. I tried not to let that show, though. 'Ha Shi'ist! Not me, Nathan, I'm winging it, mate.'

We said our goodbyes and I dragged my box to the self-check-in computers. Do you have a visa to enter America? The screen read once I'd scanned my passport and ticket. YES, I ticked, relieved there was no one standing over me to check. And with that my boarding pass was printed. I wouldn't receive my ESTA until I reached Los Angeles, only moments before I was asked for it.

• • •

We all have our bugbears in life, those little annoyances that grate on us more than they should. Mine is the people who walk around airports with inflatable pillows, especially when they pre-deploy them, blowing them up long before they're needed, and then flaunt them, braced tightly around their neck, often with a serious glare in their eyes, as if they had indeed broken their neck and this pillow was all that was left to keep them upright. These pillow people have an air of having their shit together in a way I could never imagine, particularly at an airport.

I stood depleted. Getting ready for the longest flight and potentially the biggest rest of the trip, pondering whether to buy one. It would be the only luxury I could have on this flight, which was a 17-hour two-parter: New Zealand to Los Angeles, then Los Angeles to Alaska, with a five-hour layover in between. I didn't have a whole lot of money to play with at this point and two days ago, as I lay in the motel room still too sick to move, I had rebooked the cheapest one I could find with the quickest overall time. I'd never travelled on a really cheap long-haul flight before – I might have made a different decision otherwise – but the difference in flight prices was significant, so this and a random seat selector decided my destiny.

Because of the ESTA fiasco, I didn't ask the help desk for a seat with extra legroom in case they asked some awkward questions. The only hope I had to gain a little bit of comfort was to spend $15 on one of those neck pillows sitting in the window of the shop directly across from me – but I found it incredibly difficult to justify. What would I do with it on the other side? Carry it with me all the way to Halifax – 8700 km? I had nowhere to store it, my systems were already bursting at the seams. Okay, so I could leave it at the other end and maybe someone would want it (doubtful if they had one look at me and my dribble-stained pillow). So, what, I just chuck it away? A perfectly good pillow? I worried about the environmental impact of this tiny little pillow, entirely missing the irony of being about to board a plane and fly halfway around the world. A pillow should have been the last of my environmental worries.

This level of decision-making was too much for my heavily fatigued state of mind. When I was on the bike, life was simple: must eat, must sleep, must keep pedalling. Anything more than that was a lot and now I was off the bike with a small amount of time to spare and a decision that was of no immediate consequence. Walking away was the only sensible option.

I had managed a sink wash and changed into the lesser of my smelly clothes: Ronhill Lycra shorts, BaaBaa merino wool long-sleeved black top, my Haglofs down jacket and my new grey wool neckwarmer which had been in my life for only one week and which, I was fairly sure, had saved my life every single freezing cold day of it. I finger-combed my hair and smeared Vaseline over my weather-beaten face. I had no spare shoes with me, so my cycling ones remained on. When I reached the plane, the plan was to swap them quickly for my bed socks and stuff my sweaty, dank shoes into a dry bag before offending anyone with the smell.

I craved comfort. I had imagined buying PJ bottoms just for this flight. The thought of fleece-lined pyjamas from FatFace had kept me going through so many cold mornings crossing Australia. I used the idea of them as a bartering tool to keep me motivated, but along with the pillow those dreams collapsed as I wandered on to the plane in my same old Lycra shorts.

It felt cruel that we were made to walk through the serene space of business class before opening the curtains to the hive of activity in economy. I took a deep breath. I'd never suffered in small spaces before, but after eight weeks on the open road this cramped little cabin bustling with people left my chest feeling tight. Why were the seats this close together? Life choices ran through my head. I should have paid extra, should have got legroom. I made my way up to my seat number, then stared at the empty middle seat. There was a woman already sitting next to the window. She'd made herself a comfy little headrest against the wall. The aisle seat was occupied by a man. He sat bolt upright, stony faced, with a neck pillow – true to form. As I shuffled past I tried not to make any sudden movements that would let out some of the ghastly smells I was keeping in by constraining my limbs and slid into place, carefully removing my shoes and jacket. My bed socks were tiny down slippers that my mum had bought me for my birthday. I had almost not brought them, believing instead that I should remember wool socks offered a dual purpose, but the sentimental value meant that every night I slipped them on it was like having a hug from Mum.

I packed my little down jacket into itself, creating a sausage shape that I wrapped around my neck. My body ached to lie down and rest. The picture on the seat in front showed that there was a board we could pull out from under the seat to make a kind of bed. The family in the picture had infants, and as I assessed the area we had to play with I realised that a huge amount of spooning would be needed to cram three adult bodies on to the board. I mean, I was game; the thought of being spooned in-between these two complete strangers sounded dreamy if it meant I could lie down for a while. It might even be fun! I looked around at them both, hoping to make eye contact, but nothing. They both looked extremely comfortable and happy not to be speaking, and so that's what we did. It was a restless flight with sporadic hours of sleep and an overall sense of relief not to be riding my bike.

The layover passed fairly quickly. I'd taken all my electricals to charge, so found some new socket adapters, ate, washed and video-called home. The Alaskan Air flight was a much shorter journey of five and a half hours and to my delight I'd bagged a window seat, so I could rest my head up against the wall and get some more sleep. After 10 weeks of losing hours in my day as I rode across timelines heading east, I had now shot back in time by 21 hours after crossing the international date line between New Zealand and LA. So, I'd left New Zealand on Saturday evening, travelled for 34 hours and would arrive into Alaska on Sunday morning! Bizarre!

ALASKA

ANCHORAGE

YUKON

BRITIS
COLUM

PART IV
THE NORTHERN HEMISPHERE

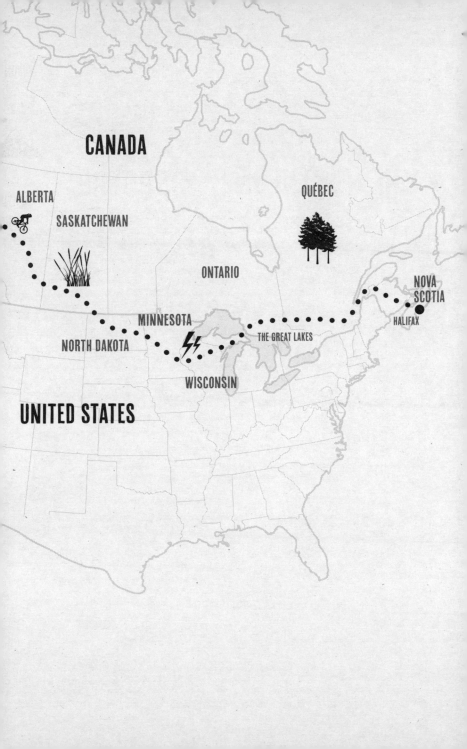

CANADA

ALBERTA

SASKATCHEWAN

QUÉBEC

ONTARIO

NOVA
SCOTIA

MINNESOTA

THE GREAT LAKES

HALIFAX

NORTH DAKOTA

WISCONSIN

UNITED STATES

Day 72: 26 August 2018 • **Anchorage Airport, USA to Matanuska Glacier** • **10 hours 16 minutes** • **168.76 km** • **ODO: 17,283.81 km** • **Bivvy at campsite**

Arriving in Anchorage was exciting, not in the 'yahoo!' manner I was accustomed to, but more in the 'smiling on the inside' fashion. I couldn't muster up any form of overt excitement. I felt dulled, fuzzy around the edges. My 38-year-old body was ageing dramatically – from the ride and now a whole day of crammed flights. I could see from my movements that I was no longer a flexible, fit woman in her prime. Instead, I was slow and considered, moving with great concentration and limited flexibility. My bones would have been sighing if they could, letting out great big gasps of air. It was hard to know if this was from the flight, the ride or the illness. All three, I suspect.

The airport was a modest affair, but I found a small kiosk selling coffee, then dragged my gigantic cardboard box into a corner and set about building my bike. Wheels on first, handlebars, then pedals. Blow tyres up. Attach bags and stuff full with all the kit that's currently scattered across the floor. It was raining outside, a heavy storm battering down. I sat and stared at my phone, answered all my WhatsApp messages, replied to some social media posts, scrolled... for just a little longer. Struggling to motivate myself to move, I remembered Audible. Yes, a new book was just what I needed to get me out of my own head and into someone else's world.

I cycled away from the airport with all my bits now attached to the bike and the cardboard box neatly piled by the bin. I had Adam Kay blasting through my earphones, narrating *This is Going to Hurt: Secret Diaries of a Junior Doctor*. It was a laugh-out-loud book and laughing out loud was just what I needed as I pedalled the empty streets with the rain lashing down. I'd actually made it to Anchorage... Go, me!

• • •

There was 9520 km to ride on my North American leg, from Anchorage in America in the north west to Halifax Nova Scotia in Canada in the east, and my first trail angels (impromptu one-off support from strangers) of North America appeared just 80 km into my day, when I rolled through Palmer and met Tony, the owner of Backcountry Bike Shop. I'd called the previous day from LA Airport, but my credit ran out and the call was cut off. We had long enough for me to hear that they would check if I could take my bike in the following day, but with the time difference and the fact that I never called back, Tony wasn't expecting me. He wasn't expecting anyone, in fact, and had closed for the day. My heart sank as I arrived in the car park and saw the shopfront in the dark. I'd been riding with no rear gears since the north island of New Zealand. There would be no other bike shop opportunity until Whitehorse, over a thousand kilometres and a whole lot of accent away.

Tony was walking across the car park and into a house as I called out to him, 'Hey, is this bike shop going to open today?' 'No, we're closed...' I didn't listen to the rest, something about renovations. Instead, I launched into my Round the World story. I didn't often play the Round the World card, but I really needed his help. 'Ah, you called yesterday, but you were cut off,' he replied warmly. 'Let's get you into the workshop and see what we can do.'

Tony was a long-distance rider and knew some of the big names in the endurance world. We were soon sharing stories of the Arizona Trails and our favourite two-wheeled memories. He was passionate about bikes, community and people. He'd set the shop up years before to support his wife and her friends when they got into biking, and now it was clearly a thriving business. Before long, Nathan arrived. He was holding pizza and set about making coffee. Lots of it. Nathan was the mechanic at the shop and had coincidentally (and loosely) been following my dot as I pedalled around the globe. It felt so comforting to be there. Finding your people so far from home is special and was quite the contrast from how I'd felt just a couple of hours before.

Tony fixed all the usual stuff: chain, brake pads, tyres, gear cables (inner and out). I had thought it was a broken cable affecting my gears, but at the end of all the work he realised the spring in the shifter had worn itself out. Nathan's kindness hit the next level when we realised there was none in stock and he offered me the lever from his own bike as a replacement. I was riding with Shimano Ultegra components; he had the Shimano 105 model, which would be compatible for now. Such a gem. Tony said it would take about an hour to do as the brakes would need to be bled etc., and he offered me a shower and bed in the motel that he owned across the road. A nap would be so good. I lay on the bed feeling safe and cared for by the warmth shown to me by these complete strangers.

Nathan woke me a while later and the two of them then packed me off with my new Franken-bike and a good supply of bear spray, which had been wedged into a water bottle for easy access on my bike. I had budgeted for these fixes, but Tony would barely take a cent for them, the spares or the bed. It was so kind of him and helped towards the rest of the ride.

● ● ●

This would seem like an appropriate moment to give special mention to the bike shops in my world. Throughout the Highlands of Scotland you will find some exceptional bike shops and mechanics working in them. I spread my work between three of these places – Orange Fox Bikes, Bike of Inverness and Velocity Bicycle Workshop – and used them regularly (and I mean very regularly!) in the lead-up to Round the World.

I found keeping on top of maintaining my bike a bigger task than normal during preparation for the trip, which is understandable as I was spending 20 hours a week riding it, including through the winter, and that's harsh on the components. I was also trying and testing so many options when it came to tyres, saddles, tribars, gearing systems, bartape and pedals that there was a never-ending stream of work to be done on the bike as I searched for my perfect set-up. I'd repair and maintain what I could, but the speed and skillset of a mechanic would be invaluable to me during this time.

Forward planning didn't often come into the equation though, so Friday afternoons would arrive and I'd appear at the shop in a whirlwind with a new emergency, making a plea for a quick fix, a special bike part or just a skilful eye to be cast over my bike, so I could go on some 'million mile mission' at the weekend. 'When do you need it by?' became a bit of a standing joke as I'd always need it with immediate effect.

There were times when I wouldn't even make it as far as the shop and instead I'd call them up and they would arrange parts to make it to me via another customer or a mechanic dropping it off on their way home. I'd receive discounts, freebies and even be allowed to use the workshop to do my own fixes when the store was closed.

Writing this I can see how annoying I must have been, but at the time I'd never have known by their reactions and they gave their time patiently. The conversations we could get into about rubber tyre compounds, rolling resistance, tubeless repairs and on and on and on... This was their artform and a good mechanic is an invaluable source of information.

I assumed this was something unique to the Highlands of Scotland, as the cycling world is fairly tightknit up this way, but having been so well looked after all around the world, I could see that bike shops spoke a global language. Bike shops of the world, I salute you!

🎧 *I'm just lying in my bivvy bag feeling slightly silly for being so scared of the kangaroos, seeing as it's the first night in Alaska and I'm lying next to my bear spray! Oh, there's a bit of perspective for ya.*

Oh wait, what? Aw, it's just my bike light still flashing – phew, I feel a bit jumpy. It's just the first night on any new continent, when you're not sure what to expect, isn't it?

I went into this shop earlier. It was going to be the last shop for the next 160 km or so. The woman was giving me all the chat. 'You've got a gun, haven't you?' 'No, I've not got a gun.' 'Whaaaaat? Are you crazy, going out without a gun? You do know it's bear season?' 'Ohhh, do bears have a season? I don't think I knew it was bear season!' She said this is the time they all go down to the river, although all the rivers are in spate just now, so it should be okay if they're still up in the high ground, eating berries.

As a result, I clutched my bear spray and bear bell, which definitely wasn't loud enough that night. I rode with it attached to my fingers and ringing for about six hours. By now I was definitely a bit twitchy. I had looked behind me earlier and felt my saddlebag and screamed, thinking it was a bear. Yeah, definitely feeling a little nervous, but it was good to be getting the first night out of the way.

The woman in the shop did give me some really good advice, though. I forgot that everyone carried guns out here and was thinking I'd just rock up and sleep on a veranda or roadhouse porch before they opened up, but she told me her shop was covered in cameras and had an alarm, and she'd come out with a gun if it went off. Then she told me about Christy down the road: 'Now Christy would come out with a gun and I just wouldn't trust her because she's a little bit edgy.' Jeeez, she wasn't the only one.

Day 73: 27 August 2018 • Matanuska Glacier to Red Eagle Lodge, Glenn Highway • 11 hours 32 minutes • 219 km • ODO: 17,502.81 km • Bivvy beside a toilet block

The initial relief of opening my eyes and finding myself alive and well was short-lived. Reality soon struck: I was still in the woods! I looked around as I tried to unzip the net on my bivvy bag. How would I have ever been able to spray a bear from inside this bag when the zip took so long to open? At World Record speed, I was out. The area I stood in was a fairly dense woodland, apart from a dirt track for a car and a picnic bench. You wouldn't necessarily see an animal coming at you in this place. A stream of these unhelpful thoughts ran through my head.

The slightly terrified, alone and mildly panicking feeling was now fairly familiar. I made as much noise as I could when packing up my kit, saying aloud what I was doing. 'Here I am, packing away my sleeping bag. Here I am, packing away my bivvy bag. What a goooood sleep. I'm going to be gone soon. Just need to tighten these straps up.' Finding my way back to the tarmac road lifted some of the tension and turning those wheels felt like I was back in control, pedalling my way to safety.

I climbed and climbed that morning on the Glenn Highway with a feeling of vast emptiness all around. To my right the Matanuska Glacier came tumbling out of the valley in all its glory. I knew Alaska was home to some big game – caribou, moose, bison, and bears, both black and brown – but as so often before, reciting that list from the comfort of my home in Scotland felt very different to the reality of living among them. The thought of daily wildlife encounters was making sleeping out less attractive than ever before, but choices for accommodation were limited. Anyway, I might be worried about nothing. What's the chances of having any sightings at all? Well, quite high as it happens, but according to the National Park Service website you are more likely to be killed by a bee sting than by a bear, so I would hold on to that and repeat it to myself when needed.

Two moose. Great, big, majestic beasts holding their fat, flat, furry antlers proud as they moved about their day. The first was casually wandering across the road. I, along with some cars, stopped way back from it. I felt relieved to see some of the drivers with their phones out recording. I took that to mean it wasn't a regular occurrence, which fitted with the story I was telling myself about probably not having any/many wildlife encounters. I'd been warned about the moose. Apparently they could be aggressive if agitated, but right now it was difficult to imagine anything but grace and goodwill from this godly beast. The second was grazing on the verge. I didn't stop. Instead I took a wide berth. In a way it felt good to have some big game sightings under my belt. They were both calm and respectful, and it felt like neither the moose nor I felt threatened at any point. I was gaining confidence as I stopped to eat in Glennallen and fill up with some supplies from the local supermarket, where I also found some nice packable chargers.

Leaving the village as the sun set felt a little eerie, though. Along with a fear of loud noises I think a fear of the dark must probably be our deepest rooted concern. When you think back to our hunter-gatherer ancestors, you can see why we urge ourselves to find shelter and safety. When I started on my journey into endurance sports I was always aware of this feeling as the sun went down. I'd do mental checklists to make sure I had everything I needed to stay safe – tent, stove, torch, etc. – rationalising to confront the fear. Over the years this urge has lessened, but occasionally I'll feel that ancient tug to find safety. Tonight was one of those nights and perhaps for good reason.

That night I was leaving the perceived safety of civilisation and beginning down the long road to Tok Junction. I was reminding myself of the kangaroo situation and the big deal I had made of them and how that seemed laughable now, and assuring myself that one day the wildlife of Alaska would be laughable and that overthinking was just down to exhaustion. Mustn't get caught up in the hype of dangerous animals... CRUNCH, a branch broke. It came from the woods on my left. The noise was magnified, so loud, maybe down to the empty roads or maybe down to the sheer fear I was feeling. It was as if someone had munched on an apple, right in my ear.

Looking up, I locked eyes with a baby black bear as it froze, halfway up a tree. Neither of us had wanted to be seen by one another, yet here we were and time, just for a second, had stopped. All the wonderful words of advice came pouring through my thoughts: DON'T RUN! STOP! MAKE A LOUD NOISE! DON'T PANIC! But all I could do was pedal and pedal. Faster than I had done for months. The only sound was of my heart beating. Shit, shit, shit, shit, shit! What if Mama Bear was chasing me? A glance behind told me she wasn't. Okay, but what if she was tracking me? I'd heard that's what bears did if they were hunting you. Unsure whether that was the best or worst decision of the trip (and maybe my life), I kept pedalling. With urgency! Until well after dark.

'Noise, Jen, make plenty of noise and this will be fine,' I told myself. I kept pedalling at a slower pace as I armed myself with jingles and jangles. I moved the bear bell, which had been sitting fairly discreetly on my frame all day, to my finger, where I could rattle it like a great big tambourine all night long. I switched my head torch on to the strobe setting. I selected a playlist that I had made for long training rides and listened to all year in the preparation. I now knew nearly every word to every song and pressed the loudspeaker button to blast the music from my handlebars. I sang and sang, then sang some more. If nothing else, it helped drown out my own unhelpful thoughts. I was quite the picture, riding along the lonely highway.

I hadn't passed anyone for hours, but some lights ahead caught my attention. The car passed slowly – unsurprisingly, given the scene I've just described. The truck then began reversing as I continued riding forward. A lone man began speaking out of his passenger's window, leaning over from the driver's side. He began talking about moose. Had I seen any, did they have horns, etc.? I stopped riding and momentarily felt safe to be in another human's company, knowing the car engine would have scared away any animals lurking around. I happily shared my sightings, thinking they were weird questions to be asking, until I realised he was a hunter. Of course. I then felt bad for telling him about the antlers, but that was hours ago and hopefully my girls were well gone. Fairly quickly, being alone with the bears became appealing again, so I wished him a good night and cycled on, relieved to hear him drive off in a forward motion and not continue with the reversing.

I didn't feel in a good state of mind at this point. I was tired and scared and slightly overwhelmed about how the next few weeks would play out. Then there was that guy, who I didn't have a good feeling about now. Just a couple of kilometres up the road I found the Red Eagle Lodge Campsite. Although I couldn't see the park in all its glory, I did find the toilet block, a gorgeous wooden cabin bigger than most of the hotels I'd stayed in. It smelt so good, crispy clean like it had just been washed with disinfectant.

I sat, taking in my new surroundings. It was well gone 1 a.m. by now and I was relieved to be somewhere off the road, away from drivers and bears. Then the conversation with the woman yesterday came back to me. Oh god, the security cameras and the guns. The thought of being woken up by some angry American pointing a shotgun in my direction was a bit much to handle. I'd rather take my chances with the bears. So, once I had washed and changed in the comfort of the changing rooms, I laid my bivvy down the side of the block, cursing myself for not being brave enough to stay inside for fear of trespassing. The feeling of fear wasn't for immediate danger; it was more the fear you experience when watching a thriller; the kind where you're waiting for someone to jump out. It rained a bit, but I just lay there, motionless, and soon fell asleep.

Day 74: 28 August 2018 • Red Eagle Lodge, Glenn Highway to Tok Junction • 8 hours 25 minutes • 147 km • ODO: 17,649.81 km • Motel

I woke with that familiar relief of being a survivor and retreated to the nice, clean wooden bathroom to sort out all my kit. I packed up the clothes I had sink-washed the night before. They were still pretty damp, so I packed them in a dry bag to keep them separate. It looked like it was going to rain, so I'd take them out if it dried up later. I packed and made my way back to the entrance. I could see the main house was an impressive three-storey wooden structure with carvings and wood that stood out bright against the dull morning.

I knocked on the door as I went to leave. 'Hullo, I sort of camped here last night. I just wanted to let you know and pay what I owe.' What I actually meant was: 'Please don't hunt me down with your guns for sleeping on your porch!'

I was welcomed with the greatest fuss by Julie and Richard, who insisted I stay for breakfast. I gave them my usual chat about being in a hurry, can't stay too long, blah blah blah, then I spent the next hour and a half being fed, caffeinated and connected with. They laughed when I told them I was too scared to sleep in their bathroom and Julie got a little cross with the woman with the shotgun story: 'Jenny, you will be welcomed in Alaska. Don't you worry about guns and Christy characters.' I was relieved to hear that. We were half joking as we talked, but it had been playing on my mind.

During breakfast Julie asked if I had needed anything washed or dried. I gave her my bib shorts, knowing it would make for a nicer start to the day. More guests came down and the conversation, like the coffee, kept flowing. When the tumble dryer beeped, Richard passed my bibs across the table. I was so embarrassed by the distinctive smell of warm, sink-washed bibs, still slightly damp and ingrained with Sudocrem, wafting over breakfast. I left my new friends feeling rejuvenated from our meeting and took on the day with a little more ease.

The roads were the quietest so far on the trip. I thought of the heavy traffic of Russia: the warmth I would feel from the lorry exhausts as they passed so close at night, the constant flow of people living on that highway. Now there was nothing. There was literally no one on these roads. Occasionally the odd car would pass or an RV – a motorhome that would have seemed gigantic anywhere else in the world, but which out here fitted into the scale of things. This section was definitely remote and I was hyper-aware of having no company.

Over the last few days I had learned that asking hairy Alaskan men, normally wearing tartan shirts, about bears was a bad idea. They all had stories of practically wrestling their heads from the jaws of a grizzly, which wasn't helping the paranoia. I promised myself I'd stop asking, because I was never going to find the answer I was looking for.

Then I met Brian propping up the knife display outside the restaurant I would eat in and I just couldn't stop my mouth. As soon as he made eye contact, I was rattling out my brown bear worries. Brian had everything from pocket knives to machetes. Dressed in full combat, he was a larger-than-life character who warned me about the dangers of not being protected (with one of his shiny blades) from the big bad grizzlies, who would be licking their lips as they saw me pedal towards them. I laughed nervously as the stories came flooding from his mouth.

After dinner I left the restaurant, Brian and the knife display behind. The sun was going down and I had spooked myself again. I couldn't help feeling that to still be riding as darkness fell would be easier than leaving the nice safe restaurant to go riding into the dark night at dusk.

I cycled past the town motel to the end of the road and stopped with my head in my hands. It was all too much. I felt like a mess. It was only 9 p.m., which was early to be stopping, but I needed to recharge, rationalise these fears, buy more bells and not sleep out tonight, which was my only option now I'd filled my head with gory bear stories. So I stopped, the immensity of the whole trip weighing heavy. I now had no idea how I was going to get through the next bit. I needed a plan that could keep me moving late into the night, every night, for the next 8050 km.

Day 75: 29 August 2018 • Tok Junction to Koidern, Canada • 13 hours 13 minutes • 234 km • ODO: 17,883.81 km • Tent inside camp ground

🎧 *I had big plans to get up at 4 this morning but blah, blah, blah, of course it did not happen! It's eight now and I've just hit the motel breakfast cabin, which is very cool. So, I am filling up with waffles, because there's nothing for another 100 miles. Actually, it has all just worked out fine. I would have just been hungry, so yeah, I think this is all right. Well, it's going to have to be all right because I've done it now.*

I swung by the Tok local hardware store to pick up some bear protection paraphernalia. The wooden building stood alongside the road on the way out of town and had been decorated with bright forest green paint. The sign had a picture of a bear and a gun, along with 'The Three Bears Outpost' written in bright yellow.

Inside, the walls were lined with trophy animal skins and heads, mostly bears, moose and caribou. The aisles had an endless supply of sporting, fishing and hunting gear. I had my eye on a big bright flare and then a blow horn with a gas canister attached, but in the end opted for three bells and a bright orange whistle with rope attached, which would from that moment forward live around my neck. Surrounded by blades, gun barrels and carcases, it felt like the most modest of choices, but the whistle would become my talisman: I'd leave it clasped between my teeth and blow for hours on end as I rode along the empty highway.

I rode out of Tok with my new bells jangling, having attached them to my bike with zip ties. The road was rough and finished with a gritty asphalt coating, not the smooth glide riders are usually looking for, but it did make my bells ring even louder. I was now on the Alaskan Highway, a long tarmac corridor that sits among 58 million acres of wild land. It would be my home for the next two weeks and would guide me for 2232 km into the city of Dawson's Creek, British Columbia.

For today, though, my mind was on a more manageable distance and my target was to reach the American/Canadian border crossing, 170 km away at Beaver Creek. Occasionally the road would climb above the tree line and I could see out over the vast expanse of wild land, untouched and impenetrable. Everywhere I looked another 'Wow!' slipped from my mouth. The scale was so intimidating, yet I felt as if Alaska was cupping me gently in her jaws, the way a lioness would carry a cub. She had the power to crush me, yet I felt safe. A deep sense of belonging had been missing for me in the southern hemisphere. Alaska always sounded so romantic and for me it was, in a rough and rugged sense.

It felt tense at times being here and the wildlife was definitely freaking me out, but I was fairly sure that reaction was caused by fatigue. I didn't want to be scared. I wanted to embrace and respect all parts of this land, including the wonderful, unique presence of big mammals. I hadn't actually even seen that much wildlife, despite it being omnipresent in most of my thoughts; loads of squirrels, a couple of moose and that bear. I had nearly passed through the region now and felt grateful to have some meat on my North American bones.

The border between Alaska and Canada was marked with two great big wooden signs. One read 'Welcome to Alaska' in lemon yellow writing, contrasting well against the chocolate brown background. It continued: 'The historic Alaskan Highway. Gateway to the 49th State' and featured a silhouette of the Alaskan state map with little moose migrating across the land. Standing opposite and facing towards Alaska the second sign welcomed you to the Yukon. The word 'Yukon' was spread the whole way across the face of the board, in bright blue writing with a sun rising over the top of it. Along the bottom it read, 'Larger than Life' with the French translation below: 'Plus Grand Que Nature'. I took a picture at both, feeling this was a monumental moment.

The untamed, mountainous territory of the Yukon now demanded my attention. I already loved it and I'd only seen the sign. The official border control, where the guard gave me a great big blue stamp in my passport reading Beaver Creek, was a further 16 km down the road. I rolled into town and headed straight into Buckshot Betty's Restaurant and Café. I tucked into the diner food as the waitress asked lots of questions about my ride. She was horrified to hear I was going to sleep out that night. She insisted on finding me accommodation. 'It's too early to stop here,' I told her, 'but what's further down the road?'

'There's tents, but they're at Discovery Yukon,' she said, 'another 40 miles away.'

'That's perfect!' I said and she set about booking my bed for the night.

Soon after leaving Buckshot Betty's I was benighted. The temperature dropped significantly and by the time I arrived at Discovery Yukon at 2 a.m., frost lay on the ground. The sky was beautiful, the moon once again taking centre stage. A shadow was cast across the top of its now oval shape, suggesting it might dissolve in front of my very eyes.

The waitress had given me instructions, the first being to turn right up the driveway with the big flags, where there would be a long building with a green roof. I couldn't see the colour of the roof, but continued following the convoluted directions, weaving along pathways until I reached my designated tent.

It was like a yurt, only rectangular in shape with a double bed, wooden-effect flooring and electric points, but crucially no heating. My breath was visible as I pulled all my spare layers out of my bag, swapping my bibs for my shorts with no chamois before layering up with all my clothes – every single piece, including my hat. Then I lay in the foetal position, doubled up in the sleeping bag and bed covers. I was uncomfortably cold, but grateful for my fake walls and the peace of mind they brought.

Day 76: 30 August 2018 • Quill Creek to just south of Destruction Bay • 10 hours 41 minutes • 184 km • ODO: 18,067.81 km • Bivvy in rest spot

Chewing on a chocolate muffin I had left over from yesterday's buffet, I wheeled my bike out of the driveway, googling my most popular search: 'Coffee near me'. Nothing appeared, other than the frustrating whir of little dots trying to make a connection. I had no reception again – not surprising in a place so remote.

I zoomed into my GPS map. The maps were preloaded and would have shown any town I was approaching. The smaller screen meant a lot of scrolling to find it. Nothing. Just a whole lot of nothing (or a whole lot of everything, depending on what you're after). I settled into the saddle, rested on my tribars and continued along the long empty road to Destruction Bay, 130 km away. I was still in awe of the sheer grandeur the Yukon was delivering, though waves of frustration took over every now and then.

I had ridden 50 km when, with no warning, I saw two flags waving in the wind. The blue, white and red bands of France and the unmistakable maple leaf of Canada flying proud. I beamed at the sign 'Pine Valley French Crêperie'. What? How wonderfully bizarre. The smell of fresh pastry and coffee hit me as soon as I opened the door of the wooden cabin. This was the stuff dreams were made of, certainly *my* dreams! I ordered a can of lemon fizzy juice, an Americano, a ham and egg crêpe and a homemade cinnamon bun to take away (which actually got eaten with the second coffee I ordered).

I went through my usual charging routine: GPS, lights, phone, battery packs, camera were on constant rotation. I had picked up three tiny USB plug adapters, back in Tok Junction. They were satisfying to use, their prongs folding away when in transit, making them sleek to carry.

I had a brief conversation with an elderly couple who had come in for lunch. The woman seemed a bit agitated that I was riding alone. 'What are you going to do if it snows?' she asked in a hostile tone. Right now, the sun was beating through the window and, although cold, this was only September. I was fairly flippant in my reply: 'Well, it's not snowing, but if it does I'll just deal with it.' It annoyed me when women in particular showed this unconscious bias towards other women travelling alone. She didn't say what she actually thought, though it was obvious enough from her demeanour.

Back out on the road the landscape was changing. The tall pine trees that had been lining the road were now set back and the woods not nearly as dense. Causeways and bridges crossed rivers and often opened up to panoramic views of the wide meandering waterways that poured from surrounding mountains.

Today's bear prevention strategy included blowing my whistle on repeat each time the road bent and I couldn't see around the corner. Bears just need plenty of warning, I kept thinking. I had just about reached Destruction Bay when I saw, on the stony verge bank, an unmistakable and gigantic paw print left in the mud. Triggered!

• • •

Standing in the doorway of the Talbot Arm Restaurant and Motel, the weight of my choices hit me. I'd been inside for two hours and now, looking out at the storm-tossed waters of Lake Kluane, I watched the night fall. By the time I'd got on my bike and cycled out of Destruction Bay, it was sure to be pitch-black. Frustrating! After Tok Junction, I'd planned never to get into a situation of having to leave a safe space at twilight again.

I had two options: turn around and go back inside or step out into the dark. Through the door behind me was the warmth of the fire, the safety of families chatting to one another, the comfort of beds that lay empty in rooms and food – oh, lots of warm, yummy food. Behind me was the cheery waiter who had brought me endless pots of tea and then there was that woman, the one with the eyes. Peggy. Peggy would have loved to see me walking back through the door. To be sitting behind the long glass-paned windows that lined the walls and to chat the night away with her and her husband Dutch.

I hadn't planned on oversharing with Peggy; I hadn't even planned to make eye contact with her. Walking in, I'd made an attempt at keeping my head down and not chatting to anyone. I was sick of hearing my own voice banging on about grizzly bears. It was all-consuming and all I could think about when I had some airtime with anyone who might have some different information for me.

It would be easier if I just sat alone and kept myself to myself, but I couldn't avoid Peggy's gaze. She could have been my aunty, my mum, my friend or neighbour. With a slight and athletic build, she had a familiar empathetic face and long dark hair that hung right past her shoulders. She struck up a conversation, asking what I was doing. I told her about the record and tried to change the conversation back to her own trip, but soon we were talking toilet block bivvies, the bear paw print and my new information: wolves in the area! An article online described a cyclist being chased along this stretch of road only a year before. So much for keeping myself to myself.

I recognised the look in her eyes, the mothering concern. It should have felt a comfort to be cared for all the way out here, but I was carrying a sackful of my own worries, heavy enough, and I didn't need to carry hers too.

And now it had just gone 7.30 p.m. Not carrying on would have a dramatic effect on the rest of the trip. I needed to keep going, but on this doorstep I was magnetised to the mat. Out in front of me was the only place I could make forward progress, but there were so many unknowns. The only thing I could be sure about was I'd spend the next few hours overthinking on high alert and blowing my whistle into the night.

The storm blew in from the bay as I zipped up my many layers. Wearing this many clothes doesn't exactly make you feel athletic – I couldn't have felt less so – but this wasn't about athleticism, it was about keeping going and that was proving to be the biggest job of all.

Despite what its name suggests, Destruction Bay was a really pretty spot, standing on Lake Kluane. In daylight I could see the far-off side of the lake enclosed by mountains so eroded that deep scars had been carved out and ran the length of them, from the sky to the shore. The lake was so big it had a separate arm that stretched out for 30 km, creating its own fjord. Lake Kluane translated as 'Big Fish Lake'. It felt apt; everything was so grand and had a real presence. I'd keep the lake to my left for the rest of the evening.

I'd downloaded some podcasts in the restaurant. Since being in North America I'd already listened to the whole of *S-Town*. Immersed in the quirky story, I finished all nine episodes in one day. The same production company had produced another series, which I thought was bound to be a winner, although I hadn't fully appreciated the topic before committing to it. It was called *Serial* (which perhaps should have been a giveaway). It was a crime story; a murder, to be exact. I pedalled through the first episode, listening to the circumstances that led to a young, lone female being murdered in her town as she walked home.

I pulled out on to the middle of the road, so as not to be too close to the bushes that lined the edge of the tarmac. I felt edgy. Was I being followed? I swung my neck around, expecting someone or something. Of course, there was no one; there had been no one since leaving the restaurant over two hours ago. I continued listening as the young girl's boyfriend was revealed as the prime suspect for her disappearance. I was going uphill now and had become more aware of my heavy breathing. My surroundings were completely dark other than the five-metre light bubble coming from the Sinewave dynamo frontlight attached to my tribars shelf and the Exposure Links flashing from my helmet. I pulled the buds from my ears – pheeeew. That was too much. It was also too late. Too late for serial killers and too late not to be freaked out.

After 11 hours' riding, I pulled over at the next toilet stop, wheeling my bike to the metal bearproof bin with the special catch that was supposed to keep them out. I wished I could climb into the bin; it looked so safe. Instead, I threw in my two feedbags and emptied my pockets of any half-eaten biscuits. I then wheeled my bike in through the three-quarter-length wooden door of the long-drop cubicle. It was far from bear- (or murderer-) proof, but I was drawn to be inside an enclosed space; that primal instinct to find shelter, a momentarily safe spacc.

Day 77: 31 August 2018 • Just past Destruction Bay to South Whitehorse • 13 hours 14 minutes • 251 km • ODO: 18,318.81 km • Bivvy in rest spot

Canada does a lot of things well, but the cinnamon buns are exceptional! I'd never been a fan of them at home. Too dry and far too many raisins.

Plus, they're all drowning in thick tasteless icing. The Yukon, though, takes them to a whole different level.

The Village Bakery at Haines Junction served up the best cinnamon bun of my life. This title would, by a slim margin, be taken from them in two days' time when I passed Johnsons Crossing at Teslin Lake – they added nutmeg and you could ask for it to be heated in butter, just to add to the gooeyness! But for the moment, right now, I'd never tasted anything like it. The roll itself was a squircle and sat about three inches high. The dough was soft, the thin swirls of pastry were packed with plenty of cinnamon goo, the golden raisins were scattered sparsely, and top to bottom it was finished off with a brushing of cinnamon sugar. Best of all, it was still warm as I tucked in.

The village had a striking backdrop: glaciers came tumbling from the jagged mountains. The foothills that I'd followed all morning were just the guardians to the giants lying in the Icefield Range, home to 17 of Canada's largest peaks, all over 5000 metres in height. I missed the mountains...

I used the post office to send my pedals home. I'd been carrying them since Brisbane and this was the first proper post office I'd passed. I didn't know it at the time, but in three months from now I'd end up paying £90 in customs charges to release them. I would have just held on to them if I'd known.

The next two days went by with mountain passes, cinnamon buns and frosty nights. Feeling much braver through the day I continued with the *Serial* podcast, thinking that I'd most likely stopped listening at the scariest part. If I didn't finish it then, dread would be the feeling I was left with all the way down the Yukon. Turned out I was right and I was glad to shake off the creepy vibes. Occasionally, I'd leapfrog my Yukon buddies Peggy and Dutch. They'd hang out the window of their RV waving and would leave snacks on my bike when I went to the toilet. I continued bivvying out, singing as the sun went down and wearing every single bit of clothing I could... except for a pair of bright orange Endura arm warmers. That was the only piece of clothing I hadn't yet used.

Day 79: 2 September 2018 • Morley Lake to Watson Lake • 12 hours 10 minutes • 224.9 km • ODO: 18,732.71 km • Stayed with warm shower family

'JENNNNNY GRAHAMMM, IS THAT YOU?'

I was wandering around a laundrette outbuilding, holding my phone in the air trying to find some signal, when I heard my name bellowed from the other side of the car park. Until arriving here into Nugget City (not actually a city) just 10 minutes before, I'd barely seen another soul all day. 'Um, yeah, that's me.' I laughed nervously, walking towards the voice. I'm not sure what caught my eye first – his shiny white smiley teeth or his shiny bright police badge.

'I'm J.M. Sauve. I've been following your dot. Thought I'd drive out to say hi and see if I could buy you dinner?' I was touched. I looked at the badge he was holding out. 'I'm an officer with the Royal Canadian Mountain Police.' A Mountie!

I'd already placed an order in the restaurant, though, so I invited him to join me. From the outside, it just looked like a little wooden shack built on the side of a campsite, but inside was vibing. The small space was crammed with people, sharing tables. The food looked incredible. I ordered the lamb chops with mash potato and green vegetables. The chef and owner was everyone's friend and he juggled conversations and orders as he was cooking up.

J.M. knew lots of people too. It felt nice to have a buddy and be part of something – it was so unexpected. Dinner took ages to arrive and, in the meantime, J.M. offered me a bed at his family home in Watson Lake. 'I have an RV in the driveway you can have to yourself, and my wife and kids would love to meet you.'

I was planning on staying in Watson Lake tonight anyway and he had already confirmed he was a Warm Showers host. Still, I had apprehensions about staying with people on this trip, knowing that extended conversations would take so much out of my energy reserve; knowing too that I was such a chatterbox I'd spend hours there in the morning, feeling too attached to leave.

I was just about to refuse and book a motel when he hit me with the deal maker: 'And we have a washing machine. You can wash and dry your clothes if you like.' Oooooh! Now that was tempting! I'd only had sink washes and the occasional tumble dryer since Melbourne; another machine wash would be good. My white string vest looked in the worst state, the fabric ingrained with dust, dirt and grime, but my bibs weren't too healthy either.

After dinner I followed my route for 50 km, then made a small detour when I reached the town of Watson Lake to find J.M.'s house and a welcome on the street, just as he'd given me in the car park. It was already late and everyone else was in bed.

I showered and lathered my hair with their conditioner, hoping it might help with the matted dreadlocks that had been building up over the past 10 weeks, mainly on the back of my head and behind my ears. I had never even considered taking a brush with me given how tight space was. Instead, after washing my hair I threw my head upside down to give it a finger sweep, but by now that was having limited success.

J.M. took care of my clothes, washing and drying them all for the morning. He was a true trail angel and I certainly wasn't the first bedraggled cyclist he'd picked up and cared for. He knew exactly what I needed and with all the warmth he generated made me feel very comfortable in his presence.

An early rise in the morning was followed by bottomless pancakes and coffee, really fun conversations with the whole family, and lots and lots of bear reassurance. J.M. was a hunter and knew so much about bear activity. He laughed hearing about my antics, but also put me at ease. 'You'd need to be really unlucky,' he said. 'It's very rare.' I was beyond pleased to hear that.

Day 80: 3 September 2018 • Watson Lake to Liard River Hot Springs • 11 hours 35 minutes • 208.43 km • ODO: 18,941.14 km • Bivvy in woods by hot springs

🎧 *I left J.M.'s amazing family very, very late, all packed up with a lunch and clean clothes. He fixed my waterproofs by sticking duct tape on with the hairdryer to stop my trousers ripping any more; they'd been flapping about endlessly! It was just lovely.*

And then I saw something not so lovely. I rode through the area where there had been some forest fires. The devastation is just massive, like the amount of trees that had been burned down, the people's homes, townlets that had been burnt out. I couldn't quite get my head round how it must have been. There were still some bits in the area on fire and it was still quite smoky, so yeah, that was pretty sad to see – just to think how vulnerable it is, I suppose, this sort of landscape. I think it was the biggest forest fire they had in a very long time, if not, ever.

British Colombia had been devastated by wildfire that year. A dry summer was followed by severe lightning storms, causing an incredible amount of damage. Over 3.2 million acres burned within four months. That's a landmass almost the size of Wales. Riding through charred surroundings made for a reflective start. No one had been killed, amazingly, but thousands of homes were evacuated and the habitats of wildlife across the country were ravished by the blazes.

I weaved my way back and forth over the Yukon/British Colombia border, following the Liard River all the way down to the hot springs, 220 km away. The river stayed hidden for much of the day as my sight remained blinkered by the large trees lining the road. When my view did open out, it was such a treat to see the turquoise-green waters among the scenery. Its vastness takes your breath away.

Throughout my whole journey, I had met only a handful of other people out on active adventures. Lots of folk in cars and motorhomes, but very few out facing the elements, day and night. This would change by mid-afternoon at an arbitrary lay-by, where my path crossed with that of Richard Zier Vogel.

Richard was a tall, slender man with long silver hair tied back in a ponytail. He wore a full-brimmed beige hiking hat tied around his neck with two long pieces of string and beige cargo pants, his well-tanned knees sticking out proud from them. They looked strong. The thing that stood out the most about Richard Zier Vogel, though, wasn't his appearance or the fact he had been the only hiker I'd seen in months; it was the large cart he was pulling behind him. His home. It was attached to him by a lime green, padded waist band, like you'd expect on a good-quality rucksack. This was attached to poles stretching all the way back to his cart.

I was fascinated. He was soon telling me all about his home-built contraption. The base was made of spruce lengths with wheels salvaged from a bicycle and child's stroller. The material used to create the structure was Coroplast®, a corrugated plastic similar to cardboard. The front end was rounded, designed to be effective in the wind. The lower half had been painted lime green and he'd been collecting stickers along the way. I scanned my eyes over one side: the Canadian Flag, a fox, a bunch of two-finger peace signs and my favourite: 'My Plod Pod', referring to the cart.

The inside was like a spaceship. He'd lined the walls and roof with silver reflective material for warmth. Four porthole windows let in a tremendous amount of light. Inside was his bed, kitchen and spare clothes. We compared our living spaces and laughed. Looking at his cart, I wondered how much safer I'd have felt in it... I mean, the bears would smell the food, right? I decided to keep that thought to myself and try not to pass on any of my worries.

Richard was on a trek from west to east Canada – 8455 km. We had followed the same route from Beaver Creek, but while I would cross back into the United States before reaching Halifax in Nova Scotia, he would stay on this side of the border and finish up in Newfoundland, the most easterly province in Canada.

We talked about our adventures so far and life back home. I must have waited a whole three and a half minutes before bringing up the wildlife. Richard was so cool. I mean he was from the Yukon, up in Whitehorse, this stuff wasn't new to him. The hot topic wasn't bears, though, it was the wood bison we had both come across that day. I'd passed a couple of individual ones only an hour ago and switched to the other side of the road, but neither was bothered about me. Richard told me simply that there was one bison which didn't like him, so he got out of its way. I imagined what my own reaction would have been.

Richard also carried a bunch of small worry dolls that he'd made himself out of wool and cloth. He was giving them out to people he met along the way, along with a card that read:

Adopt-a-doll

Donate to YOUR favourite charity.

If you don't have one then my charity of choice is: Little Feet, Big Steps. They work to protect vulnerable children in Haiti.

I accepted one of his palm-size beauties. She had been wrapped in a bright blue yarn to make her outfit and had wild orange hair. I stuck her in the side of my feedbag, so she could watch the world go by. We spent half an hour chatting and that would be the last I'd see of Richard, but throughout my trip he'd message to tell me he regularly shouted out loud to the wilderness: 'Go, Jenny, go!'

I carried on riding, feeling blessed for these recent interactions. Since speaking to J.M. and now Richard, I felt way more at ease. I'd even seen another black bear, at a distance, down by the river fishing. See, she wanted to eat fish, not cyclists. Finally, I was regaining some calm and enjoying my surroundings – just as I'd imagined I would.

The temperature would drop to just below freezing when the sun went down. Tonight felt particularly frosty. I was having an issue with the button on my helmet light, so I decided to ride with just the glow from my dynamo. This was fine, but as the beam was directed in the direction of your handlebars, not your eyes, it could be limiting.

I was riding up a gentle hill when I first got the whiff. Hmm, cattle. I didn't have enough time to really think what that 'cattle' might be and had completely forgotten what Richard had told me earlier about there being a herd of wood bison ahead of us.

I was resting on my tribars when I realised I was now eye to eye with a bison bull, so close I could see the definition of fluffy dark balls of fur across his thick, flat face, his shaggy fringe dangling down in between his horns to reach the empty hollow stare of his widespread eyes. My light cast a shadow and he was gone again, but the rest of them were not. I was now surrounded by around 40 bulls. My bells jangled gently as I tapped my feet to keep both momentum and my light going, but still give me time to react to any space ahead of me. Softly I heard myself say: 'Heeeey, you guuuuys... just passing on through' (jingle jingle jingle).

The average wood bison bull weighs around 890 kg, stands two metres tall and three metres long. They are front-heavy, their strong shoulders rising up to their highest point, giving them the strength they need to use their head as a snowplough when searching out food in the winter. They taper towards the rear and have a small little toosh (although I wouldn't tell one that).

How much trouble was I in? No idea. My freehub whirled as I continued gently tapping the pedals, navigating my way around the bodies. I didn't want to take a wrong turn and have to stop in the pack with this dim light. And then, as quickly as I rode into them, I was out again. Just like that, I'd been allowed a safe passage. What a blessing.

My light illuminated the road ahead as I upped my pace significantly to get some distance between us, adrenaline pumping through my body, thinking of that big beastie staring back at me. I was elated, riding on a high with a twinge of nerves, knowing I was lucky to have made it through the herd with no issue. Had that been daytime, I'd have been so cautious, passing them with a wide berth. They have notoriously bad eyesight, but their ability to smell and hear are heightened. So, given that I was both loud and a bit pongy, maybe I hadn't sneaked up on them as suddenly as they had seemed to sneak up on me.

I turned to look back and was hit by vivid green waves of light high above me, skipping playfully, forming a solid rainbow shape before re-morphing and starting again. The aurora borealis, the Northern Lights. Wow, could this night have been any more Canadian? I'd seen the Northern Lights from home in Scotland a few times, but nothing as vivid and bright as this. I stopped to take them in for a moment.

I was at the highpoint of the climb now and had a 4-km descent down to the Laird River Hot Springs Provisional Park, home to some of the largest natural hot springs in Canada. I wondered if I could get into them when I arrived. I reached down for my bear spray – for the first time, surprisingly. Riding into the bison had brought home how quickly encounters can happen. I was feeling a strange mix of excitement and nerves, and wanted to hold it in my hand for a bit, a sort of North American comfort blanket. It would make the ride into Hot Springs a bit more carefree.

To hold the metal canister, I'd taken off my mitt, and by the time I'd reached the village my hand and body were freezing. The big wooden lodge where I'd hoped to grab a bed had a sign at the door: no vacancy.

I stood in the porch fixing another puncture and trying to warm up again. It had gone 1 a.m. but still lots of people were milling around. 'You should go down to the hot pools,' one woman told me excitedly, having just walked back from there. It sounded wonderful – but all I wanted was a bed.

I made my way through the thick forest, following signs to the springs and past a campsite. This would be the second time on the trip – after the whales in Australia – that my mission took precedence. I knew the warm water and bright sky would be a pinnacle moment, but continuing through the woods alone (and past potential bears) to find the pools seemed too stressful. Plus, I couldn't face having to take all my clothes off while I was already shivering with them all on. Next to some tents and a toilet block, I got out my bivvy bag and lay down to sleep.

I woke in the morning still cold and could see a sign telling me I was 20 metres from the pools. I'd been so close, but didn't really mind. I bypassed them again and went for a hot meal in the lodge.

🎧 *I woke up shivering this morning with all my clothes on. I could barely take off my sleeping bag. I've got down sleeping socks, but my feet were like ice cubes.*

I just came into the café where I was hoping to stay last night and just got a really nice breakfast there and warmed up. And now everyone was saying, 'Oh, you been to Hot Springs?' And I had to tell them no. Aw, gutted! Anyway, doesn't matter, that's not what I'm here for. Bit annoying, though.

Day 81: 4 September 2018 • Liard River Hot Springs to Tetsa River Access before Fort Nelson • 12 hours 56 minutes • 213.55 km • ODO: 19,154.69 km • Bivvy in the woods

I woke after four hours' sleep, just as it was getting light, wondering where I was. This didn't happen every morning, but lately I needed to run through the story so far: okay, there was the world... and then Canada... it had been dark and wet last night... I was at the RV parking site.

In the early hours of this morning I'd followed a sign (saying it was closed) waaay further into the woods than I'd have liked to go, but I found a BBQ area with a canvas cover and walls. There was a wide open space where the door should have been, which meant a breeze I could feel from behind.

I heard two deep voices getting louder. Then their boots came into sight. I closed my eyes. They were making plans to replace something. No one mentioned that I was lying on the ground by the wood stove. Their voices became more distant again and I drifted off back to sleep.

The next time I heard footsteps near me, it was just one set. I woke more startled this time. 'Sorry,' I said, jolting upwards. The woodsman was about the same age as me and looked just as feral. He too had forgotten his hairbrush. 'You're freezing,' he said. 'Why didn't you put the stove on?' 'No, no, I'm fine,' I said, readjusting myself stiffly. 'I didn't want to disturb you by lighting the fire.' This was only half the truth. I'd been so tired and even more relieved not to be sleeping *out* out that I didn't want to do anything to jeopardise that by drawing attention to myself. It was pretty cold, though.

He left me to get up and called over as I wheeled my bike out of the big doorless space. 'Come on in, kettle's hot.' He was standing at the door of his RV, which was so big that it resembled some sort of Transformer with sides extended out. Inside, the warm heater blasted and he made strong black coffee from real beans. He was the park ranger and stayed here for the winter. The park was pretty much closed now. We chatted for two cups' worth.

'Have you seen any grizzlies?' he asked casually. I was relieved someone else had brought it up before I did for once.

'No, only black so far. I think I would die if I saw a grizzly!'

'I'm surprised you've not seen any. This is prime country for grizzlies, especially that pass you went over last night.'

It had been a murky evening climbing up and over the pass. At an altitude of 1300 metres the fog hovered around the ground like something straight out of a *Scooby-Doo* cartoon. My light had struggled to make a path through. I didn't need my eyes to sense the great empty void to my right where the mountain fell away and occasionally I'd glimpse the tops of a tall skinny tree. I hugged the left side where I could feel the dense presence of rock jutting upwards.

'I passed something last night,' I told him. 'Near the highest point. It was small, dark. Big in girth. Way bigger than a badger, maybe up to my knees on the bike.'

I hadn't got a proper look at it, but we skiffed past one another. It moved quickly out of sight again. I was speaking calmly to the ranger now, but last night I moved as quickly as my weary, weather-beaten body could while going uphill.

'It was too small for a bear cub,' I said confidently.

'Oh, that's exactly what it was,' he came back, crumbling my confidence. 'I've seen a mum with two pretty small two cubs up there recently.'

There wasn't much more I could say. I was at capacity; no more advice or near-miss stories. I just had one more day left and I'd be dropping into civilisation, something I usually dreaded, but today, after that latest piece of information, the safety of noise and the presence of people was really appealing.

The temperature was around freezing when I set off, but the hefty climb to get started helped warm me up. The low-lying fog continued through the morning and traffic works were scattered along the road – a welcome bear-deterrent noise on the quiet highway.

On a long, empty stretch of road, I tried to do some body maintenance. I had felt so weak since arriving in North America. The dulled, fuzzy fatigue that I felt leaving the airport in Alaska hadn't gone yet. I wondered if I was still feeling the effects of the New Zealand bug. A big ride followed by a long flight wasn't the ideal recovery. Since arriving on the continent 10 days ago, my average riding speed had dropped to 202 km per day, whereas overall it was 241 km per day, but I'd been sitting on the saddle for too many hours and my body was seizing up, particularly my glutes and quads.

●   ●   ●

Although I love the outcome of a good stretch, until then I didn't have very good daily stretching habits. It was an activity I usually endured, but by this stage of the trip I had hit a wall with overall stiffness, so most mornings I'd stretch and massage my tender muscles while riding along slowly.

Firstly, I'd run my water bottle down my quads and IT bands. I'd continue pedalling and as my leg rose it would apply more pressure to the bottle. These muscles were the tightest. I'd arch my back like a cat and drop my chin to my chest. Then I'd run two fingers around the little hollow at the bottom of my skull and gently knead that area. My neck was working hard at the moment and sometimes I'd do this a few times throughout the day. My massage therapist, Lindsay, had told me – repeatedly – to stretch in the opposite direction to how I was crouched each day. This meant sitting upright, balancing with just my fingers on the handlebars, sticking my chest out proud and pinching my shoulder blades together – aww, *they* hurt too – and then beginning to rotate my neck around slowly, using my fingers to manipulate the tightest parts.

The end of my saddle was excellent at getting right into the pressure points of my glutes. Because I could get so deep into the tissue, this massage hovered more than the others between pleasure and pain, but it was very satisfying. Dropping one pedal at a time and pushing my heel to the ground, I worked my calves into a big long stretch before unclipping my feet and rotating my ankles. I'd twist my wrists in the same way, although they always felt tender, especially since my padded handlebars had been stripped back in Oz.

Although I'd have loved to be feeling a bit sprightlier, I was amazed at how well my body had adjusted to the added strain. It would work a bit more efficiently if the muscles weren't so tight, but being able to warm up and settle in each day was reassuring. The first couple of weeks through Russia I had been dreading an injury, aware of every twinge. Now I was feeling that all the conditioning work I'd put into training was worth it.

●　●　●

The day was punctuated by two events. The first was pulling into the little town of Fort Nelson and coming across my first Tim Hortons. I'd be drawn to them for their ease. They served pretty decent coffee and mini doughnuts with various toppings, which fitted perfectly into my feed bags. They also sold savouries like soup and burgers and breakfasts, and there was always free Wi-Fi. I used the stop to book some accommodation for that night. I just had one more evening left in this remote mountainous landscape and was heading towards the much flatter lands of the prairies and out of Bearville – well, certainly, Grizzly Bearville.

It was mid-afternoon now and my two accommodation options were Profit Lake, 90 km away, or Buckinghorse River, 190 km away. I always aimed to ride for 15 hours a day in the hope of averaging 300 km, but it had been a long time since I'd achieved either of those targets. Today the first 100 km had taken me six and a half hours to ride; the going was hilly and cold. To meet my target average speed I'd need to be covering that distance in five hours.

Physical fatigue was playing its part, as was my obsession about the wildlife in the evenings. I needed a few more daylight hours to gain a larger daily distance. The remote location also meant I was sleeping outside a lot and woke up every morning shivering, hardly the sign of a restful sleep.

If I passed Profit Lake but didn't make Buckinghorse River then it would be another really draining night. Perhaps I could take the hit on distance tonight and get a decent sleep? If I got efficient, I could reach Profit Lake with only one hour riding in the dark. The next day, once the terrain changed, I could refocus without the stresses. That's what I decided on.

There was a beautiful golden glow in the air as the sun set, striking every tree in its path. A single truck drove towards me on the long, straight road. A black chunky vehicle pulling a trailer with a motor boat. Slowing down, a young man – stereotypical Canadian, strong jawline – leaned out of the window. 'There is a massive black bear up there.' He gestured with his head to the direction I was going. I stopped the bike.

'Where?' I asked, as if it mattered. *Up there* was enough to make me want to ride as far as I could in the other direction.

Pointing to the far side of the road he said, 'Three hundred yards up there.'

Damn yards – who still uses them? I couldn't picture 300 yards, but it sounded closer than I'd choose to be to a 'massive black bear'. I straddled my bike with my gaze fixed in the distance, having no idea what my next move should be.

'What are you going to do?'

'Hmmm, I'm not sure. I guess I'll ride past it on the other side of the road and make loads of noise?' I couldn't believe that was the plan and I was saying it out loud. My inside voice was saying, 'We're not going to do that, though, are we?'

It was clearly an unconvincing pitch. The driver had now pulled over and was unhitching his trailer. 'We can go together,' he declared. I explained that I couldn't get into the car because of the World Record attempt, so instead he drove to my right, in between me and the 'massive black bear'. It was so sweet of him – and fascinating to see the bear behind the safety of the truck, just minding her own business foraging for berries. The driver was right: she was massive! He carried on with me to the top of the hill before wishing me luck and turning back.

And then it was just me – well, me and my flashing lights, jingling bells, music on loud speaker and whistles blown frequently. It took one and a half long, tense hours to get to my motel room that night.

I was meant to be tough, fearless and an adventurer, challenging society's perception of the dangers facing women, embracing my wild soul, but as the trip progressed I felt I was becoming more and more fragile, as if I had ridden all this way to discover that the truth was quite the opposite.

Day 83: 6 September 2018 • Prophet River to Mile 101 • 12 hours 34 minutes • 207 km • ODO: 19,552.15 km • Camping pod

🎧 *Morning. I can't believe it's the 5th of September, or no wait is it the 6th today? Yes, it must be…*

What happened? I left a B&B in the morning and, yeah, pretty decent riding and a pretty good overall ridetime actually, hardly any stops. That was twelve and a half hour's ride time and my overall time on the bike was 15 hours, so two and a half hours stopping time – that is ideal!

And, it was like nowhere near as bear-scary. It feels a lot more urban, which is sad in one way that the big mountains are gone but I'm holding onto the fact it's getting less beary. Although I did make the mistake of looking it up on the internet on the Grand Prairie Bears – don't google it, whatever you do.

Day 85: 8 September 2018 • Dawson Creek to Valleyview • 11 hours 14 minutes • 244.26 km • ODO: 19,960.66 km • Motel

Little Pig was hanging limply from the bike rack. Just moments before her crank arms had been removed to reveal the empty space in her bottom bracket where a ball bearing cartridge once sat. Bearings always wear out eventually, so the fact they'd disintegrated after 20,000 km wasn't a huge surprise. Still, this was a fairly catastrophic moment for two reasons:

- The bottom bracket acts as a connector between the frame and the pedal arm. Without any working ball bearings, the bike could no longer make progress.
- The closest replacement part was 600 km away.

I had limped to the doorstep of Griffin Source For Sports in Dawson Creek first thing that morning. It was a general sporting goods store as opposed to a bike specialist, but they did some repairs and stocked some parts. I followed the store manager Mike (insisting on calling him Kevin for the duration – no idea why, perhaps sleep deprivation – sorry, Mike!). Followed him all the way through the shop, passing the wall of ice skates, array of caps and an impressive quantity of baseball goods to reach the rear of the store, where there was a small workshop and bike stand. Mike's first word on seeing the state of things was: 'Yikes!' In my world 'yikes' is an underused word, but it seemed to sum up the situation well.

We already knew the store didn't stock the part I needed – a whole, sealed, bottom bracket unit – but they might be able to pinch some of the necessary ball bearings from another product. They had a model with the same size of ball bearings. I needed Mike to extract these compatible bearings from a sealed unit of an incompatible bottom bracket and then make them fit into my bike, despite the damage now caused by the corroded cartilage. This wasn't a standard procedure! To get moving again, I needed more than a mechanic; I needed a grand master in bike bodgery.

I didn't mean to seem ungrateful, but I wasn't convinced that Mike had the experience to pull this off or that he realised the time pressure I was under. He had even told me I could come with him to a restaurant opening that night if I was still in town. An innocent and kind gesture, but it filled me with panic: 'Mike, I can't still be here tonight, mate!'

After an hour of close proximity to me offering as much 'helpful' advice as I had and Mike bashing bike parts with a big mallet, he suggested I go for coffee. I didn't blame him, I was sure I was being very annoying, so reluctantly I left him to it.

The weather was still wild outside. It had been like this for the past 48 hours and, I was sure, had accelerated the damage to my bike. Once there is movement in the ball bearings, the seals become loose and begin to leak. All the water and grit from the road would have been getting inside. Everything seemed to be breaking this week. I had a list of fix-its and to-dos:

- Change rear gear cable
- Pick up new tyre
- Look out for new bibs (the zip had burst open on the bum)
- Get a hairbrush
- Replace bottom bracket
- Get more glue for the sleeping mat or perhaps just a new sleeping mat
- Get new cleats for shoes ASAP

My gear cable went about the same time as my bottom bracket began to wobble. Without lower gearing at the rear of the bike, I had spent the past day and a half zigzagging my way up all the hills. I did leave Berlin with a spare cable, but now couldn't remember if I'd already used it or lost it.

As for the drop seat part of my bibs, I had sewn these together before coming into the shop this morning. Luckily they'd burst at the end of the day and not on a busy highway, revealing my bum to all the passing traffic. This was just a bit of a nuisance, because the zip made going for a wee so easy. Without it, I needed to take lots of my top layers off and pull my bib braces down.

My hair and the sleeping mat were ongoing issues. I had as many dreads in my hair as I had holes in my mat. I was concerned I'd need to get a crew cut when I got home if I didn't start working on the knots now... Knot funny!

The half skeleton mat was a fairly specialist piece of kit, which no one in their right mind takes on a long journey. I'd chosen it for barely using any space inside my saddlebag. I was never going to find one so packable in an outdoor shop and now I figured I could try to slather glue across every seal as they, I was fairly sure, were the source of the leaks.

The cleat is an external attachment used to connect your feet to the bike. It had been the first thing to go. A small lip that slots into the front of the pedal had worn off, and I'd spent the last 10 days chiselling little notches into the now-flush plastic block on the bottom of my shoe. This was in a bid to stop my left foot violently jutting forward into my front wheel and it worked, as long as I was concentrating on keeping my foot balanced during each pedal stroke. A more robust solution was tying my foot on to my pedal with a doubled-over, elastic hair bobble. The downside was stopping in an emergency: I couldn't put my foot down without extracting it from my shoe.

Returning to the store fully caffeinated, unsure of what to expect, I was welcomed by Mike's smile. He had actually fixed it! Wow, I'd completely underestimated this man. I had lucked out finding him today. I was literally hundreds of miles in either direction from anyone else who could help. He was my Dawson Creek hero!

There was just one small issue. A piece of tubing was now sitting in the hollow of the bottom bracket, blocking the crank spindle from going all the way through. We were both scratching our heads over this one. It didn't make sense, but now it was in there we didn't want to take it out in case it was a crucial part.

Mike had been juggling the shop floor with this mend all morning. More customers came in and I stayed with my bike and began googling images: 'Bottom bracket... Bottom bracket tubing... Bottom bracket extra spacer'. I wasn't sure what to call it, but nothing that matched what I could see was appearing on my screen, so I flicked through Messenger to see who was online back home. Nash Manson had a green dot next to his name. Nash was a renowned bike mechanic in the Highlands – if anyone would know, it would be him. I sent him a video. He called back from his store and quickly confirmed that the extra spacer was most likely just a cut off from the floor and had nothing to do with the bottom bracket. Result!

I may have slightly offended Mike by getting Nash involved. It was simply the time pressure and the need to get rolling again that made me call, but rolling I now was and Mike's master bodge saw me all the way to Edmonton, where I was able to get a full replacement (and complete a long list of other fixes).

Day 88: 11 September 2018 • Red Deer to Morrin • 8 hours 11 minutes • 147.7 km • ODO: 20,616.36 km • Room above a pub

I've spent most of my adult life being inspired by mountainous landforms, drawn to the contour lines on a map as they rise off the paper and fill my world with ridges, glens and peaks. Their texture excites me. They pique my curiosity and I want to know what it would feel like to be there, touching them, moving through them. However, until this trip I'd never given much thought to the flatlands that cover so much of the planet's surface.

This would be the fourth plain I'd traversed: the East European Plain across Russia; the Mongolian steppe; Australia's Nullarbor Plain; and now the Canadian Prairies. Bound by the Rocky Mountains and the Great Lakes, this high plateau stretches out across three provinces – Alberta, Saskatchewan and Manitoba – and is covered by grasslands and sweet meadows, with very few trees and even fewer peaks. It's pretty, with a subtle enchantment.

Without a summit to be drawn to, though, these plains could be a repetitive undertaking. The lack of a dynamic terrain could allow you to underestimate these crossings – and I'd made that mistake before. It's easy to assume this is a ride that won't need grit, but the enormous stretches of endless horizons and big skies leave you exposed and at the mercy of the elements.

The charming Yukon seemed a distant memory. Things stay the same for so long when you're riding your bike through huge landscapes that it's almost a surprise when suddenly they are quite different.

• • •

Leaving a motel in Red Deer, I had a 100-km ride down to Three Hills. The weather forecast was looking bleak for the week. The TV screen over breakfast had shown strong easterly winds sweeping across the prairies, black clouds and lightning flashes – and single-digit temperatures. But I had the warmth of the sun on my face for now and was feeling optimistic. How bad could it actually get?

In this moment anyway, I didn't care. My mind was on Lachlan. I'd had a video call with him this morning. It felt so good to see him, his lips moving and that familiar voice spilling out stories. 'You're looking rough, Mum,' he laughed. I did: tired eyes and scruffy, bushy hair that I'd tried to pat down when I saw myself on screen. He looked handsome. He'd had a haircut. He'd shaved it a bit shorter than normal around the back of his neck, but kept his wispy fringe long enough to tuft up into a peak at the front. He was in our home, wearing the down jacket I'd given him before I left. Didn't he have a clean T-shirt or was he cold?

'You've been in the papers! People keep coming into work asking if I'm your son and am I proud of you?!' Lachlan, with his dark humour and glint in his eyes, went on. 'The next one that asks, I'm going to say: "Not really, I wish she'd come home and make my dinner."' He was chuckling, but he did look thinner than normal. 'Are you eating okay?' I asked. 'You look Skinny Malinky.'

His appendix had burst the year before and since then he had never filled out in the same way, was always a bit too slim. A chunky child, he'd never been overweight, just filled his own skin. Now this young man, with the fresh haircut and jacket that I assumed was covering a dirty T-shirt, told me he was eating fine.

Remote parenting felt like such a cheat. I knew that in my absence Lach had the whole clan looking out for him, but still it was a battle between the guilt of abandoning him and following my own yearnings. I wondered if 19 was still too young to have left him. It wasn't just my absence worrying me; the reality of the burden that Lachlan and the rest of my family carried was hard to accept. They were supportive, caring and always encouraging, but to honour a loved one's burning desire to be somewhere else, explore, adventure and push their limits must come with stress.

We left the call making plans for Berlin and the finish line, in a month's time, where I'd get to hold this special human in my arms once again. Only 8050 km to go.

• • •

The sky above me dazzled with rainbow after rainbow. I played music through my headphones and sang along as I arrived into Three Hills. The horizon was as flat as the Nullarbor in every direction except for three subtle lumps in the distance.

It stayed this flat until the road surprisingly dropped down into a canyon-type valley, then crossed the Red Deer River, enclosed by dry, tanned eroded slopes. Emerging after 8 km, the road was once again as flat as the eye could see. I looked back at where I'd come from and there were no signs that there was even a canyon, nothing at all. Weird.

A dark, grey, menacing sky lay ahead. Soon it was lit up with great jets of lightning cracking down across the plains. It was an impressive sight from a distance, but if it came any closer there wouldn't be very much protection. Nothing stood taller than me for miles around. The only break from being at surface level was the drainage ditches running the length of the fields on either side of the road.

I figured that I'd need to dive in there if the storm reached me. They were less than a metre deep, but I could lie in one of them. I zoomed into my GPS map, checking for anything with more cover. There was a small cluster of trees nearby. I leaped under them in complete darkness as multiple forks of light jutted out of the sky, followed by the sound of thunder crashing.

As a child I counted elephants in between seeing the lightning and hearing the thunder. Each elephant equated to one mile. The more elephants there were, the further away the storm. So, five elephants equalled five miles, etc. This was my 'Quick, hide from the storm' evaluation system – not very scientific, but it seemed to work.

When I first started counting that night, they were way up at 13 or 14 elephants, but crouched in the wet woodlands, they were much closer. One elephant, two elephants, three elephants, four... the loud rumble of thunder rolled out, filling the sky. My helmet light had a dodgy button on it, so I couldn't get it off the strobe setting. The flashing from my bike only added to the already dramatic atmosphere, like a scene straight out of *The Blair Witch Project*. Soon there were no elephants left to count and the storm was straight above me. It lingered for a bit and gradually made its way past. I'd been in the trees for an hour and in that time I'd got steadily colder, sitting still in my wet clothes.

From under the trees I began checking for accommodation in the next town, Morrin. I wasn't sure I even wanted accommodation. I had planned for a much longer ride tonight, but it would be good not to be sleeping out in this, so I called the only place available. The barmaid was happy to give me a room until I told her I was cycling and it would be another 30 minutes before I got there. Her tone turned and she began backtracking: 'Oh, actually I'm not sure we have any rooms left.' The change in me happened just as quickly as I switched from enquiring to really wanting the room. I sat out the awkward silences and with a little haggling, the 20-dollar, smoky room above the dimly lit pub was mine.

Day 89: 12 September 2018 • Morrin to Kindersley • 11 hours 52 minutes • 270 km • ODO: 20,886.36 km • Hotel

🎧 *I just can't do early mornings anymore. I'm so annoyed. I actually got up when I was meant to – it was still dark outside. I got out of bed, got dressed and packed up my stuff and then kidded myself that I could have another half an hour in bed because it wouldn't take long to leave now I was dressed. . . Well, that's me just woken up and leaving now. It's just gone 9, agh. Annoying, but riding on!*

The next two days passed with the wind at my back as I crossed over into Alberta and beyond. The weather was much colder than I'd expected and every time I stopped for food the news would warn of snowstorms, which were following me down from the north. I seemed continually to be 300 km ahead of them, but I thought back to the elderly woman in the French Crêperie in the Yukon, who had warned me about snow. I had probably been a bit flippant about her concerns.

My average distance over the last two days had increased dramatically, so when I lay down in a field in Keeler at just gone 1 a.m., having clocked over 306 km that day, I felt deeply satisfied. I looked up at the stars momentarily and fell fast asleep. A few hours later, I woke up in a downpour. I'd drifted off before I'd even pulled my bivvy bag up around my shoulders. The top of my sleeping bag was exposed around my chest. There was nowhere to hide from the weather, so I pulled everything up and around my head, snitching the hood tight, then rolled on to my front so as the rain would pour off me and on to the ground. I woke up in the wet bag as the sky was getting light.

If I had been in a tent I'd have struggled to open the zip and leave it this morning, but to be honest, the most comfortable thing to do in a bivvy bag in the rain is to get out of it. I stuffed everything into my bags and began cycling, still wearing my damp clothes. The thermometer on my GPS read 2°C with drizzle and low-lying fog – yuk. There were 45 km before I'd reach Moose Jaw and could find a café to dry out.

I was pitiful that morning. My mood was low and I felt irritated. My hands and feet were both in pain. They were so numb with the cold they felt as if they might shatter into little pieces if anything hit them too hard. I blew into the cuffs of my gloves to try and spread a little warmth into my fingers. I shook them one by one, then gave them a rest from the wind by hiding them behind my back. I unclipped each foot and shook them out too. Nothing helped. Even my toenails ached.

'Please don't get a flat, please don't get a flat,' I said to myself, over and over. I couldn't imagine having to deal with anything worse right now and doubted anyway that my numb fingers could cope.

I thought back to Apsley Cherry-Garrard and *The Worst Journey in the World*. 'Frozen eyeballs, shattered teeth…' I'd say, trying to bring myself back round, but I had gone beyond the point of perspective, so deep I was in my own discomfort. The most it did for me was stop me from crying. Each time I warmed my fingers up enough to use them, I'd zoom in to the map just to check there were no towns sooner. I hung wild hopes on there being a surprise café along the way. Each empty junction I passed, I'd yell out in frustration.

I had to stop myself from erratic pedalling. Going hard, then stopping to freewheel and wallow in some more self-pity, going hard again…

I was a sorry state as I rolled into Moose Jaw. I followed the first road into an industrial estate and found a diner behind a gas station. It looked a bit scummy from the outside. The only reason I was bothered was in case this had a direct effect on the quality of the coffee. I needn't have worried. Inside was an absolute gem!

There were seating booths with their own charging points opposite the window, so I could keep an eye on Little Pig. Perfect. I picked a seat closest to the door with no one behind and used the space to drape my sleeping bag, bivvy bag and roll mat over the edge of the seating. I went to the bathroom and changed into dry clothes, and then hung the rest of my wet kit on the other side.

The waitress brought my Eggs Benedict served on a muffin, with a side helping of hash browns – actually just chips cut into cubes. It was a bit like a crouton, but tasty. The breakfast came with two pancakes, both bigger than my head. Fluffed up, still warm, eggy pancakes. I had completely lucked in. I thought back to this morning's headspace – a bit scary, actually. I'd not felt so angry before.

I promised myself accommodation for that night. I went to pack up my booth, which now resembled a laundrette, and asked for the bill. The waitress told me someone had taken care of it. Wait, what? I looked around for any clues. Another cyclist perhaps? 'We had a phone call from a guy called Ian. He paid for you.'

In that moment, it felt like Ian had just reached out of the phone and given me the biggest hug. It could only have been Ian Fitz, fellow endurance lover, all-round good guy and affectionately known as the

House Elf at the Adventure Syndicate, because of his ability to 'know stuff' and his willingness to help. When my social media plan for regular posting about the challenge broke down in the first few days, Ian stepped up as one of the media heroes, and committed to collecting pictures and posting once a week for the whole trip. He also continued to regularly check in with supportive messages.

He couldn't have known quite what a boost he gave me by reaching out that morning or how low I had been. I was feeling so alone that day; alone not from being on the ride, but alone with my mind, the fatigue, the cold and the discomfort. And now here was Ian – he'd just looked up my dot, called Canada and paid my tab. In this bikepacking world, this is the act of a trail angel – an impromptu, one-off act of kindness shown to someone out on the trail. He never admitted to me that it was him, but the waitress had told me the name on the payment card and this was very true to form.

Fuelled, feeling more positive and thoroughly warmed up, I continued the day riding south-east. I was riding directly into the wind for the next 14 hours. The long grass that filled the fields danced in my direction. At points the wind was so ridiculous it was almost funny. The place names were amusing, though: Drinkwater, Eyebrow and Brownie were among my favourites, as well as finding out that locals of Moose Jaw are called Moose Javians.

I wanted to get as close to the American border as I could that night and booked into a Super 8 hotel in Estevan with a 24-hour reception. I arrived at 3.30 a.m. to a really grumpy receptionist, who cared more about me messing with her accounts than she did about my bedraggled state. I stared blankly back at her as she ranted about not being told about me, already cashing up and blah blah blah. I had no words or condolences for this woman. I just needed to lie down.

She eventually gave me my key and I took a paper cup full of broccoli and Stilton soup that had been sitting on a warm hob for far too long and wheeled my bike along the corridor, up the lift and finally reached my bedroom. I climbed into the shower to try to warm up, but the water cut out halfway through, so I crawled into bed with the bubbles still in my hair and slept.

Day 92: 15 September 2018 • Estevan to Foxholm • 11 hours 23 minutes • 162.7 km • ODO: 21,643.66 km • Bivvy behind a pub

🎧 *The flags are flying taut (in the wrong direction) outside the hotel this morning, so I'm in for a headwind and I've just heard on the news about that awful hurricane that's down south in Carolina. It's coming up the coast and it's expected to hit the Great Lakes and Halifax in the middle of next week, so I'm expecting a really wet few days.*

The border at Portal was just 38 km away, but it took a soul-destroying three hours to ride as I was continually buffered by the wind. Rerouting was my worst nightmare. I'd calculated distances at home when my mind was fresh. Here, eating in the town of Bowbells, I decided a detour out of the wind would be beneficial. It was 500 km until I reached the next city of Grand Forks. The current route would have me cycling directly into the relentless gale. I plotted a new way on my phone. A dog-leg to get to the same destination, via Carrington – 30 km longer but, I figured, faster and less draining, especially as the wind was forecast to continue from the east for a while.

My head was immersed in the numbers all day. I'd ridden for 12 hours and covered a little over 160 km across fairly flat terrain. All I could do was keep steady and hope the plan paid off. The Sleepy Monsters came on strong that night too. I had two naps between 10 p.m. and midnight. The first was on the doorstep of a corner shop and the second against a tree, sitting in the middle of a flat green, with the most finely trimmed lawn. The grass felt almost warm and this was the first time since the morning that there was no wind howling in my face. The tree was in the middle of a housing estate, so I moved on and rode for another hour before settling for a bivvy at the back of a pub. I woke up with rain pattering on my face. I was lying on my back, my arms spreadeagled with 90-degree bends at the elbows, as if I was about to start a robot dance. I was frozen there for a moment, shoulders locked in place. Around my head was my GPS, with my phone beside rather than plugged into the battery pack and cables. I must have fallen asleep before connecting them. Annoying.

Day 93: 16 September 2018 • Foxholm to Finley, USA • 13 hours 19 minutes • 343.22 km • ODO: 21,986.88 km • Bivvy in a toilet block

🎧 *Stats for 16 September were absolutely banging! I ended up having a great tailwind – so good! Covered a distance of 344 kilometres. I needed that, absolutely buzzing.*

Day 94: 17 September 2018 • Finley to Mahnomen • 13 hours 58 minutes • 243 km • ODO: 22,229.88 km • Hotel casino

I had a small shopping list when I reached the city of Grand Forks. On the outskirts I found a shopping complex and then wheeled my bike through the doors of the Columbian Mall.

I roamed around the department store, passing shops selling clothes, trainers, books, bikes, pet wear, jewellery, vitamins – the choice was endless. So. Much. Stuff! Right at the back of the store I found Scheels Sporting Goods. I could smell flowery shampoo and sharp aftershave as people passed me. The chattering of slightly stressed-out voices was loud and I could see gleaming white trainers and matching, pristine tracksuits.

After so many days by myself on the open road I felt out of place, but not at all envious. There is a freedom that comes from carrying your home with you. Up every incline. Into every headwind. You soon whittle down your wants and settle on your actual needs. The pressures of maintaining a life within mainstream society are gone. The suffocation of consumerism is gone. The endless choices about what to do and where to be are gone. My life had been stripped back and felt so simple, and my needs on this shopping trip were modest, but vital: insoles, socks, puncture repair kit.

The balls on my feet were aching. Each bump on the road created a pressure point where my cleat was screwed into the cracked sole. These shoes were trashed. Still relying on the layers of duct tape I'd inserted in Australia to act as a barrier from the wet road, I hoped some thick new insoles would make all the difference.

I'd worn these socks every day for the past three months. They carried sand from the Gobi and grit from the Nullarbor. They'd been sink-washed and radiator-dried every few nights for three-quarters of the world. Now the ingrained dirt made them cold, stiff and abrasive on my feet.

The puncture repair kit was for my sleeping mat – please let it inflate!

Items ticked off, I wandered across the road for the final thing on my list: fresh food.

The Panda sign advertised an all-you-can-eat Mongolian buffet. The food selection was as overwhelming as the Mall. The hot plates were filled with every type of cuisine. Noodles, buffalo chicken wings, curries, beef, sushi, pizza. I went straight to the veggies – oh man, how I needed some vegetables! Bamboo shoots, grated carrot, mixed pepper slices, mushrooms, broccoli. So much broccoli! Without a doubt, the *best* broccoli ever.

My sugar laden palate benefited from the cleanse after months of eating fast food and as many calories as I could pick up at a garage.

Over the next few days, the wind would become my biggest problem. It was swinging around so much that either riding into it was a crushing battle or I enjoyed a fairground ride with it on my back. There was little in between. When the rain came, it came hard. My accommodation switched between toilet blocks and a recycling shed to a beautiful four-star hotel plus casino, but really by 2 a.m. I was grateful for any dry place I found.

Acceptance is the greatest mindset of all on the road. You don't have to be gloriously happy in a storm, but accepting *it is what it is* makes for an easier passage. Sometimes this was the most natural way of being; other times I battled for every single pedal stroke. During the next few days I flipped between the two, going from utter contentment to out-and-out restlessness.

I had noticed that I was feeling more reclusive than normal recently. Usually I sit somewhere in the middle of the extrovert/introvert scale, drawing energy both from time on my own and from others around me. Now, though, I'd begun resisting conversation, even if it meant that I was coming across as a bit rude. My state of mind was eroding. I wasn't unhappy; I still laughed at podcasts or funny thoughts and had long times of contentment riding, but communicating with others had become very difficult, even draining. My audio diary explains these feelings far better than I can now, five years on.

🎧 *Warning – I'm being a bit of a knob! So, I've become really unsociable, but Americans and Canadians are not! Here's the thing, on an average day, I'm not exaggerating, I get at least 20 to 30 people speaking to me, asking about my bike and what I'm doing. Every. Single. Day.*

So, along with working out the shortest answer I can give this person to get them away from me I also give a bit of an eye roll. I don't do it outwardly, at least I don't think I do, but I do it inwardly and think, 'Aw please, no!'

Honestly, I'm really not like this normally. I am just so exhausted. All I have the energy for when I stop is food, shelter and warmth. I have nothing to give. But today, I caught myself out big time.

I'd stopped at a service station and was packing up the bike when I heard this guy's voice behind me, saying, 'I've got a bike.' I did that internal eye roll, then turned around and this bloke, about my age, started telling me all about his own Trek bike and how he's got a crate on the back of it to do his shopping. After a bit he switched the questions to me: 'Hey, how many miles have you done?' I've stopped telling people because it makes them ask more questions and you're there for another 10 minutes at least. At first, I just said I was riding from Anchorage to Halifax and he was so excited that then I told him I was trying to break the female World Record.

Well! He was like, 'Oh my god, this is amazing.' So, I got him to sign my witness book for me and I wrote him a really nice note, gave him ride details and all that. He was fair chuffed. I turned away, packing up, but when I turned back, he had 20 bucks in his hand. He wanted me to have the next meal on him. I said it was fine, but he insisted and said if I needed more money he could go and get some.

Obviously, I was taken aback, mainly because I had been so stand-offish to everyone I'd seen and then, regardless of that, he'd just shown this lovely act of random kindness. So now I'm like 'Have a word with yourself, Jenny Graham, this should not be doing this to you.' So, I need to think of another way to deal with this, because it's not nice of me.

I found podcasts, music and audio books a great help through some of the tougher days; a place for me to escape to. Dan Holland was a Content Producer alongside Pennie Latin at the BBC Radio Scotland and was part of the team collecting my audio for the *Out of Doors* radio show, so he knew all the ins and outs of the trip. I'd never met him, but he'd been in touch with words of encouragement from the beginning and at some point in Australia he had asked if I needed any podcast recommendations. He soon became my No.1 earworms supplier, sending episodes every week to my WhatsApp, making it super-easy for me to download them. He'd also put 'health warnings' on to them if they were particularly sad, in case it was too much for me and I needed something cheerier.

My top five podcasts:

- *Soul Music* (BBC Radio 4)
- *S-Town* (Serial/This American Life)
- *The Dirtbag Diaries* (Duct Tape Then Beer)
- *Brainwaves* (BBC Radio Scotland)
- *The Ricky Gervais Show* (TheRickyGervaisShow.com)
- *Desert Island Discs* (BBC Radio 4) (okay, that's six, but it's really good!)

My top five audio books:

- *Endurance: Shackleton's Incredible Voyage to the Antarctic* by Alfred Lansing
- *This is Going to Hurt: Secret Diaries of a Junior Doctor* by Adam Kay
- *The Worst Journey in the World* by Apsley Cherry-Garrard
- *Scott's Last Expedition* by Robert Falcon Scott
- *A House in the Sky* by Amanda Lindhout and Sarah Corbett (harrowing!)

Day 97: 20 September 2018 • Northfield to Pepin • 5 hours 19 minutes • 107 km • ODO: 22,858.47 km • Hostel

The day had been spent riding through a spectrum of grey tones. As I crossed between Cannon Falls and Redwing, Minnesota, a dull blanket of thick cloud lay further than I could see and single bolts of lightning had been dropping effortlessly and sporadically from the sky – soundless energy in the distance. A few times, an electrical storm got close enough that I dived into some shelter, but thankfully I was a lot less exposed than I had been on the prairies. Now there were woodlands, undulating roads and small hillsides. The terrain had a lot more depth and the towns were closer together.

Night was falling when I stood on the banks of the Mississippi River by Maiden Rock, watching as the skies roared with another thunderstorm. The enormously plump clouds darkened and gathered, circling the skies like a pack of school bullies. Using my trusty method, I calculated the storm to be seven elephants away. I'd become used to the drama the skies had thrown at me today and now fancied myself as a bit of a meteorologist. I began calculating wind direction x speed of storm x distance to travel. I made a fairly confident conclusion that this lightning storm would be blown away from me, so I settled on to my tribars and committed to a fast spin with the village of Stockholm in my sights. I've played Russian roulette with a small number of storms in my life and was feeling lucky to have avoided being struck. I made it 3 km before scrambling down the wooded bank for some shelter.

A large beech cathedral swayed above me as the sky erupted with energy. The deep, rhythmical bass line of the roaring thunder was layered with booms and bangs, hurled violently, directly above my head. The treetops became an amphitheatre and the sky was alight with the greatest display of blues, pinks and white flashes. It felt reckless, like a train of storms bursting my path wide open, yet it was calming and humbling. I'd been stopped in my tracks by something so much bigger than me and my mission – the power of the earth taking over from everyday life. Nestled into a thick beech trunk, blocking myself from the wind, I felt blessed for the ringside seat as I looked out over the water.

• • •

M-I-SSI-SSI-PPI – the Mississippi River. I must have been seven when I learned how to spell that with a little jingle. Now, 30 years on, I couldn't see the word written out without humming it. I wonder what seven-year-old me would have thought if she knew this would be her encounter with the M-I-SSI-SSI-PPI?!

I lost track of the time I'd been sitting in the woods, but with the rumbles now in the distance I made my way back on to the road. It was eerily calm. Debris was scattered across my path as I weaved my way through branches and leaves. It felt so dark, almost black. Sirens began, an airhorn pulsating through the sky. A warning?

The town I'd been riding towards was empty. It was only 9 p.m. I turned up a street looking for signs of life and saw a candlelit window. It was the Humble Moon Folkstead and Saloon, where two friends were merrily chatting while drinking red wine from tumblers. They welcomed me in. The wooden cabin felt homely in this warm, flickering light. I could make out red diamonds painted across the tiled floor and a bar that was lined with mirrored shelves holding bottles of spirits.

They fed me with soup from a flask and made a very convincing argument for me to stay. 'If the house is on fire, get warm from the heat,' one of the women told me. It was fun being here. I imagined passing a night here with laughs and tales and lots of wine. In another life this would have been my dream scenario, but I was so stripped of the woman I once was. Now forward progress was my only purpose. So, I left and cycled another hour up the road to find a hostel for the night.

The storm was due to come in again overnight, the receptionist in the hostel explained, and the sirens warned of a tornado. He said it was only 10 km away and hundreds of them had been recorded in the area over the last few hours. I'd managed to ride only 107 km today and wondered if it had been worth all the effort.

It wasn't normal for me to be in accommodation by 10 p.m., so I made the most of this early night and bought a small hairbrush and a mini travel conditioner. I showered and left the conditioner in my hair before starting the huge task of untangling the dreadlocks that had formed on the back on my head and behind my ears. The image of a haystack sprung to mind as I wasn't able to make even a dent in the tangles.

Day 99: 22 September 2018 • Mosinee to Island View • 14 hours 1 minutes • 301.98 km • ODO: 23,402.27 km • Bivvy by Lake Michigan

🎧 *So today I'm heading towards the Great Lakes and should make some good headway if I can leave the coffee pot. I'm on my third. It's taking me so long to wake up in the morning, I have noticed. I'm getting quite bad at waking up now. Always need a few more moments, just to gather myself.*

My temperament had relaxed over the last couple of days and I was finding I was able to manage my moods a lot better. I was still deeply tired, but the black cloud that seemed to be lingering over me had lifted – just in time, because the next few days would be sociable. A couple of dot watchers came to cheer me on and I actually enjoyed some garage forecourt chats.

I also had the joy of two familiar faces join me for some miles. I'd met Jim Hertel and Dave Bach the year before when I was guiding a mountain bike trip in the north-west of Scotland for Wilderness Scotland, a company I did some work for. The promise of these trips is a luxuriously adventurous week in the Highlands. Hand-picked mountain biking trails are fuelled by high-quality picnics, the best coffee and excellent evening accommodation. They are a joy to work on, showing people from all over the world the very best of Scotland. They are particularly wonderful when you meet characters like this pair and it didn't take long for these clients to become friends. The quick bond that can develop between complete strangers who share a passion for two wheels and wild places always fascinates me, but it's a connection that could take years to build in an indoor environment.

Jim had been passing through Wisconsin on a business trip and came to find me on his bike. It was such a wonderful coincidence that we were there at the same time and it was fantastic to share those miles. Dave didn't happen to be passing by, so instead made the six-hour round trip to see me from his home in Houghton, Michigan. I was so touched and super-relieved not to still be in my eye-rolling phase – would have been awkward!

The common ground between Dave and myself the last time we met was a love of good food and even better coffee, so he was probably pretty shocked when I turned down his offer of a local roastery café. It was going to be a detour of a few kilometres each way and I was saving every ounce of energy. Instead, I pulled into a Subway and enthusiastically explained how out of all the fast-food chains I was eating from Subway was one of the best: free refills, salad and the crisps that came with your sub as standard. There was a split second when I could see in Dave's eyes that perhaps this wasn't normal, but after three months on the road, it was my new normal. Dave had never even been in a Subway before – I'm not sure he'll ever return.

We shared some great chat on the bike. I hadn't actually talked to anyone about Mongolia and China properly, so it was lovely to cast my mind back and share some of the wonderful moments. We discussed the wildlife – of course! And, ridiculously, I found out there were actually bears and wolves in these parts too. It seemed like a long time since they had consumed my every thought and now they didn't fill me with quite the same fear, probably because there were no grizzlies, 'just' black bears. After a few hours we parted ways and I continued well into the night, before camping on the shores of Lake Michigan.

The Lakes Superior, Huron, Erie, Ontario and Michigan make up the huge body of water known as the Great Lakes – a fitting name because they collectively hold one-fifth of the world's fresh water. They felt so familiar after months of looking over the maps. Once I rode through them I'd re-enter Canada for the final stretch to Halifax. There I really would be on the home straight – well, kind of.

**Day 100: 23 September 2018 • Island View to Roberts Corner •
10 hours 50 minutes • 209 km • ODO: 23,611.27 km • Motel**

🎧 *Oh yuk! So, the last few days I've been like, 'Is that a snake? Is that a
snake?' and I'd be like, 'No, hardly, you don't get snakes out here, you're
just paranoid! That'll be a bungee cord', because often straps would be
laying on the ground from falling off trucks, so I just thought it was that
at the side of the road.*

*Well, today there was no getting away from it, right in front of me. I
am not joking. It must have been about a metre long. I am cringing even
just saying it, like, aw yuk! Dead snake! Right there!*

*Why have they got dead snakes and bears and wolves in the same
place?! That just doesn't make sense. One or the other, surely, guys,
not all of them. And I've been diving about the woods getting out
of thunderstorms and camping down by the lake and just like, you
know, snakes.*

I still can't think much about that incident. I have shivers running
down my spine just beginning to cast my mind back to it. What did
surprise me was how quickly I managed to let go of the fact that my
nemesis was lurking. Anywhere I travel in the world, it's my No. 1
fear. I overthink, worry endlessly and the thought of coming face to
face with one means I have never been able to relax. I was completely
grossed out by seeing this dead snake, but had so little spare energy to
give, I had no choice but to let it go.

A friend, Mark Edmonds, from back home, had messaged with some
golden nuggets of advice after listening to my audio postcards on Radio
Scotland:

Listened to your piece from NZ on suffering in the cold. Made
me laugh. Don't know anyone who does it better. In the Canadian
Arctic back in the day suffering started when you ended up
eating your own boiled-up leather boots. Trust the recent weather
challenges haven't taken you that far. If not, there is more in the
tank... This is the crux of the route now so keep focused and
ride smart.

Mark has a natural ability to be super-supportive as well as a really straight talker. He doesn't cushion his words. He has a logical brain, great humour and is an all-round excellent adventure buddy. I'd shared many a messy night with him riding bikes in silly conditions. Hearing him call this the crux felt such a great relief. I hadn't seen it, but of course he was right.

I'd come so far yet still had a 4825-km chunk to go, which felt like a really long way. Focus was coming and going, time was frittering away and most days felt like a continuous uphill battle. Yes! He was right, this was the hump for me to get over. Once I'd made it to the end of this leg and got back into Europe, it would feel a lot more manageable. Now this part had been labelled, I could use that to gain perspective during tough moments. I kept in touch with Mark for the next week. I assured him I had a stream of people sending caring and loving messages, so not to worry about my feelings, just help get me to the airport ASAP. He sent little quotes like:

> More time could be saved off the bike than on at this point. Repeat the mantra: Slowly, slowly, catchy monkey. Stick to your plan... it was a good one and has got you this far.

He was right, particularly about time I could save off the bike. It was easy to let that bit slip. At home it had been impossible to imagine what on earth I'd do with the nine hours per day I had planned to be off the bike for, but 25,000 km later I knew exactly what I could fill my time with: charge equipment – lights, GPS, phone, camera – keep a diary, record film footage, message home, download listening material, plan flights, do a bit of scrolling (Facebook, Insta, Twitter, Strava), chat to people at petrol stations, deal with the daily logistics of finding food and shelter, log daily stats, maintain bike, maintain self, sleep, eat and battle with procrastination tendencies.

There were many distractions to busy myself with, some were urgent and needed my attention, but others just allowed my mind to engage in something other than my pedals going around. Despite wanting those hours on the bike, more than anything I found it difficult to always prioritise them and nothing falls away quicker than minutes in the day.

🎧 *It is funny how people get in touch at just the right time, eh? I'd have never thought of messaging Mark but, as soon as he wrote that, I just knew: He's thinking what I'm thinking!*

Day 101: 24 September 2018 • Roberts Corner to Iron Bridge, Canada • 14 hours 3 minutes • 234.81 km • ODO: 23,846.07 km • Bivvy in shed

It was 10 a.m. by the time I set off today, after a five-hour sleep and a quick call home to say hi. It had been weeks since I felt energised enough for a phone call, rather than a text. It felt good to hear Mum's voice.

Before I even started riding each morning, I'd calculate my estimated bedtime for that night and 3 a.m. had become normal for me, although the hours after midnight were becoming much tougher to deal with. To reach my 15-hour ride time target today would mean riding until 1 a.m. That didn't include any stops I would have. I felt re-focused now I realised this bit was the crux and was meant to be a struggle, so in the bid for a high mileage day and an early-ish night I made it my mission to minimise my stop time today.

The Canadian/US border was my first target, at 120 km. That was sure to be an energy boost, having a landmark to tick off. I was pedalling with a new determination. The wind was making for some tough miles, but I continued counting them down and trying to stay on track. That focus was broken when a friend of a friend came to meet me, 60 km in. He pulled in ahead of me, got out of his car and started chatting. I felt pretty frustrated at the mandatory stop he was imposing on me. I'd already used up my chat time this morning, but was trying my best to be polite.

It's a gamble when people just turn up. It can either be a welcome distraction or a head-messer. He was called Dave and he was really excited to see me. He brought food and coffee, but stopping for it would completely blow the plan. To keep moving, I reluctantly arranged to meet him in the next town, where I needed to do a supermarket sweep for a whole day's worth of food. He left and I saw him again an hour later when I pulled into Strongs Corner (Minneapolis) General Store. I went straight into the shop and bought what I needed, so I could pack up while chatting to him. I knew I wasn't giving him 100%. The overriding urge to stay focused and keep in control of the day's hours was too much.

'I'm so sorry, I've really got to go,' I said after only a few minutes.

'Well, wait a second, then.' He went into his pocket and pulled out a 100-dollar note. 'Get somewhere to sleep for the night,' he insisted and put it in one of my bike bags.

It turned out Dave had been visiting his dad out here and had made a three-hour round trip to come and meet me. And all I'd given him was a 50% welcome and some clear vibes that I wasn't in the mood for a chat. I would feel bad about this for the rest of the trip... and actually maybe the rest of my life.

• • •

The US/Canada border control at Sault Sainte Marie Port is halfway down a hill, so I arrived at the barriers with pace. A group of people started gathering with their cameras and were cheering. I was so confused.

'Hello, what's going on here then?'

'Oh, a guy came through earlier and told us what you were doing. We've been waiting for you.'

Oh, the guilt!

One of the men asked where I was from and when I told him he said, 'Oh, I've been to Inverness three times, I'm in the Clan Macpherson and I go over there for Clan gatherings.' Ha, what a coincidence, my family clan is also the Macphersons. We did some selfies and I crossed back into Canada for the final time.

🎧 *Windy, windy, windy! Headwind all day, like, jeez, I turned at one point just before I came into Canada and had it on my back. It was so lovely, but it was only for about 5 km and then it was straight back into it! As I came into Canada the rain started bucketing down and that was it for the entire night. Rain bouncing off the ground.*

Despite the rain, the temperature had risen and was now up at 12°C, higher than it had been for a long time. I needed to tap into some extra determination when I passed a lovely-looking motel in the town of Bruce Mines at midnight. The headwinds meant that I'd covered only 182 km, despite having ridden for 12.5 hours. My maps told me that in another 50 km there were another two motels, so I carried on past the welcoming 'bed for the night' sign and rode till 3 a.m., when I reached a little village called Iron Bridge.

Because it was so wet, I hadn't wanted to keep my phone out to book a bed back at Bruce Mines and I couldn't imagine them being busy as the roads had been so quiet. The two motels were on the same street. The first one was in darkness. I rang the bell, wincing and a little embarrassed that I'd be waking someone up, but no one arrived. The second motel had lights on so I confidently arrived at that door, only to find a sign reading: 'Sorry we're full'.

Cycling into the village, I'd passed a large green with a really big beech tree in the corner, so I backtracked and was happy it would give me enough shelter from the weather. The tree was lit up from the street light nearby, so I rested my bike against it, stripped off my top layers and walked into the shaded section of the park for a pee. I was now almost naked. As I pulled my bib shorts down and squatted, a massive security light came on across the whole park. I got such a fright, but was now committed, so had to stay there in the spotlight, bare-bummed and in just my bra.

The light did mean I could see a little further into the park and just before it went out, I saw the edge of a bridge, which might offer a bit more cover than the tree. I got dressed, collected my bike and went to investigate. Under the bridge was room to sleep, but the slats of the walkway were letting in lots of water. There was a little outbuilding that was probably originally used for water gauging, but inside looked like a local party den. The walls were covered in graffiti and the floor was full of empty lager cans and wine bottles. It was tiny. If I slept on the built-in shelf that spanned the width of the room, there was just enough space for the Piggy on the floor. I slept well considering how squashed it was, and I was glad I'd found a roof as it had rained all night.

Day 103: 26 September 2018 • Sudbury to Deep River • 15 hours 10 minutes • 292 km • ODO: 24,337.77 km • Motel

🎧 *I rode straight into a stop barrier on the road today. No rhyme nor reason. It was low-lying but still an extremely visible wooden cross covering half of my lane. I hit it at pace. My bike stayed put as my feet unclipped and I flew through the air and across the pile of wood, landing on a piece of newly tarred road that had been protected by the sign.*

I slid along the road enough to tear my leggings, gloves and toe covers. It is funny to think what I must have looked like but a bit sore mostly with the thud of landing. How on earth hadn't I seen it? I took a bit of time to get sorted afterwards.

I found a motel at 3.30am, so much for trying to finish earlier at night, it just never works out. I'm so tired, I fell asleep fully clothed in my chair, woke up at 8.30 - it's mad how my body is waking itself up after five hours even though it clearly needs more! Anyway, was gutted not to have made it to the bed but had a shower and breakfast, although I'm still hungry. And my shoulder is still a bit sore from falling off the bike… ooft that was so silly!

Day 105: 28 September 2018 • Kemptville to Saint-Jean-sur-Richelieu • 12 hours 17 minutes • 276.89 km • ODO: 24,864.66 km • Motel

🎧 *SO PRETTY! The trees are changing colour and are really vivid reds, yellows and oranges. Plus, the rocks are cool, they're a bit like The Flintstones. Quebec province is quite different to the Canada I've been travelling through up to now. I knew it was a French province but I didn't expect it to actually look French. There's been a brilliant light and loads of churches! I only realised I'd entered the province when the guy in the garage greeted me in French. I have the very basics to get by. So annoyingly I left my second pair of bibs in the motel room the other day! One set to the end… Is that a bit minging? I'll see if I can pick some up but I just really like the zips on the bum.*

Awww, I know I keep saying it but I am so tired! I sat down on a bench at 2 a.m. to sort out shoes I had some stones in them. And fell asleep for an hour, so ended up having to cycle until 4 a.m. (yawn).

Day 106: 29 September 2018 • Saint-Jean-sur-Richelieu to Saint Nicolas • 14 hours 10 minutes • 297 km • ODO: 25,061.66 km • Bivvy in a play park

The scenery was striking, as autumn was setting in as I skirted around Quebec City. In the afternoon I called into a petrol station for a resupply. It was a massive store, but every shelf was filled with crisps and sugar-laden snacks. I needed some healthy food. My mouth was beginning to blister again from the lack of sleep and the amount of sugar my diet was enduring at the moment. Some days I actually worried that I'd end up with Type 2 diabetes after this trip or scurvy from the lack of nutrition and the sheer number of doughnuts.

I was sick of the contents of these shelves, so I left the shop with tea from the vending machine and a pack of cheese puffs, assuming I'd pass somewhere more nourishing soon. My Canadian SIM card had run out of data and I couldn't use my UK bank card to top up my credit. This was a bit of a pain. I had been relying so heavily on my phone to make plans for the evenings, but I'd be all right if I found somewhere with Wi-Fi. I could download a few maps then too. At the time, I was working from a previously downloaded line on my screen to navigate with no detail of terrain or towns I might pass through.

My route quickly left the main carriageways and wound around some country B-roads. This continued for the next 12 hours. The country lanes were nice to ride on, really quiet but not fast rolling. By midnight I had passed no shops or towns.

I raked about in my food pouches, hoping for something remotely edible to eat. If you don't empty your bags regularly enough, they can get a bit wet and fusty. I rummaged through the wrappers and wet nuts, and found the end of a packet of mint polos and a cereal bar that I would nibble on until I lucked out by passing an orchard. Apples and pumpkins. I picked an apple from the tree and crunched my way through it – a satisfying find that kept me going for a few hours.

That night I slept in a play park in Saint Nicolas, underneath a double chute after the young man in the 24-hour garage tried hard, but failed, to get me accommodation. Bless him, he called around four different places. It had been raining quite a lot, but at least I'd found a dry patch and a bit of shelter is always good.

Days 108 and 109: 1–2 October 2018 • Rivière-du-Loup to Fredericton • 21 hours 41 minutes • 406.52 km • ODO: 25,675.59 km • Kept riding

I'd woken up with 843 km to ride until I reached the airport in Halifax. Having this achievable target excited me. I hadn't booked my flight yet, but there were evening ones from Halifax to London to Portugal with minimum flight time on Wednesday and Thursday evening. And with all my transit times included in my overall time, the most efficient flight would make a big difference. Of course, I wanted to believe that the one taking off in 58 hours would be achievable, so here began the classic 'airport smash'.

🎧 *So, I'm conscious that if I do two overnighters – which I don't even know if I'm capable of right now, to be honest – then I've still got 10 to 12 days to do in Europe, so I'd like to arrive there fresh. Well, as fresh as possible. But equally, I'd like to get there as soon as possible. It's a hard one, but by the end of today I'll know what I'm doing.*

It's just about to get hillier and I'm turning into the wind that I have had behind me for the last couple of days, so there's quite a lot of external factors to take into account.

I'll have to give it some to make either of the flights, but if I get a miracle tailwind, then I could make the Wednesday night one – but it's really pushing it!

I wouldn't be able to sleep between now and then. [Laughter.] 58 hours away! It's funny how I'm still thinking that could be an actual option, isn't it? Excellent. Okay, I'd better go. Bye.

My first proper stop of the day was at midnight: the Best Western at Grand Falls. I'd stuck my head in the door to check if I could use the bathroom and maybe grab a coffee? The receptionist Tina welcomed me in and had soon rustled me up some dinner: chicken and sweet potato fries. We sat and ate together. It was calming being with her. As if I'd been riding in the wind all day and had now found a lull, where all was silent – which was actually what was happening today, her vibes adding to the calm. We had a very truthful conversation. She had a son too, so we chatted about families and compared notes on the similarities between Scotland and Nova Scotia. I left feeling very grounded.

I found a Tim Hortons open for a quick 5 a.m. muffin, then continued cycling until 7 a.m. I had only come 260 km and I hadn't slept all night. I'd been napping on the bench of JP's Café in Heartland when the owner Dave came to open up. Instead of being horrified at the state of this smelly, weary traveller, he insisted I come inside for a proper nap. I was adamant I'd just have 10 minutes, then woke up in the closed-off bar out the back of the café an hour later. The café was full now, but when I reappeared, he found me space, and sat me down with a coffee and bacon roll. He charged up my phone and refused to take any money for my breakfast. Just sign my visitors book, he told me. When I was writing him a message, he gave me advice about taking it easy and not blasting it too much at the end, when I could be exhausted.

Usually I'd have rebelled at this kind of advice, but he was so lovely and I actually really appreciated it – even if I wasn't going to pay it any heed. I continued to ride until 9 p.m. that evening, when I arrived at Fredericton in an horrific storm. Other than the hour's nap in the café, I hadn't slept for 36 hours. I had completed 400 km within that time, which was a satisfying number, but I was sure the lack of sleep was going to cost me in the next few days. I'd been moving at an average of 18 km/h, which was a bit slower than normal, and I had a massive stop time included in there too. This hadn't been the best plan I'd ever had, but I was committed now. I'd have a good sleep and then do the same again tomorrow.

Days 110 and 111: 3–4 October 2018• Fredericton to Halifax Airport • 23 hours 59 minutes • 439.4 km • ODO: 26,114.99 km • Kept riding

Over breakfast I booked a flight for the next evening, which would give me 36 hours for the final 439 km of this stage. This time around I paid the \$30 for some extra legroom and then emailed Mark Beaver of Cyclesmiths bike shop in Halifax. Mark already knew about me from a friend who used to live in the area and who had contacted the shop to let them know I was coming.

He was very helpful as I chopped and changed the days and times I was due to meet him. Mark was a long-distance rider himself, having completed classics like Paris–Brest–Paris (1200 km, self-supported) multiple times and audaxes (organised long-distance cycling events, which are non-competitive, but you ride within a predefined time limit), so he seemed to take my changes in his stride. 'I'll follow your tracker and take a box/tape/pedal spanner – let me know if you need anything else.' The logistics done, all (all!) I now needed to do was ride the next 434 km and make that flight.

I knew I wouldn't be able to lie down and sleep between now and then. I couldn't trust myself to wake up again. I imagined if I closed my eyes that could be me for weeks, so slow and steady did it. Throughout the day I felt focused and was steadily ticking off the distance needed. Things would get a little messier as night fell…

🎧 *5 a.m. Tim smash! My kit and I sprawled across a Tim Hortons seating booth. I've just ridden for 12 or 16 hours? And I've got another 10 hours to go – my flight's another 200 km away. I can't trust myself to go to bed; I keep sleeping in, unsurprisingly. I've just filled up with coffee with a shot of espresso in it – yup. In fact, breakfast has been:*

Large coffee plus shot plus three creamers; OJ; bagel and Philadelphia; Hash brown meal with egg and cheese muffin. It's a fake egg really. [Yawn.] And a bag of TimBit (bite-size) doughnuts.

I need to get going now, but putting it off. It's still dark outside. I've got a guy coming to the airport from a bike shop. I can either go to him – it's an extra 35 km that I could maybe take off the route when I get to Spain if I can work it out – or he said he'd just come up and meet me at the airport. Mate, just come and meet me right now. [Laughter.]

It's funny not being able to get a lift off anyone! I wouldn't obviously, but sometimes I dream that I have. I wake up and gasp: Awwwwwwh, have I taken the bus? I haven't taken the bus! I've not even seen a bus, to be honest with you. [Laughter.] But when I wake up really tired, I have to run through the process of where I am and how I get there. It's not too hard to figure it out – it's bike every time!

As the sun came up, my rear tyre blew out, completely ripping itself from the rim. I was trucking along at the time, but held the wobble and refitted the spare I'd been carrying from Red Deer. I could ask Mark to pick me up a spare.

Coming into Nova Scotia felt like I could be riding through the west coast of Scotland with its scattered bedrock and lochans. Along with the landscape, the place names and weather were also very familiar. The drizzle had hardly lifted all day and coming across the Cobequid Pass in a ferocious wind I could have been on many a training ride back home!

I'd be much later than planned arriving into the airport – a feeling I was quite used to – but still on track for my flight. My main concern was missing Mark. He was bringing me a box and missing it would be disastrous. Just like in New Zealand when I felt I was giving it my all, I punctured only 20 km out of the airport. I was already cutting it fine, so out of nowhere began the hilly time trial to the plane. I promised myself that one day I'd arrive somewhere with plenty of time to spare. Yup, one day, just not today.

● ● ●

After 24 hours on the saddle I swung into the airport, with just enough time spare to meet my final bike shop angel, Mark. He was lovely! He'd taken along tools and spares as well as a couple of bottles of beer. I hadn't drunk alcohol in months, never on this trip. Tea and coffee were the go-to comforts, which suited me as I felt so rough each day as it was. I didn't need a beer hangover added into the mix. We did a quick turnaround on the bike packing and then ran out of time, so there was no need for me to decline his lovely gesture.

Mark waved me off as I went through security and I felt a little emotional thinking of Laith, Nathan and now Mark all going out of their way to make sure I had a smooth passage.

My flight was split in two. Halifax to London Gatwick, then Gatwick to Lisbon, with a short layover. The first journey passed, unsurprisingly, with a lot of sleep. I managed to get the seat by the emergency exit that always comes with a little extra legroom and a window, so I could rest against the wall – small points but extremely satisfying. I was on my way back to Europe to ride the final 3220 km into Berlin...

🎧 *When I got off the plane in London, there were so many delays. We were late in leaving Halifax and there was bad weather when we went to land – so bad that the whole plane screamed. It was like we got caught in one of those air bubbles or something, and the whole plane just went up! I thought it was going to flip, honestly. I was like, 'Oh no, this is it?!'*

When we landed it was so foggy, it was as if they didn't see the ground. And we landed with such force everyone screamed again, oh my god! Then we were stuck on the plane. I was already late for my connecting flight. We must have been sitting on the runway for a good 20 minutes and then I'm making my way through Gatwick, where getting your luggage is a trek and a half, especially in cycling shoes.

I picked up Little Pig fine – but my flight was due to leave from the South Terminal and I was in the North Terminal. I wasn't going to make it. I legged it as fast as I could to the desk with my bike. And the young lassie just burst out laughing – I can only imagine the state I must have looked.

I was babbling by this point – 'my connection flight, blah, blah, blah' — and she was so brilliant: 'Don't panic, your flight to Lisbon is late anyway, it doesn't board for another 1 hour, 40 minutes.'

Phheewwwww.

I checked in Little Pig for the next leg of the journey, and went for breakfast. Back into Europe, – yay!

It's roasting by the way, it's 29 degrees. You don't know how happy this is making me, so happy.

PART V
BACK TO EUROPE

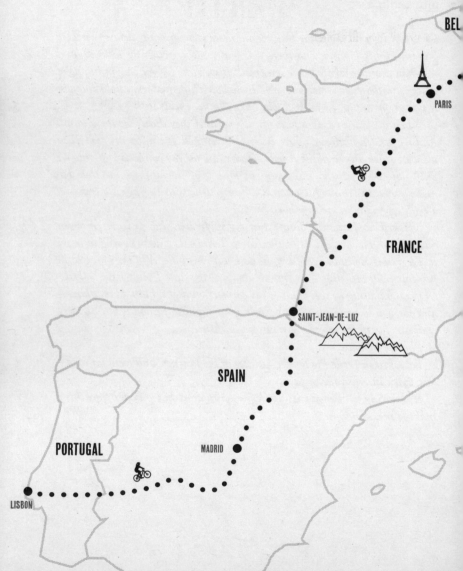

Day 112: 5 October 2018 • **Lisbon, Portugal to Mora, Spain** • **6 hours 44 minutes** • **130.9 km** • **ODO: 26,245.89 km** • **Bivvy on park bench**

It was late afternoon when I arrived in Lisbon, Portugal. My planned route left 'only' 3220 km between me and the finish line, the Brandenburg Gate in Berlin. I admit that back in the planning stages of this trip I hadn't researched this section at all. I had no idea how remote it would be, the type of terrain to expect or the busyness of the roads. There had been so many more pressing jobs to do that I'd allowed myself to be fairly blasé about this part. Perhaps because I'd been working with such big distances up until now, knowing I was down to the last few thousand kilometres gave me the confidence to think, 'If you make it that far, then you'll be able to wing this last bit.' Time would tell.

Being back on familiar soil was a huge boost. The great wilderness crossings of the world were behind me and I'd spend the next 11 days ticking off relatively 'bite-sized' countries as I traversed Europe: Portugal, Spain, France, Belgium, the Netherlands and back into Germany.

The relief of not having to worry about losing my passport was immense. I'd clung to that tattered bumbag of precious documents the whole way around the world, searching under layers, double- and triple-checking that it was still attached around my waist after every single stop. Each night I slept out, it was tucked down my front to keep it right next to me. I didn't care that losing it now would cause issues getting home to Scotland as my only focus was Berlin and making it this far without leaving my passport in some far-flung toilet block felt like a huge achievement in itself.

Leaving Lisbon, I looped around a nature reserve and headed east towards Merida, where I'd cross into Spain the following evening. The sun went down and I was surprised how quickly I was into wilderness. In all the excitement of landing and setting the bike up, I'd forgotten to get any food for the evening. I passed through lots of sleepy little villages, where the only signs of life came from the dogs barking and yelping from behind their fences. I thought a few times how annoying it would be when you were trying to sleep if the dogs were barking all night, and it took me a few days to realise that I was the one causing all the havoc and making the dogs lose their minds! My bear bells jingling from my bike had become a familiar backing track to my ride, but the cobbled streets through Portugal and into Spain heightened their effects and woke up every canine in the vicinity.

I was skirting around the old streets of a town called Mora at 2 a.m. when I was hit by the smell of fresh bread. I had been descending fast as I spotted the lights and three elderly bakers at work. I turned immediately and climbed back up the hill. I had to stop myself from physically drooling as the man in the string vest bagged up a warm pan loaf for me, fresh from the oven.

A few kilometres later, still munching on my fresh bake, I found a bivvy spot on a park bench on the top of a hill. The southern European temperature warmed my bones. I hadn't felt this comfortable sleeping out in such a long time. For much of the trip, it had been a few degrees colder than I'd have chosen. After spending the first few weeks cruising through Asia, building some impressive tan lines, I'd been bundled into my Gore-Tex waterproofs for the rest of it – first for the extreme wet conditions in the southern hemisphere, then as a wind block from the cool air while crossing North America. Now I could finally begin to thaw out.

Day 113: 6 October 2018 • Mora to Merida • 9 hours 36 minutes • 190 km • ODO: 26,345.89 km • Hotel

The autumnal orange and mustard hues went some way towards distracting me from the discomfort I was feeling on the bike. Gorgeous twisted and complex rock formations rose from the side of the road. The weather was good, the tarmac mostly fine and 1400 metres of climbing made for a pretty average day, but I was churning out each kilometre with great effort. The heaviness of my legs weighed me down, as if each one had filled with concrete in my sleep, and I was now left with the burden of carting them around.

It wasn't just my body that was taking time to adjust after the flight and the cumulative kilometres of the trip; my mind had slowed down too. I punctured twice, something I was used to by now – by my reckoning, these were Nos. 26 and 27, but finding a spot to stop, getting all my repair stuff to hand and taking the wheel off took me twice as long as normal. I felt lethargic, unmotivated and I just wanted the faffing to end. I'd decided that I was happy enough riding, but fixing things as well felt unfair and I got a bit moody about it.

By midnight I was on the outskirts of Merida, on the Spanish border, when my gear cable snapped. I had everything I needed to fix this except the energy. I cycled for a bit with limited gears until I found a really fancy, exclusive hotel, where I was quickly assured they had no vacancies. It would have been so expensive to stay I imagined, but I'd have paid anything not to have to stand on the street at midnight and deal with the cable.

Now that I had the idea of finding accommodation in my head, it was difficult to let that go and just find a bivvy spot. The urge to sleep indoors was so great that it would become my sole mission. I backtracked, downhill into the town of Merida, and spent the next 40 minutes finding a room. I convinced myself I needed a bike shop to deal with the cable and that this was the sensible thing to do.

The next morning was a Sunday and nothing in the town was open. Reluctantly I found coffee and sat on the street, fixing my gears. Removing my old broken cable and rethreading a new one took me 10 minutes and gave me a bit of a wake-up call. I'd haemorrhaged so much time. First with the punctures and now the cable. Why hadn't I just fixed it last night? That frustration motivated me through that day and the ones to follow. As I had been taught many times on this trip, the riding was the easy part. Dealing with unknowns along the way was where the skill lay; having the resilience to accept what has come your way and get on with finding a solution. The time on the clock felt like grains of sand slipping from my hands. Some moments I carried them so carefully and meticulously; other times I just threw them in the air.

I passed over another time zone today too, losing another hour as I looked down at my GPS. FFS! I had to catch myself, remembering the moments just months before when I had felt like a time traveller crossing these zones.

Day 115 : 8 October 2018 • Luciana to Arganda del Rey • 12 hours 34 minutes • 232 km • ODO: 26,878.89 km • Bivvy in an olive orchard

🎧 *Morneeeen! Word on the street is that Lee Craigie is in town. She's just texted, so I think there's less than 100 miles between us now, so we'll get together today or tomorrow, which is nice.*

I've got an absolute thumper of a hill coming up. It looks like a 40-degree angle from here, sure it's not. It'll be nice, though, will warm me up! My Achilles are a bit twingey today. I'm walking now, then I'll ride for a bit and get some stretching done. Okay, then, adios.

The decision didn't come easy about whether to meet Lee en route or not. She reached out to me as I neared the end of the Canada leg of my trip to suggest joining me in Europe to collect some media content for sponsors and share some kilometres along the way.

I tussled with this for days. I mean, I tussled with most decisions for days at this point and making them was becoming increasingly harder. I worried that having a familiar face along for an extended period would tear apart the integrity of my solo, self-supported ride. On the other hand, I had done all the big crossings alone: Russia, Australia and Canada. I'd battled through winter with no support in the southern hemisphere, so maybe sharing a few kilometres at the end would be okay?

Lee had been a great support on the lead-up to the trip. She was generous with her time and contacts, and listened to my endless amount of chat about kit choices and visa issues. I wanted her to feel that she had a place on the ride, that her time had been appreciated. There was also the draw of her character. She has a unique perception on the world which I find thought-provoking. She's never one to shy away from a deep and meaningful conversation, and I had plenty of thoughts to explore. She's also humorous and light-hearted, and comes with an energy I find easy to be around. There were very few people on the planet that I could have shared those days with, but I was confident Lee was one of them. After a few days of thought I agreed. She could join me for sections of a few hours a day on the pretence of collecting content. We agreed on the rules and she wrote them up:

- Lee cannot ride in front of Jenny at any point (Lee can draft Jenny all she likes).
- Lee cannot buy or offer Jenny any food or equipment (Jenny is welcome to behave as generously towards Lee as she likes).
- Lee must not assist with any navigation or mechanical issues (Lee didn't even bring a GPS and is encouraged to ride on to the next coffee stop rather than watching).
- Jenny must not be woken in the mornings.
- Lee must not ask the following questions: Where are we? How are you? What's the plan?
- Lee must never interpret or speak for Jenny.
- Lee must not be too entertaining (neither Jenny nor Lee think this is likely to be too much of a problem).
- Lee cannot offer Jenny a hug or any other emotional support, unless Jenny is in full control of her emotions and the hug is more beneficial to Lee (probably the most likely scenario anyway).

So, in a lay-by on the outskirts of Madrid I watched a familiar silhouette ride towards me. In that moment, I couldn't have been happier to see her. We embraced (instantly breaking the rules) and laughed at the absurdity of it all. We rode together for a while and, still nervous about the decision, talked more strategically about how we would manage the next week of riding.

My route was the most direct, often using busy roads, and bypassing towns and cities when possible. Lee would spend some time with me in the day or night, then take herself off on a bit of a more scenic route – sightseeing, if you will – and intercept me throughout the week. The same went for sleeping. I didn't want to have to discuss sleeping arrangements or venues; she could do her own thing. If it meant we slept in the same field, fine, but it was important that I was given space at those times.

There were pros and cons to this plan: Lee's company was really comforting, familiar and easy. We enjoyed long chats and connected on a much deeper level than ever before. We were unfiltered, having both had life-changing summers. She also collected riding shots that would be a brilliant addition to my selfie world tour. But the downside was I now had someone to compare myself to. Lee was sprightly; she looked strong and healthy. Even her hair was all nicely plaited and brushed. When she went off on her 'sightseeing tour', it could be draining knowing that she could go – or had been going – much faster that day. Sometimes I felt bad that I was holding her up, which was ridiculous as it was my ride.

There was also a readjustment I needed to make every time she left or came back. To keep me planning my day as a solo rider, we agreed that I wouldn't know when she would appear, but with that came suspense and tension – knowing she was out there and nearby, but unsure when she would arrive. These were trivial emotions on a normal day, but a good helping of exhaustion meant they would take some managing.

That evening the rules were put to the test as I chose a local fish restaurant for dinner, instead of my usual burger stall. I had no idea it was a fish restaurant at the time, but Lee being proficient in Spanish did, and had to sit back and watch awkwardly as I ordered a full fish platter for my dinner. A dish large enough to feed a family for a week arrived – of raw fish.

From now on, I will mention Lee if she was with me. Otherwise, assume I am alone.

Day 116: 9 October 2018 • Arganda del Rey to Gómara • 12 hours 52 minutes • 244 km • ODO: 27,122.89 km • Bivvy in wash room

My £100 Motorola phone had lasted me well. Throughout the world it had collected all the video footage for the film, audio diaries and photos for the Guinness World Record team; navigated me through cities; kept me in contact with home; and allowed me to run two SIM cards at the same time. A star buy, for sure. It was incredibly robust, surviving utter drenchings day after day with just a plastic sandwich bag to protect it, as well as being flung to the ground on countless occasions. Finally, as I made my way towards the north of Spain, I put my phone into semi-retirement.

I'd been riding with a Quad Lock® system on my bars to hold my phone. Until now, it had worked brilliantly, but I'd removed the back of the phone so often to dry it out and change SIM cards that it wasn't as secure as it had been. I often held it together with a hair bobble, which I had to remove when using the phone because the pressure affected the (by now) smashed touchscreen.

I was going downhill at speed when I heard the clatter of my phone bouncing across the road. The important bits had gone flying off, leaving the rear still attached securely to my handlebars. It took me about an hour walking up and down that hill, trying to work out the exact spot it had come off. Either side of the road was deep vegetation and I had almost given up when I spotted it lying by the bottom of a bush with the battery beside it.

I couldn't believe how lucky I was. The screen had seen better days, but it switched on at least. I could still send and receive messages, though I did have a limited view of what the other person had said. The two main functions that were no longer in use were the selfie button to switch your camera around – heartbreaking – and the audio recorder. The position of the app on the screen meant it would take forever to open up, an annoyance I had little patience for at this point of the trip, so now my audio recounts and diary stopped. As a result, I've pieced together the rest of my story from memories, messages I sent, media collected by Lee, Tom and others, and by following my GPS route.

Day 117: 10 October 2018 • Gómara to Saint-Jean-de-Luz, France • 12 hours 16 minutes • 234.7 km • ODO: 27,357.59 km • Bivvy on the beach

Just south of the city of Pamplona, filmmaker Tom arrived in a hire car. He had found a cheap flight from Scotland, booked it on a whim and come to collect some film footage. Tom's such a cheery, enthusiastic guy and it's always nice to be around him. I felt a real high being in his company again.

He leapfrogged me in the car throughout the day, getting some riding shots from the side of the road. I kept on riding with little vocal contact, but knowing he was there and seeing him smile or wave was enough. As I cycled into the Pyrenees with the most stunning sunset behind me and an orange sky, Tom called it a night and left me to enjoy the most glorious climb up and over the pass to Irun with only the stars for company. The descent was incredible down to the coast before crossing the French border and spending the night on the beach in the town of Saint-Jean-de-Luz. I fell asleep with the sound of the waves, thinking this had to be one of the best bivvy spots I'd had the whole way around. (It's easy to feel like that when you've found a peaceful place to lie down.)

The next morning, Tom found me after breakfast and stayed with me until the afternoon. Then he flew back to the UK. It was strange knowing I'd see him again in less than a week to film the end.

Lee joined me that evening and we soon found our rhythm, playing French shopkeepers as we cycled the quiet roads. Languages have never been my strong point. I have very little retention for words, but after four years sitting through French lessons in high school I had a tiny bit still rattling around my brain. So, with a lot of patience from Lee, the shopkeeper, I'd pretend to be a customer greeting her and then ordering food.

Great hilarity came at the welcomes – with long, drawn-out 'Bonjour Madam-mou-selles' being exaggerated for effect before I ordered the 20th pain au chocolat of the night. The next day I went into a real shop and confidently ordered two oranges, an apple, a pain au chocolat and a coffee, hoping the guy wouldn't try to engage me in conversation. I was all out of French!

Day 119: 12 October 2018 • Libourne to Chauvigny • 12 hours 53 minutes • 235 km • ODO: 27,859.59 km • Ibis hotel

It was a Sunday morning when I hit the suburbs of western Paris. I was riding with Lee, having set out from a barley field that we'd slept in the previous night. I was having a slow start to the day, tired after hefty kilometres the day before, but a chance meeting with a bunch of road bikers on the outskirts of Versailles revived my energy. Two of the group, Sina Witty and Victor Decouard, had ridden as a pair in the Transcontinental Race the previous year so they recognised the bikepacking set-up and wanted to know what I was up to.

They were delighted when they found out about the record attempt and guided us along the most wonderful riverside road until we reached Saint-Denis, a northern suburb of Paris. Being among a group of friends (even if they weren't actually my group of friends), hearing them laughing and chatting away, was so lovely.

Not long after they left, Lee and I rode into a hipster part of Paris I didn't even know existed. There was street food, music and an international vibe – the Camden Market of Paris. I wandered around the stalls picking a large corn on the cob that had been cooked on the grill and a burrito wrap. After lunch, Lee went away on her own and I continued on my route towards Belgium. The previous day's tailwind had helped me cover a considerable distance – over 350 km – but now it had dropped off I was feeling the complete opposite: heavy legs and sluggish roads. I wondered if I'd pushed too hard yesterday.

It had taken four days to cross France. I'd spent the nights sleeping in a barley field, a riverside park and tonight it would be the second of two Ibis hotels.

Day 122: 15 October 2022 • Saint-Quentin to Heppen, Belgium • 11 hours 23 minutes • 227.85 km • ODO: 28,616.32 km • Bivvy in a veg patch

I sat at breakfast in the hotel where I had spent the previous night, sending my boy a birthday message. I couldn't believe I was missing his birthday. I had planned to be celebrating with him, not imagining I'd be this far behind in my schedule. It was Day 122 and I had just under 1000 km still to go. Lachlan was in Scotland, but was leaving later that day to make his way to Berlin. I couldn't remember a single birthday being apart from him, but he was 20 years old so I was probably taking it worse than he was.

I sat with my back towards the door in the large, mostly empty breakfast room, and over a plate of pancakes and strawberry jam I silently sobbed, feeling completely overwhelmed, frustrated with myself for all the moments when I had lost my focus and frittered away time. I should have been finished by now. I had no control over the tears streaming down my face. I was desperate to leave the room, but felt paralysed with emotion.

Eventually I got myself together and as a couple by the door were getting up to leave, I tagged on to their momentum and walked out behind them, back up to my room, where Little Pig sat, ready and waiting for some more kilometres. I messaged Lee: 'I'm having a wee wobble. Need to be alone today. All good just need to work through this.'

Being on my own probably wasn't what I truly needed, but I was trying to resist that emotional support of a pal on the road. When it's not an option, you don't have to consider it, but having to choose *not* to embrace it is like riding past an ice cream shop every 30 minutes and choosing not to go inside. If you weren't riding past one, the idea wouldn't even be in your mind, but knowing it's there and not going in takes extra trying.

Hiding most of my puffy face behind my sunglasses I left the hotel and rode along the main street to the traffic lights – and straight into Lee, who was trying to leave town before she saw me. We both laughed, said an awkward hi and she rolled off in the other direction. It was weird; there was nothing normal about this way of being around each other.

The cycle of self-criticism I'd found myself in this morning was exhausting. I continued crying behind my sunnies, disappointed with my perceived failure on the ride and with my shortcomings as a mum – despite the fact that I was on target to beat the record by three weeks and Lachlan was delighted to be on his way to Berlin. It was just somehow a difficult moment to get any sort of perspective.

On top of these woes I was carrying an underlying anxiety that I was losing control of the project. I'd been on my own with it for so long and now there was a buzz around the finish. Family and friends were making plans, the media were being alerted. People were talking about me, the ride, the ending. It was as if life (although not physically) was suddenly accelerating, spiralling out of my hands. I wanted to clutch it tight, pulling it back in close.

Over the next two days I'd find myself getting involved with conversations, distractions that I really didn't need, micro-managing in the fear that the only life I knew now was about to stop.

By mid-afternoon I rounded a corner to find Lee sitting by a bench. I stopped and we spoke for a bit, aware she couldn't ask me anything without me offering it. I began explaining how I had felt and broke down again, sobbing on the kerb as she watched on helplessly.

I think this was a hard moment for Lee. She couldn't do or say all the things a friend would normally do or say. I didn't want to be talked down or comforted. It was just part of this roller-coaster I was on, where the highs were getting higher and the lows were bringing me crashing down. Keeping momentum was the only thing I had control of right now. Keeping my legs turning. We cycled silently for a time together until I regained some hold of myself.

That evening as I came into Belgium, endurance rider Florian Ponzio came out to share some time on the bike with me. I'd ridden with him the previous year on the Highland Trail 550 race. A few more kilometres down the road, Emma Russell, a good friend of my friend Mary, was standing on the side of the road with a big sign saying 'JENNY'. I suggested we all go for pizza. It was my way of saying thanks, I guess, for everyone's efforts and I was hungry. It was such a nice idea, but I regretted it almost instantly. The others were drinking beer and looked quite relaxed, understandably, but the 'relaxing with friends' vibe filled me with dread and I told myself I mustn't lose focus now.

We stayed just long enough to have a good chat, but not linger. I went to pay my share of the bill, only to find the restaurant didn't accept cards and I'd run out of euros. There was a cash machine around the corner. I went, but it was out of order. I looked down at my phone and the battery was dead too. I made my way back to the restaurant. I'd managed to get myself out of these situations the whole way around the world, but there was a new pressure now with people watching. The others paid as I stuttered my way through a conversation with the waiter, seeing if there were any other bank machines and if I could charge my phone to find my way back to them. The restaurant was closing and he didn't seem to have much time for my dilemma – I assume because I was with others, so he didn't see the issue. It was less than 10 euros.

As everyone else walked away, I looked down to see a 20-euro note on the ground. Without saying a word, I reached down, picked it up, paid for my dinner and put the change in my pocket. Lee and I spoke no more of it for the rest of the trip, although I played it over and over in my head. All that effort of battling through weather, darkness, borders and language barriers, and I just picked up money that I know was dropped for me. All the way around the world and I felt like I'd blown it in a pizza shop in Belgium.

Days 124 and 125 (the final day!): 17–18 October 2018 • Batenhorst, Germany to Berlin • 23 hours 56 minutes • 474 km • ODO: 29,352.2 km • Kept riding

I woke early in the B&B that I'd managed to talk my way into at 2 a.m. that morning. The man had been leaning out the window, clearly not wanting to get up and saying there was no card machine, only cash. Cue a lot of pleading from me. I assured him I'd pay in the morning and gave him my passport. It was now 6.45 a.m. and the bank machine was 3 km away. I passed the reception desk on the way out of the door and spotted a card machine. I debated whether to go or just wait for him, because he clearly did take cards, but I wanted there to be no hold-ups today. Breakfast wasn't until 7 a.m., so I had time. When I arrived back with the cash, he took it sheepishly. I couldn't blame him, to be honest: 2 a.m. is 2 a.m.!

Now I had 474 km until the finish line in Berlin. Touching distance. The excitement, nerves and reality were replaying on a loop, hitting me throughout the day. Sometimes I'd be marvelling at the fact that I was about to actually do it! In fact, I had basically done it! Then the reality would kick in that actually I'd still need to ride my bike for 30+ hours to get there. I love that about endurance racing – the fact that you can be so close yet still nearly 500 km away. Quite bizarre, really.

Tom, Mike and Mike's girlfriend Sherrill were all in Germany. They met me mid-morning, full of enthusiasm. I just had to keep riding while they hid in fields and bushes, pointing their cameras, flying the drone and sometimes driving along beside me, Mike leaning out of the window with the video camera. There would often be 40 to 50 minutes between seeing them as they would pack up, race to the next location, set up the cameras until I rode past – and then repeat.

At one point in the early afternoon, as I made my way through west Germany, my route took me on the autobahn. The police saw me before I could find a way off it and blue lighted me to the nearest exit. Unbeknownst to me, Lee was tucked into the back of a lay-by at the bottom of this exit slip, recording a video for Cycling UK. Friends and peers were collaborating to celebrate the ride and my efforts, and would go live as I crossed the finish line. Lee was mid-sentence as the police car and I rolled into her frame, their lights still flashing. We burst out laughing seeing one another and she started filming before being stopped by an understandably annoyed and confused German policeman. It would take a little time to talk my way out of this situation, but I think the difference in languages probably helped me avoid a fine and take a telling-off.

Apart from that blip the riding was fairly straightforward, with long sections of flat terrain. Some of the small towns and villages I passed through were charming, but today I had other motivations to keep me going.

My CatEye computer, which had been totting up the total distance as I went along, had passed the 29,000 km mark as the sun was setting. It was the magic number – the same distance as the circumference of the world. In actual fact it was more than that as both computers were running under due to battery failures throughout the trip. There would also be some distance to cut from the overall total, once I took into account detours and times I'd backtracked. My planned route to the end was still 300 km. I was sure I could have cut it a bit shorter – in reality I could have cut it in half – but I did not have the ability or belief in my maths to work that out there and then. It's easy to say with hindsight, now I've been verified and all the counting has been done, but I just couldn't bear the thought of coming all this way and my distance being too short. I stuck to the plan and rode the mileage that meant there could be no doubt.

The media crew left for some sleep and I met up with Lee for what would become one of the funniest and most bizarre nights we would spend on the bike together.

'I'm not sleeping tonight,' I said as we rode away from the crew.

'I know,' she replied with a grin.

We were no strangers to riding all night and both knew just how messy things were likely to get. The end of Canada and those last few nights trying to reach the airport had been incredibly tough on me mentally and I wondered whether I actually had another one in me.

My sister Nic had made the logical suggestion for me to get a good sleep tonight, wash and really enjoy the finish line the next day, but the thought of coming all this way to be as fresh as I could at the finish line horrified me. I'd be so disappointed in myself if I arrived anything other than completely delirious! I wanted to be 110% sure that I had left nothing out there on the ride. That gut reaction was enough to assure me that I probably still did have one more overnighter to give.

Alan Goldsmith – a founding father of the UK bikepacking scene and creator of the Highland Trail 550 and Lakeland 200 (both thrilling yet gruelling routes) – had been making his way over from the UK by bike to join me for the final day. I felt touched. The Highland Trail 550 was the spark that had initiated my infatuation with endurance riding, undoubtedly leading me to this very point. Regardless of how gushy I felt towards him when he messaged to say he was camping just outside Wolfsburg and to let me know when I was passing through, I knew I wouldn't make that call. There was an assumption that I had a clue where I was, but in reality I never really needed to know. I worked in distances, days, towards food or shelter – but town names were usually pretty much off my radar.

But I was sure he would be able to find me. I was carrying the GPS spot tracker. True, it's great for the big picture view, but not always accurate when dealing with finer distances (there's sometimes a lag in the signal uploading to the webpage), but he was a master at this stuff, so I expected to see him at some point before Berlin.

At 2 a.m. on 18 October, the yellow gleaming light of the golden arches shone in the sky. I couldn't hide my excitement. McDonald's! A reason to stop turning the pedals just for a moment. To be inside. Drink coffee. And awh, just stop. Even Lee, who often protests about fast-food stops, looked quite pleased. Coffee and fries and an apple pie. I had become fond of the apple pies, although when I ate too many (which was often), they gave me ulcers on my tongue.

I plugged my phone into the mains and lay down on the padded seats. 'Just 10 minutes,' I said, setting my alarm and resting a jacket over my eyes to block out the harsh lighting. My alarm came and went with repeated hits on the snooze button that I barely remembered making. I had no idea how much time had passed, but I could hear familiar voices close by me. I pulled myself up and slowly opened my heavy, puffed-up lids, wincing at the intensity of the strip lighting across the ceiling. I saw two lenses pointed towards me and some great big smiles coming from behind them. Tom, Mike and Sherill, who had been resting in the back of the car, had now arrived at McDonald's. Lee looked like she'd been asleep too, but was now sitting up. She shuffled over and for the first time since meeting her in that lay-by in Spain she gave me a hug. 'Get off me,' I said, leaning into her. We laughed and she shuffled back. 'That was longer than 10 minutes!' I said to her. It had been about an hour. I rested my head on the table a little longer and contemplated how this was going to work.

It was now 3.30 a.m. in the outskirts of Fallersleben. I had 200 km to the finish line. The immediate tasks of getting up, collecting the possessions that were scattered around the table and then leaving the comfort of this inside space was the unimaginable bit right now. There was chat happening around me from the others. I was shivering a bit. It wasn't that cold, just my body's way of telling me I should sleep some more. Staring down at the floor, I saw the tape on my waterproof trousers, which J.M. had so carefully mended, back in Watson Lake. He had done a good job: all those kilometres and not one corner of tape was flicked up or coming loose. I made some slow and methodical movements to get my layers of clothing back on and tied up my shoes, which I'd loosened off. I was now wearing everything I owned; everything I had carried the whole way around the world. I stood up and made my way, crouched over and waddling, to the door. There was nothing heroic about this scene.

Outside, I used the kerb to mount Little Pig. I had next to no mobility or strength, so getting my leg over the frame was becoming increasingly more difficult.

My left cleat had worn again and it was a struggle for me to unclip my foot without turning my heel inwards towards the wheel, instead of out in the traditional fashion. It's more difficult to make an inward movement when you're off balance and your foot is in the wrong position for a quick tap of the ground to stabilise yourself. When I was clipped in – I was in! Clonk, clonk – I turned the pedals and heard that failure sound as I tried to change into an easier gear and I began wobbling around the road. I changed it quickly, hoping I could stay balanced long enough for the chain to move and pedals to turn. I just made it. Perhaps the cameras filming me gave me the extra power to stay upright, but it was close.

The winding country lanes were as empty as you'd expect for the middle of the night, and there was a low-lying fog on the ground and a constant stream of drizzle. I had no idea of my bearings as I followed the line on my Garmin. Lee cycled behind me in silence. I drifted in and out of alertness. I'd pedal hard, then freewheel. Then hard again. That's usually a sign that I'm deeply uncomfortable and fatigued – not exactly breaking news – and I did find it difficult to regain control.

I'd focus on having a steady rhythm for a few minutes, then stop for a handlebar nap. Lee would pull up beside me and just copy my actions. When I woke after a few moments, she would wake too and we'd go again. I couldn't work out if she was actually tired or just doing it so I wouldn't feel bad (she assured me it was real sleep!).

We'd become so stoppy-starty that it was hard to tell if any progress was being made at all. 'I think I need to stop stop,' I said. We wandered over to the side of the road and Lee rested against the tree, while I leaned up against a roadside post, both bikes scattered on the grass beside us, their rear lights still flashing.

I woke first, with the screeching of brakes and the sound of people running. A car door slammed and German words were being shouted. Shit! I wondered what had happened as I came to, semi-conscious. I looked over at Lee, whose body was now crumpled up against the tree, her limbs sprawled out and her neck flopped over to the side. I saw our bikes, abandoned around us, and the red glow of our rear lights still flashing through the thick fog. And, of course, there was me, leaning up against a roadside post in a very similar position to Lee.

I jumped up when I realised the scene we had set, shouting: 'It's okay, we're okay!' at the panicked drivers running towards us. Waving my hands and arms as if to assure them I had full bodily function. 'We're fine! It's okay!' Lee had woken now as well, and from against the tree gave the German drivers a big double thumbs up. 'We're okay! We're okay!'

It was difficult to make them out in the dark (which was only just beginning to lighten), with the fog and the shock and it all moving so fast, but I remember two vehicles and people in suits. I'm so very sorry for the stress we caused when they came across what looked like such a horrific scene, but for the next 12 hours the image of Lee's double thumbs up kept returning and we laughed, uncontrollably, at the state of ourselves, doing impressions of one another's reactions, tears rolling down our faces.

Our moods had changed, from plain exhaustion to all-encompassing giddiness. We got ourselves back on the bikes and 30 minutes later were joined by the lovely Alan Goldsmith. We had pedalled right past his bivvy spot without realising. We recounted our tales of the McDonald's stop and the fake crash many times throughout the morning, getting more and more animated.

The sun was rising for the very last time on this ride just as we found some coffee. The film crew were back with us and continued leapfrogging the three of us for the rest of the day. To impress Alan, Lee and I tried to wow him with a newly acquired singing skill that had been developed throughout the trip, thanks to our friend Penny Phillips. With two-way phone conversations often being too much for me, I relied on WhatsApp voice notes to keep in touch during the ride and loved receiving long messages from home.

The song game was a simple concept, yet highly amusing. You pick a song, preferably nothing too niche, then replace all the words of the song with variations of your friend's name. For example, Penny could be Penelope, Pen, Penpens, etc. The key changes and the way you extended or shortened the name gave the clues to the song.

Once Lee had arrived, she joined in and together, over a couple of long Spanish nights, we perfected the whole of Queen's 'Bohemian Rhapsody', replacing each and every word. It was quite the masterpiece. For example (activate imagination), the opening lines became: 'Pen Pen Pen Peeenny Penn? Pen Pen Pen Pen-Pennnnn?' Much harder to write than it was to sing!

For Alan, we replaced all the words with Alan and Al. Then he rode behind us patiently throughout the morning, guessing the name of the song. Quite a feat, as there was very little in the way of tuneful singing coming from us. He threw himself into it and was extremely good at guessing. This was fast becoming my favourite pastime ever.

By midday I was getting messages to tell me that my family and friends were hovering in cafés and pubs at the Brandenburg Gate, excitedly waiting for me to arrive. I was only 100 km away. From an initial target of whopping 29,000 km, I would very soon be down to just double digits.

My mood was high. Life appeared to have a filter layered over the top of it, saturating the normally subtle tones of the day. Everything was heightened and brought alive. The giddiness continued and every slip of the tongue, sigh or sneeze would leave us in fits of hysterics. With around 50 km left, we were joined by a photographer called Stephan Haehnel. Russell Stout from Shand Cycles, one of my sponsors, had hired him to capture the moment. He cycled around us, taking high-speed snaps. He was a nice, friendly guy with a cool hipster look about him, but of course he wasn't on the same wavelength as us: we were teetering on delirious by this point.

The time passed so quickly. I'd been trying to pull myself together, aware that I should probably be slightly more professional and attempt a normal conversation. Lee had dropped back; I assumed to do the same thing. I started telling Stephan about how she had raced for Scotland in the Commonwealth Games and had been British Cross Country Mountain Bike champion. He seemed impressed.

Just then we came to a sign for Berlin – 3 km away! I stopped for a picture. Stephan and Alan stood in front of me with their cameras. Lee pulled up behind them, unclipped with one foot as she lifted her phone to start filming too. In that moment she lost her balance ever so slightly. Time slowed down for me as I watched her unable to unclip from her shoe and she came tumbling to the ground with the greatest of thuds, still attached to her bike. My shock and concern at watching the scene quickly passed and I was soon doubled over my bike, the tears streaming down my face, laughing as Lee was lifted from the ground by the others, who had missed the visuals and were able to show more compassion.

The giggles had now taken over and I was unsure if I would ever be able to stop. My shoulders shook hard as we roared with laughter. I felt I needed to lie down just to give my body a break from the jerking. Lee was fine, although it had been a hard landing. I tried to stop laughing when I realised she was hurting, but the image of her slowly toppling over replayed in my mind every time I looked at her, so I struggled. We had one last McDonald's stop, where I washed my face and composed myself. As long as I made no further eye contact with Lee, all would be fine.

Nic later told me that by this point things had become very tense at the finish line. They knew I was approaching, but didn't know exactly when I would appear, although somebody had agreed to jump up and down under the Brandenburg Gate when I came into view. In the meantime, they milled around, drank coffee, went for lunch, made phone calls and tried their best to stay warm. Tom had been interviewing people, but many of them seemed to have lost their ability to be articulate and tears were close to the surface, particularly for Mum and Nic.

For months now Nic had been on high alert, following my progress. Her phone, iPad and laptop screens would update every few minutes with my dot and she would frequently zoom in to see exactly where I was. She was so pleased if she could see I was in a café and would hope her messages would get a reply if there was Wi-Fi. When she heard the ping of an incoming audio recording, she'd pounce on her phone to soak up the information. She'd then summarise it in a spreadsheet she was sharing with family and friends. If anyone was around, she'd make them listen to the messages with her so they could unpick how I sounded in them.

The tension was beginning to build on the road too. The laughter had stopped and soon I was on the Strasse des 17 Juni, the very street where, only 125 days ago, I had ridden to the start line questioning if I could even come close to completing this. Now here I was, having done the whole bloody thing. It was busier now than it had been on that lonely morning. I could feel the surge in energy as the Brandenburg Gate came into view.

On the other side of the Gate stood the people I'd thought most about along the way: Lachlan, Mum, Nic and Donald. There'd also be friends I knew were coming and some who would surprise me. I wanted to be there with them, of course, and yet this was the end. The great unknown. I had just circumnavigated the world by bicycle and after I passed through the Gate I'd stop. Just stop. That was it.

A familiar Scottish voice came riding around the roundabout. 'Miles? Oh my god, Miles?' I thought it was a coincidence at first, but then the Scotland flag and his huge smile assured me he'd come out to cheer me in. 'Come on, Jenny,' he bellowed as I continued around, now with a group of riders by my side as some locals had also come to join me.

I could see Tom with his camera and his big grin. 'Straight through, Tom?' I shouted. 'Straight through, Jen!' as he ran behind me filming the moment. I rode through the arches of the Brandenburg Gate. And there they all were, standing by the same post where I had fixed my computer on the morning I left.

Scotland flags were waving, and the roaring of cheers and claps and whoops came from all around. I continued towards them looking for a face, for a place to stop. There were so many people and then I saw Nic, my sister, who had been there with me through every pedal stroke, making sure that not one day passed without me knowing she was thinking of me. We hugged tightly.

And Lachlan, oh my boy. So handsome, he was gleaming. 'Hi, Mum.' 'Aw, I've missed you,' I said, pulling him in close and squeezing. I couldn't believe I had him in my arms again after all that time. 'You've got a new shirt,' I said, surprised, as if it was big news. He laughed. 'Yeah, yeah, I do.' I turned to find Mum. I couldn't see her at first, then she appeared with Donald by her side. She'd been standing back, embarrassed with all the cameras and the crowd around her. I pulled her towards me. 'My girl, you're home,' she said, with such relief in her voice. Donald was next, with a hearty hug. He'd been Mum's wingman throughout and I felt so grateful for him and his steadfast support. The hugging continued on rotation.

Our chat was funny at first. No one really knew what to say. I apologised for being late and Donald told me that my car had failed its MOT. It was bizarre. Almost unreal. I knew it was them, I could see and touch and hear them, but it wouldn't sink in that they were actually here with me.

My best of friends – Mary, Fiona and Cathy – were here with huge smiles and welcome home banners: 'One Woman – One Bike – One World!' and 'Go Jenny Go'. They hadn't stopped cheering me the whole way round the world and now they were back at my side. I stood still, straddling my bike, hugging and chatting, amid the familiar faces of old friends and the absolute strangers who had made an extraordinary effort to be here and celebrate with me. There were some officials from the Scottish government, including Dr Alexandra Stein, who had been my witness at the beginning of the trip. She had now returned with more colleagues and I suspect they had something to do with the sea of St Andrew's Cross flags. It was just incredible.

Champagne was soon popped – and would continue to flow into the night. The scene was a blur, and not just for me, for everyone waiting too. The anticipation had built up to this very point which I'd made many attempts to imagine, but couldn't quite… and now we were all here at the finish line and it was really happening.

My mum had put together a post-Round the World care package. It contained everything I'd need and more to help me out of the cycling kit I'd lived in for the past four months. There were some essentials like pants (thank goodness for mums!), socks, jeans, trainers and a selection of tops, and lots of luxuries like creams, nail polish and clippers, nicely scented deodorant, moisturiser, mascara and lip gloss.

I took great pleasure in removing my cycling bibs and putting them straight into the bin. Little Pig was parked up in the corner of the room as she had been so many times before, but on that evening I walked straight past her and took a taxi to the pub, to spend the night celebrating.

PART VI
EPILOGUE

My Round the World trip had been championed throughout by the charity Cycling UK. Not only did they report on my ride, but they had taken over all of my PR. When we launched the Round the World project in London the previous year, I met Website Editor Victoria Hazael. Her background in journalism, her experience and advice had become invaluable to the project. Between her, Sam and the communications team at Cycling UK, they managed the influx of media interest on my return. It turned into a huge job, probably bigger than anyone expected.

There were a few weeks' worth of interviews – for TV, radio, newspapers, magazines and podcasts – but the one that stuck out the most was my first live interview, with Scottish *STV News at Six*. I was still standing on the finish line with my helmet on when the presenter asked, 'So, what's next?' This would become one of the most common questions in the weeks, months and years to come. What event would I take on now? The truth was, I hadn't really finished with this one and I wouldn't be for some time. My legs might have stopped turning, but this was only the beginning of my dream outcome.

I had spoken to Victoria at the beginning about my dreams of public speaking and presenting on screen. Muriel Gray had been a long-time shero of mine since she presented her witty '90s TV programme, *The Munro Show*. An engaging and educational female presenter in neon leggings and short spiky white hair – she rocked! As an adult I went to so many talks on the outdoors, watching the way each adventurer presented themselves – the subtleties in body language, the narrative they had chosen to share, each with their own style and flair. Public speaking was an art form and I felt drawn to it. More than anything, I wanted to learn it myself. I was sure that if I just had a good enough story to tell, then the telling of it would come to me.

I had my first talk booked just six weeks after my return, at Boat of Garten, a small community just south of Inverness that sits within the Cairngorms National Park. This felt like a big deal, because it would be full of my outdoor adventure peers. Old colleagues and friends, with whom I'd trained, worked and adventured, would all be there.

I spent weeks putting together a talk, Tom and Mike chopping up video footage and making some highlights into little video clips for me, and me organising practice gigs for family and friends, who let me tell the story over and over until finally I had it. Then, the week before the Boat of Garten talk, I attended the Kendal Mountain Festival and was asked to give a talk there first. The perfect practice – two nights with about 40 people each time.

I clung to my notes as the room filled with the Lake District's finest adventurers: Kate Rawles, Alan Goldsmith, Steve Wilkinson, Pauline and Phil Sanderson, and many more. I worried I'd got this all wrong. What if people were coming along to find out about the culture in Asia and I was going to get into the top tips for peeing while riding your bike? Pauline Sanderson was someone I'd long admired for her adventurous spirit after reading her book about travelling from the lowest point on the earth to the highest, Mount Everest. I caught her at the bar. 'I'm so nervous,' I told her, clinging to my belly, my face going redder and redder as the room continued filling. 'Listen, excitement and nervousness causes the same reaction in your stomach,' she said really confidently. 'You're just excited. Enjoy it – it's going to be great!'

And just like that my public speaking career began. Throughout the year I built to bigger audiences and talked to a range of people, from festival crowds to corporate events. Each time I learned more about how to craft my story, what to linger on and when to up the pace. I went from hiding behind a speaker's podium to strutting across the stage. The immediate feedback from a live audience is so very special. When it's going well, you feel like a rock star working the crowd, building the excitement. There's a flip side to that: when it's not going well and you're faced with stony faces, there is literally nowhere to hide. All of this has been great learning and a fascinating process.

My good friend Cathy, who had helped me with writing so many articles about my Round the World preparation, gave me her time and an abundance of patience to help me gain confidence with the written word. I had always had such a negative connection to my own writing. For every paragraph I put out to the world I'd have days' worth of panic, overthinking and brain fog to face. School had been a struggle. I wasn't sure how to concentrate properly when given a writing task. My brain would turn to mush and words no longer made sense. It's probably why I leaned so heavily into verbal communication. Intra- and interpersonal skills were where I shone, so I could easily hide my spelling mistakes behind my outgoing personality. But that wouldn't cut it any longer. I have no doubt that without Cathy's support I would never have found the confidence to even contemplate this book.

As well as being a great pal, Cathy was also principal teacher at the Bridge Educational Service where I worked. I had been telling her about all the opportunities that were coming my way. My plan was to go back to work until Easter and then hand in my notice. 'You need to go now, Jen. You have to jump on this train when it's passing! We'll all still be here,' she assured me. 'We're not going anywhere.' She was right, and on my first day back at work at the start of December I handed in my notice, worked until Christmas and then, after 14 years in a role that I had always considered to be the very best job in the world, I left.

While I'd been away Emily Chappell had stood down from her role as the Adventure Syndicate Director and Lee Craigie had been looking for a new partner. We chatted about whether I would take on the role in those final days of Round the World. Em's shoes were big ones to fill and I had massive reservations about working so closely with a friend. After a few days pulling apart the pros and cons, we decided to give it a shot and I spent two years working alongside Lee creating projects, finding funding and driving the Syndicate forward. We both shared a background in and passion for youth work, so naturally that was the direction we took it in, setting up bikepacking trips, challenges, races and events, with the focus on engaging teenage girls in adventure. It was a great comfort having both the Syndicate and Lee, particularly through the first few months. So much in my life was changing and this was a world I knew.

● ● ●

When I came home, I kept in close contact with Mark Beaumont, who had been so helpful in the planning stages. From him I soaked up all the information he could give me about figuring out the lie of this new land. Mark's a great connector of people, matching them up based on their needs and skill sets. It's quite a talent and one I have benefitted from greatly in the past few years.

In Easter 2019, he asked me along on a Global Cycling Network shoot with him and presenter Si Richardson. Over three days they were making a film about riding the North Coast 500 in Scotland. I cycled out to meet them on the last day. We sat and had coffee just outside Bonar Bridge and I talked nervously about all the public toilets I'd slept in on the North Coast 500. I'm sure it's not all I talked about, but it's certainly all I remembered as I cycled away from them, convinced I'd blown any chance of work with them in the future. Perhaps it was Si's fatigued state or a caffeine rush, but to my delight he got back in touch with me and later that year I started working on a new documentary channel that was to be launched as part of GCNPlus.

So, there it was, only a year after completing Round the World and with a lot of helping hands I'd created my dream life. I was a documentary presenter and public speaker. I'd made podcasts about the Round the World trip and the film was just about to be launched. I was speaking with book agents and I was part of a syndicate whose main drive was sharing stories, riding long distances and helping others believe that they too should and could dream big.

And yet, even while my career blossomed I struggled to regain my health and true inner connections. The physical effects of the ride were showing themselves in strange ways. I kept riding my bike, mainly because my car failed its MOT when I was away and ended up on the scrap heap. As a result, rather than 'training down' as advised, I just rode as part of everyday life: shopping, visiting, working. It was all I had the capacity for.

I felt sluggish when riding, as if my tyres were always flat. Perhaps more surprising, and at the time more worrying, was that for months after I crossed the finish line I lost the ability to descend. I just lost my nerve – even when the road was smooth, dry tarmac and I'd ridden it many times before. I'd freeze at the thought of tumbling off and either descended extremely slowly or dismounted to walk down hills. I had been Round the World for the past four months and now I was walking rather than riding. The weather became a big issue too: the first sign of cold or wet and my homing instinct would kick in, and I'd call it a day, retreating to the warmth and safety of home.

All these reactions left me feeling like a fraud. I was building a career out of being a cyclist, but my reality felt extremely different. The only moments that left me with a glimmer of hope that I would be okay were the days when I was riding on long, flat sections of tarmac and I'd reach down to my tribars. In that moment, leaning into my ride, I could have been anywhere in the world. I was crossing the Gobi Desert, out on the Australian straight or cruising down the Yukon. I had taken my tribars off in January, but when I realised it was the only place I could be at one on the bike, I put them back on.

My nervous system was at capacity and I wasn't sure how to cope. In the beginning I'd try and share these feelings, but they didn't match up to other people's excitement about the ride so I quickly started suppressing them and feeling fairly lonely. I took the lack of understanding to heart and pulled back. Having held on to so much of the stress on the road myself, I could do this easily enough, except I gradually felt more and more disconnected from the people and community around me. I felt misunderstood. I built a barrier around myself and temporarily lost the ability to be vulnerable and needy, pushing people away rather than pulling them closer. It took some hard work on my part to recognise what was happening and then even more to commit to change. I'm blessed with good family and friends who stuck by me and showed nothing but compassion as I worked it out. I'm five years on from Round the World now and thankfully (for me anyway!) back to oversharing every thought and feeling. I'm whizzing down hills, riding through Scottish winters and continuing to grow as I learn my craft.

On a journey to Ireland nearly 20 years ago, I read Jack Canfield's *Chicken Soup for the Soul*. It was full of heart-warming short stories about ordinary people and extraordinary events. Most of the details are long gone, but the message of one stayed with me and when I look back on my own journey becomes ever truer. The story was about a young boy, who loved music and wanted to DJ, although no one considered him capable of the job. He didn't care, he played and mixed his music, because it was his passion. Never standing on a stage with a crowd dancing in front of him was not going to change the way he felt about the process. Then came a fairy tale ending: a DJ cancelled at the last minute and the boy was in the right place at the right time, and ready – building to that moment without realising it had been the goal.

While I'm a fan of dreaming big and wild, I have come to realise that true contentment for me is actually found on the journey to the start line. It's the years of silly epics, weekend adventures and Thursday night rides. It's the mornings when I wake early to do hill sprints. It's the gym classes that I hate the thought of and then come out of with my face and heart beaming. It's the moments in life when I have no idea what the time is or where my phone is. It comes from having faith that riding and training on my bike is the right thing to be doing, because it looks after my body and mind, and brings me so much joy. If I had never made my way Round the World, I'd still be happy, content and passionate.

People often tell me about their own adventures, but nearly always end with, 'But it's nothing like the stuff you do.' Well, actually, it's exactly like the stuff I do. I built on my passion so much that when Round the World came into my vision it felt possible, because it was just an extension of the life I was already living. It's in that place of least resistance where the magic happens.

Goals and ambition are so important in life. Focus, motivation and accountability are all great disciplines to master, but as you strive to make it, wherever you are going, don't forget to enjoy the journey!

Thanks for joining me on mine.

Jenny x

BOOKS REFERENCED

A House in the Sky, Amanda Lindhout and Sarah Corbett (Bolinda Publishing, 2014)

Around the World in 80 Days, Jules Verne (Williams Collins, 2018 [1873])

Chicken Soup for the Soul, Jack Canfield (HCI, 1993)

Endurance: Shackleton's Incredible Voyage to the Antarctic, Alfred Lansing (Weidenfeld & Nicolson, 2000)

Scott's Last Expedition, Robert Falcon Scott (Vintage Classics, 2013)

The Man Who Cycled the World, Mark Beaumont (Corgi, 2010)

The World's Longest Climb: Dead Sea to Everest Summit, Pauline Sanderson (Grafika Limited, 2011)

The Worst Journey in the World, Apsley Cherry-Garrard (Picador, 2001)

This is Going to Hurt: Secret Diaries of a Junior Doctor, Adam Kay (Picador, 2017)

This Road I Ride: My Incredible Journey From Novice to Fastest Woman to Cycle the Globe, Juliana Buhring (Piatkus, 2016)

ACKNOWLEDGEMENTS

I couldn't have written this book without the support and understanding of just about everyone in my day-to-day life. They listened patiently, understood when I pulled out of numerous social events as I was running behind with 'the book' and learnt not to ask about 'The Deadline'. Thank you all; I'm back and promise to be waaaay more fun! But special thanks go to:

My sister Nic who not only supported me while I was out riding (those spreadsheets!) but also drove me to write this book and has continued to support and champion me throughout. Such a wonderful big sis!

My mum Carol and stepdad Donald, who painstakingly typed out my hours of audio diaries – unedited! Throughout the year they would jump on FaceTime at the drop of a hat so they could listen to the latest draft chapter. But mostly I thank them for their love, encouragement, and unwavering belief.

My son Lachlan, for being such a grounded soul and making sure I keep it real.

My book agent James Spackman, who kept his calming and gentle hand on my shoulder, guiding me throughout this journey.

Huw Oliver and Mark Beaumont for the initial structural support and copy edits, which undoubtedly got me the deal – yeehaw!

Charlotte Croft, Megan Jones and the Bloomsbury team. For sharing your skill, expertise and patience (with a capital P) while supporting me with getting this book over the finish line.

And a shout out to people who contributed greatly to me making it around the planet in the first place, making sure I had an adventure to write about: John Hampshire; The Adventure Syndicate; Victoria Hazel and the Cycling UK team; Steven and Russell at Shand Cycles; Leigh Day; UnitasGlobal; Endura; Tory and George and the team at Apidura; Ritchey Logic Components; Komoot; Thomas Hogben at MHOR Films; Mike Webster and Sherrill Mason at Spiral Out Pictures; Kat Brown at Broon Coo Productions; Pennie Latin; Ian Fitz; Exposure Lights; Evans Cycles; Insta 360; and Weibke Lühmann for her support in Berlin, contacts and infectious enthusiasm.

To the bike shops of the world, particularly: People of Velocity, Inverness; Orangefox Bikes; Bikes of Inverness; Glenpark cycle in Perth, Australia; Backcountry Bike&Ski, Palmer, Alaska; and Scott Morris and the Trackleaders.

And all the invisible hands along the way. Big loves x